4425 W9-AUE-310

# COMPARATIVE LEGAL TRADITIONS

## IN A NUTSHELL

### THIRD EDITION

By

**MARY ANN GLENDON**
Learned Hand Professor of Law
Harvard Law School

**PAOLO G. CAROZZA**
Associate Professor of Law
Notre Dame Law School

**COLIN B. PICKER**
Daniel L. Brenner/UMKC Scholar &
Professor of Law
University of Missouri–Kansas City School of Law

Mat #40639018

COPYRIGHT © 1982 WEST PUBLISHING CO.
© West, a Thomson business, 1999
© 2008 Thomson/West
      610 Opperman Drive
      St. Paul, MN 55123
      1–800–313–9378

Printed in the United States of America

**ISBN:** 978–0–314–18428–3

# OUTLINE

**Page**

**PART 2. THE COMMON LAW TRADITION**

# COMPARATIVE LEGAL TRADITIONS

## IN A NUTSHELL

### THIRD EDITION

*

# INTRODUCTION TO THE COMPARATIVE STUDY OF LAW

## § 1. What Is "Comparative Law"?

When the first learned societies dealing with cross-national legal comparisons were established in France, Germany, and England in the late nineteenth century, their founders took for granted that comparative methods would advance the understanding of a broad range of legal issues. In that expectation, legal scholars were in accord with the best of their counterparts in other disciplines. Emile Durkheim had gone so far as to claim that, "Comparative sociology is not a particular branch of sociology; it is sociology itself." The great legal historian F.W. Maitland had insisted that, "The English lawyer who knew nothing and cared nothing for any system but his own, hardly came in sight of the idea of legal history."

The question arises, however: Why, if the benefits of comparative studies are so substantial and obvious, did comparative law remain a relative backwater in twentieth century American legal education? No doubt there are several reasons, not least of which is the increasing burden of keeping up with developments in our own legal system, perhaps one of the most complex the world has ever known. To achieve even minimal competence in another country's legal system requires a major expenditure of time and effort, including, in many cases, learning another language. But, perhaps the main reason is probably that Americans have long tended to assume that they could get along quite well without casting their gaze beyond national borders. Like Roman jurists of old, many U.S. lawyers were convinced of the self-sufficiency of their legal and political arrangements.

In recent years, however, that insular posture has become untenable. With unprecedented global interdependence, and with commerce and instant communication linking all regions of the earth, nearly every legal field has acquired an international dimension. We live in a world where national boundaries are of diminishing significance in relation to technology, finance, trade, the environment, information, consumerism, entertainment, the arts, and ideas of universal human rights. Legal education, accordingly, has had to adjust to demands for the skills required by lawyers in the "global village". As the twenty-first century dawns, international legal studies are burgeoning to a degree that early comparatists could scarcely have imagined. Yet, as Basil Markesinis has written, comparative law is "still searching for an audience even where it has found a place of sorts in the university curriculum."

In the years to come, it is likely that comparative law will find many different sorts of audiences as it takes its rightful place among the methods required for the effective study and practice of law. Certain fields have always had a comparative dimension: conflict of laws, international business law, public international law, and area studies where the object is to become familiar with a particular foreign legal system. In those fields, cross-national studies are now assuming greater importance than ever. Contracts and commercial law teachers are having to spend an increasingly large proportion of course time on the international aspects of their subjects if they wish to keep pace with developments in the practice. Increasingly, law professors in many other fields are moving in the direction counseled by Roscoe Pound in the 1930s—exploring the approaches of other legal systems to the issues that arise "in the course of teaching the law of the land." The increasing importance of supranational law will present new challenges for comparatists as the roles of nation states and national law undergo transformation.

## § 2.  Aims and Uses of Comparative Law

It is fair to say that comparative law, as befits a developing field, is experiencing something of an identity crisis. The existence of lively debate concerning aims and methods, however, has not hindered comparatists from happily pursuing cross-national studies in a variety of ways and for a wide range of purposes. Nor has it prevented those studies from yielding important contributions to the understanding, practice, and reform of contemporary law. In all likelihood, the diversity of aims and methods among comparatists promotes the vitality of their work. In a world where national and cultural differences are often seen as posing a formidable challenge, comparatists hold up a view of diversity as an invitation, an opportunity, and a crucible of creativity. In a heterogeneous nation like the United States where empathetic understanding among groups often seems elusive, comparatists are witnesses to the joys and discoveries awaiting those who make the effort to enter imaginatively into another mental framework.

This Nutshell has been designed to lend itself to use by students and other readers with many different interests and preoccupations. Like the late Otto Kahn–Freund, we subscribe to the view that comparative law is "a variety of methods for looking at law." Those methods may be deployed toward an even wider variety of ends.* Among the aims of comparative law, we as academics would put first the pursuit of knowledge as an end in itself: comparative law responds to that characteristic of the human species which is curious about the world and wants to understand it. That curiosity will not lead everyone in the same direction. In fact, it will take most individuals down several different paths in the course of a lifetime. Thus, we expect that emphasis will vary among users of this book concerning the methods to be utilized and the aims to be pursued in comparative studies. Our objective, in this introductory chapter, is to open a window to the spectrum of available techniques and to the vast range of practical and theoretical possibilities they afford.

Discussions of the goals of comparative law often draw an overly sharp distinction between its practical and its academic aims. To be sure, comparative studies have many practical uses. Of growing interest to Americans is the way they facilitate communication on behalf of clients with one's counterparts and with officials in other countries, and enhance one's ability to be persuasive in international contexts. One day, Americans, like Europeans, may also take advantage of the resources of comparative law in federal and state law-making processes— indeed, that very issue has of late been the subject of heated discussions even within the U.S. Supreme Court. Some members of the Court are more willing than others to employ comparative law in their search for resolutions to novel constitutional problems. Others on the Court are equally heated in their opposition. Regardless of the eventual resolution of this issue, at least it is now a subject of debate.

The modern systematic study of comparative law had its origins in nineteenth century European law reform activities, and few major legislative programs are undertaken in Europe today without extensive preliminary comparative surveys. Comparative law is indispensable as well to international endeavors such as the harmonization of laws within the European Union, and the framing, application and interpretation of supranational legal norms. The chief draftsman of the U.N. Universal Declaration of Human Rights of 1948, René Cassin, was a comparatist who maintained that comparative law was a necessity for proponents of human rights.

The important practical applications of comparative law are often contrasted with more theoretical aims, such as promoting an improved understanding of one's own legal system or searching for principles common to a number of legal systems. There is nothing wrong with making such a distinction between practice and theory. The only harm comes if one forgets that the practical aims just mentioned are furthered by serious pursuit of scholarly objectives, and that scholarly exercises are apt to prove sterile if they are carried on without close attention to the way law operates in the rough and tumble of daily life. The fact is that, in law as elsewhere, theory and practice are like the two blades of a scissors, or the bow and the arrow, complementary and indispensable to one another. The best practical work is grounded in theoretical understanding; the soundest theory emerges from constant testing against practical know-how and experience.

When we say that comparative law enables students to understand their own legal system better, we do not just mean that it will move them away from assuming their own ways are the best or the only ways of doing things. We also hope that they will acquire a better sense of what is valuable and capable of development in their own system. Above all, we are confident that those of you who are embarking for the first time on a comparative venture will have new insights that would not have occurred to you if your imagination had remained exclusively within the confines of the legal systems within the United States.

What we have just said is even more true of the would-be law reformer. Investigation of the way other legal systems deal with problems confronting all societies at comparable stages of social and economic development seldom fails to help in designing research, framing hypotheses, and testing conclusions. In the law-saturated societies of developed nations, we need more than ever to know how legal norms actually work in various contexts, what advantages and benefits they offer, what risks or indirect consequences they are likely to entail.

Comparative law frequently proves its worth through significant contributions to specific, novel and difficult problems. Indeed, the stimulus for comparative investigation is often a problem that one's home system does not handle very well. When comparatists devote their attention to a vexing or unsolved problem, it is not with the idea that they will find in some foreign land a "solution" which, like a new electrical appliance, can be fitted with an adapter and plugged into the system back home. What they are usually looking for is, initially, a deepened understanding of the problem, and, if they are lucky, a source of inspiration. Our own way of doing things seems so natural to us that often it is only comparison with another way that establishes that there is something to be explained. Comparison often picks up issues or makes connections that remain invisible to other research strategies.

So far as increasing one's awareness of alternatives and testing one's hypotheses are concerned, one may say that comparative law gives us as much access to a "laboratory" as lawyers can ever have. Since controlled experimentation in law is hardly ever possible, legal scholars often use comparative law to expand their theater of observation, to see how other legal systems have dealt with problems similar to ours. The hope is that the experiences of countries at comparable stages of social and economic development will give us insight into our own situation and that they may help us to find our own paths through the maze.

Comparative law is also an indispensable heuristic method for legal and social theory. Montesquieu, Tocqueville, Durkheim, and Max Weber all used comparative study to illuminate the history and growth of the law, its role in society, its relation to behavior and ideas. Comparative law helps us to understand the dynamics of social, as well as legal, change.

Finally we should mention the comparatist's power and duty to make a critical evaluation of what he or she discovers through comparative analysis. If this is not done, comparative law can easily degenerate into a dizzying spiral in which everything is both cause and effect; different from, but similar to, everything else; separate but intertwined; and so on. Moreover, who is in a better position than the comparatist to follow up his or her research with a careful appraisal of its significance?

## § 3.  Methods of Comparative Law

If comparative law consists of a variety of methods for looking at law, what are those methods? Comparative analysis begins by working out a topic: Your client poses a problem. Or your government wishes to formulate and implement a policy. Or in the course of your studies, you encounter a puzzle. You investigate the facts and the opinions of others. You raise questions. You get an idea or form a hypothesis. At this stage, it may be the study of a foreign legal system that makes you aware of a problem; that suggests a hypothesis; or that helps you to form a research strategy.

When you move on to testing your hypothesis, comparative law may again be helpful. Modern thinking about how, precisely, comparative methodology enters into legal research begins with Ernst Rabel who put the systematic study of comparative law on a new basis in the twentieth century. Two concepts are key to Rabel's understanding of the field: function and context. You cannot compare legal rules, institutions, or systems without knowing how they function, and you cannot know how they function without situating them in their legal, economic and cultural context. It was Rabel who insisted that it is of little use to compare "paper" institutions, or rules and doctrines merely as they appear in books. The comparatist's province is the operating institution and the law in action. Comparatists are more like comparative physiologists than comparative anatomists. That functional approach, now recognized to have wide applicability, was probably comparative law's principal gift to twentieth century legal science. Several methodological consequences follow from the emphasis on functioning systems and context:

1. The study of foreign law is an indispensable preliminary step to comparative analysis. This means that one has some grasp of the essential characteristics of the systems to be compared as functioning wholes. With regard to the particular institutions and elements under study, one needs to know how their roles fit within the whole. What values do they protect and promote? Through what technical devices do they operate?

2. One has to know one's own system in the same way. That is not so simple as it sounds. In our experience, the comparative law course often provides an American law student's first opportunity to reflect on the U.S. legal system as a functioning whole. Unlike continental European law students, most young men or women beginning legal education in the United States receive no general overview of the legal system. That is something they are expected to pick up by themselves as they go along, putting their newly acquired legal knowledge together with what they remember from high school and college courses in politics and government. The American law school, with its curriculum divided arbitrarily into separate, overlapping subjects, affords very little opportunity to study the functions and relations of all the specialized parts of the legal order. Try to use the comparative law course, if you are a student, as an occasion for refreshing, review-

ing, and supplementing the understanding you are acquiring about the law of the United States. Think about what the French historian Fernand Braudel once wrote concerning the unexpected insights that can arise from comparison: "Live in London for a year, and you will not get to know much about the English. But through comparison, and in the light of your surprise, you will suddenly come to understand some of the more profound and individual characteristics of France, which you did not previously understand because you knew them too well."

3. The need to see our own and foreign legal institutions *in context* means that comparative law by its very nature is an interdisciplinary field, one that depends heavily on practical knowledge and empirical investigation. Legal norms cannot be fully understood without some knowledge of their sources: their political, social, and economic purposes; the milieu in which they operate; the role of the legal profession; the operation of the court system. The question naturally arises: How can any individual know enough languages, history, sociology, economics, and political science, or be familiar enough with practices, values, attitudes, and social conditions in another nation to be a comparatist? The answer is that comparative law is a group enterprise, characterized more than most other fields by teamwork and creative collaboration. For many of us, those cooperative endeavors are a major part of what gives the field its lasting attraction.

4. A functional approach means that legal rules and institutions at some point have to be liberated

from the conceptual categories of their home systems so that they can be seen in terms of the social objectives they serve. Sometimes this will mean that an institution has to be broken down into separate parts, as, for example, when one seeks to find out how legal systems lacking the Anglo–American trust handle the diverse problems we treat with that useful, single multi-purpose device. Sometimes, several seemingly unrelated legal institutions have to be studied together because it is only their joint operation that meets a particular social need. For example, in many legal systems, the problem of balancing freedom of testation with the policy of protecting family members against disinheritance cannot be analyzed without taking marital property law into consideration. As the German comparatists Zweigert and Kötz put it, "The functional approach of comparative law concentrates on the real live problem which often lurks unseen behind the concepts of the national systems."

5. The tasks comparatists set themselves may range from critical theory, to broad comparisons of entire systems, to narrower studies targeted to specific social problems. Macro- and micro-comparison tend to shade into one another, since micro-comparison furnishes examples and means of verification, while knowledge of legal systems in turn furnishes the indispensable context for the study of particular problems.

Comparative legal scholars working along the lines opened up by Rabel have produced path-breaking works. In the field of commercial law, they have discovered many essential similarities behind formal differences. Conversely, time and again, comparatists have shown how similar legal rules produce significantly different effects in different social and procedural contexts.

Sometimes the comparative study of law can even deepen the understanding of culture. The anthropologist Clifford Geertz has prodded comparative lawyers to "learn and contribute more" by attending to the fact that law is not just an ingenious collection of devices to avoid or adjust disputes and to advance this or that interest, but also a way that a society makes sense of things—"part of a distinctive manner of imagining the real." From that perspective, some of the most interesting comparisons among legal systems lie, first, in their manner of characterizing factual situations so that rules can be applied to them, and second, in how they conceive of the legal norms themselves. It is to be expected that legal systems compared in this manner will differ in the "stories they tell," the "symbols they deploy," and the "visions they project." Whether meant to or not, law, in addition to all the other things it does, tells stories about the culture that helped to shape it and which it in turn helps to shape: stories about who we are, where we came from, and where we are going. The stories that are going forward at a given time in a legal system seem to have a powerful influence not only on how legal norms are invented and applied within that system, but on how facts are perceived and translated into the language and concepts of the law. Indeed, it may be that law affects our lives at least as much by these stories as it does by the specific rules, standards, institutions, and procedures of which it is composed.

## § 4. The Concept of Legal Tradition

In the minds of many people, the word "tradition" evokes the image of a frozen and static past. As we use it here, however, it denotes a vital, dynamic, ongoing system. The Anglo–American common law tradition and the Romano–Germanic civil law tradition are operating examples of philosopher Alasdair MacIntyre's concept of a living tradition: "an historically extended, socially embodied argument, and an argument precisely about the goods that constitute that tradition. Within a tradition the pursuit of goods extends through generations, sometimes through many generations."

The legal systems with which we are concerned in this Nutshell belong to two extended legal "families" or traditions which historian Alan Watson has described this way: "Twice only have the customs of the European peoples been worked up into intellectual systems. The Roman tradition has served two separate civilizations. The common law, governing daily relationships in various modern societies, has developed without a break from its beginnings in a society utterly different from any of them."

Comparative legal studies in the United States have tended to focus mainly on the Romano–Germanic civil law tradition, or on the law of particular geographic regions (e.g., East Asian studies, Latin

American studies). Our decision to devote equal attention to the English legal system was influenced in part by our interest in drawing attention to the shared legal and intellectual heritage that links the two great North Atlantic legal traditions. As a practical matter, knowledge of both traditions is indispensable to the understanding of the increasingly important emerging European legal institutions which we treat separately in this Nutshell.

Despite their shared inheritance, the civil and common law traditions have developed in sufficiently different ways that they are now universally regarded as belonging to different legal families. In practical terms, this means that each system is, in important respects, inaccessible to a lawyer trained in the other system. Thus, for example, English and American lawyers unfamiliar with civil law concepts and methods can—with effort—communicate with one another, but will experience much greater difficulty in communicating with French or German lawyers. We hasten to emphasize that, even within each tradition, diversity exists and communication problems arise. That is another reason we have chosen to present the English legal system here, for England and the United States are in many ways, to paraphrase another great saying about the two nations, "two countries separated by a common law." And, as we shall see, France and Germany gave to the civil law world two very different models of codification and legal science.

Of the two major legal traditions in the modern Western world, the Romano–Germanic is the older and the more widely distributed. Its influence derives not only from the fact that it has shaped the law of many national legal systems outside the civil-law orbit, but also from the enormous debt owed to it by international law in its formative period. It is to the civil law tradition that we now turn.

# PART 1

# THE CIVIL LAW TRADITION

---

## CHAPTER 1

## HISTORY, CULTURE AND DISTRIBUTION

### § 1.  What Is the Civil Law Tradition?

When we refer to some of the world's legal systems with a common name, such as "Romanist", "Romano–Germanic", or "civil law" systems, we are calling attention to the fact that, despite their similarities to other legal systems and despite national differences among themselves, these systems share a distinctive heritage. The tradition of the civil law is characterized by a particular interaction in its early formative period among Roman law, Germanic and local customs, canon law, the international law merchant, and, later, by a distinctive response to the break with feudalism and the rise of nation states, as well as by the specially important role it has accorded to legal science.

## § 2.  Roman Law

To use the term Roman law to describe the entire Roman legal output of nearly a millennium stretching from the Twelve Tables (c. 450 B.C.) to the Justinian compilations (c. 534 A.D.) is about as helpful as describing the product of English legal minds from 1066 A.D. to the present as "common law." Thus, specialists in ancient Roman law subdivide their subject into various periods. It was as early as the third century B.C., during the Republic, that there appeared a class of men known as Jurisconsults, who made law their specialty. By the end of the Late Republic in the first century B.C., the Jurisconsults had acquired a monopoly of technical information and legal experience. In difficult cases, the lay judges began to turn to these legal specialists for advice. Through this advisory role, the Jurisconsults stayed close to the practice of law and remained in constant contact with actual disputes. They were the world's first professional lawyers (as distinct from orators like Cicero whose main skills were in rhetoric and statesmanship). What we know as Roman law evolved through the accretion of the opinions they rendered case by case. Eventually the principles thus developed by the Jurisconsults were taught and expounded in treatises, all in a distinctive vocabulary and style.

At first rather formal and rigid, Roman law eventually supplemented fixed rules with flexible standards and moved from concrete to more abstract modes of thought. It became characterized by attention to practical details, and by terms of art which caught on and endured. The law of the Classical period (which began around 117 A.D. and came to an end with the period of anarchy, invasions, plague and civil war that commenced around 235 A.D.), represents the fullest development of ancient Roman law. Of the Jurisconsults of this period, Ulpian, Papinian and Gaius are chiefly remembered. At its height, classical Roman law constituted a body of practical wisdom of a kind the world had not seen before. It was therefore of the highest interest to Byzantine jurists after the fall of the Western empire, and, through them, had great influence on the development of the civil law systems.

Centuries later, Roman law would be called "written reason" by the medieval scholars who "rediscovered" it as Europe began to emerge from the Middle Ages. The Roman law that they "found" when Western society began to be ready for law to play a prominent role once again among the norms that govern human activity, was not the law of the Classical period in its original form. Most of the ancient sources had been lost. What survived was the monumental compilation of Roman law that was made at the direction of the Byzantine Emperor Justinian in the sixth century A.D. By that time, the Roman Empire in the West had been breaking up for more than a century, its fall symbolized by the sack of Rome in 410 A.D. The significance of the work of the Byzantine jurists in preserving the Roman legal heritage would be hard to exaggerate. From Justinian's times to the present, the term Roman law, except to specialists, generally has meant Roman law as it appears in the sixth century Corpus Juris Civilis of Justinian.

The Corpus Juris Civilis included four parts: the Institutes, the Digest, the Code and the Novels. The Digest was by far the most important in terms of its influence on the civil law tradition, particularly in the areas of personal status, torts, unjust enrichment, contracts and remedies. The Digest was a treatise representing the distillation of what, in the judgment of Justinian's jurists, was most valuable from the best Roman legal writings from all previous periods. Since virtually all of the books they used in composing the Digest have been lost, the Digest itself became the principal source of knowledge about what the Roman law of earlier periods had been like. The Institutes were simply a short introductory text for students, the Code was a systematic collection of Roman legislation, and the Novels were the imperial legislation enacted after the Code and the Digest were completed. Together, the Digest and the Code were meant to be a complete and authoritative restatement of Roman law.

Byzantine Roman lawyers did not merely copy the law of earlier periods. The Corpus Juris was the product of a careful process of selection and rejection. In general outlook, as well as in matters of detail, it differed from the law of the Classical period. It continued the movement away from formalism, but this move was accompanied by a decline in technique. Equity, which in the Classical period was regarded as a principle of justice animating the whole of the law, degenerated into mere impatience with legal subtleties. Byzantine legislation exhibited, according to Roman law historian Anthony Jolowicz, "an almost pathetic confidence in the power of law to do away with evils of an economic character ... and a taste for excessive regulation by statute of matters to which fixed rules can hardly, by their nature, be applied with success." After the Lombard, Slav and Arab invasions that followed the reign of Justinian, the Corpus Juris Civilis fell into disuse for centuries.

## § 3.  Roman Law Survival Amidst Medieval Customs

The fact that Roman law and legal science were left stranded by the collapse of the way of life that had produced them did not mean that Romanist legal influences disappeared altogether during the Middle Ages. Certainly the sophistication and technical perfection to which ancient Roman law had been brought over the centuries was not maintained during the legal and political disorder that followed the disintegration of the Roman Empire. For five centuries after the fall of Rome a series of raiders and settlers overran the areas that had once been Roman. There were no strong, centralized states. Kingdoms rose and fell. The condition of the people was one of local self-sufficiency, and local customs displaced formal law. It would be centuries before scholars again would be capable of putting to use the technical instruments left behind by the Classical Roman and Byzantine jurists. When a reawakening of interest in Roman law did occur and when attention turned to the Corpus Juris in the eleventh century, the process became known as the "revival" of Roman law.

There was, nevertheless, a considerable "survival" of Roman law within the diverse customary systems that prevailed from the fifth to the tenth centuries. Roman conquerors once had been all over Europe, and many of the Germanic settlers, legionnaires and migrating peoples who eventually overran the former Empire had been, to a certain extent, "Romanized." As conquerors and conquered changed places, Germanic rulers used Roman law to govern their Roman subjects, while applying their own law to their own peoples. Over time, however, the distinctions between these groups disappeared. By the end of the tenth century, the rules were the same for all persons within a given territory. Crude versions of Roman legal rules had intermingled to varying degrees with the customary rules of the Germanic invaders to the point where historians sometimes speak of the laws during this period as "Romanized customary laws" and sometimes as "barbarized Roman laws". Thus, though Roman legal science and Classical Roman law disappeared in the welter, diversity and localism of the Middle Ages, a Romanist element survived and served both as a strand of continuity and a latent, potentially universalizing factor in what we now think of as the civil law tradition.

The widely disseminated Germanic customary laws that began to be written down as early as the fifth century A.D., (as well as particular local customs), formed part of this tradition too, particularly influencing aspects of marital property and inheritance law. Many of the most ingenious and useful legal devices of the modern civil law of property and commercial law derive not from Roman, but from customary medieval origins, and thus remind us that the legal confusion of the Middle Ages had its fruitful and creative, as well as its fragmented and disorganized, side. The Germanic element evolved through the Middle Ages, as tribal laws became territorial laws, to the point where it produced the beginnings of a legal literature and a new legal culture that was quite different from the Roman. But its further development was arrested, partly because of the crudeness of its procedures (e.g., trial by ordeal), and partly because of its limited potential for adaptation to the social and economic changes that were beginning to transform feudal society.

## § 4.  Canon Law

With the break-up of the far-flung system of Roman administration, the Church took over some of the functions of government. Indeed, after the fall of the Roman Empire, and until the revival of Roman law in the eleventh century, the single most important universalizing factor in the diverse and localized legal systems of the civil law tradition was canon law. But canon law itself was a hybrid of sorts. It had been produced by Christian notions interacting reciprocally with Roman law after the Christianization of the Empire, a process during which the reign of Constantine (d. 337 A.D.) was an important marker. The sixth century Justinian Corpus, in particular, was affected by Christian ideas, but the Church, for its part, had borrowed freely from the structure, principles and detailed rules of ancient Roman law. Furthermore, just as there was some degree of amalgamation everywhere of Germanic customs, indigenous customs and debased Roman law, there was a certain penetration by canon law into the codes promulgated by German rulers and, later, into the legislation of the Carolingian (c. 800 A.D.) and Holy Roman Empires (c. 962 A.D.). During the Middle Ages, the Church sought and acquired jurisdiction for its own tribunals over matrimonial causes, and over certain aspects of criminal law and succession to personal property. Many of the rules and procedures it developed in these matters were accepted in secular tribunals long after the Church had lost its civil jurisdiction.

## § 5. Revival of Roman Law

Europe entered a period of political, economic and cultural transformation from about 1050 A.D. onward. The gradual return of political order established conditions that facilitated speculative learning. Economic expansion, too, with its requirements for predictability and efficient methods of dispute resolution, led to a renewed interest in law. Along with scholars in other fields, jurists began to turn, with the excitement of discovery, to the accomplishments of antiquity. The revival of Roman law that took place in northern Italy towards the end of the eleventh century was a rediscovery, through the Justinian legacy, of Roman legal science.

The University of Bologna became the principal legal center to which students flocked from all over Europe to hear learned teachers (including some nuns who were the first women law professors) lecture on the Corpus Juris Civilis. Irnerius, who is said to have given the first lectures on the Justinian Digest, proclaimed its intellectual superiority over the legal inheritance of the Middle Ages. But the ancient text dealt with so many institutions and problems that were no longer known, that it was difficult to understand. The first generations of scholars to study the Digest therefore made it their task to try to accurately reconstruct and explain its text. They became known as the Glossators because of their annotations (glosses) on the Digest. But their approach to interpretation in time gave way to the new methods of the Commentators (or Post–Glossators) of the thirteenth century, who saw their work as adapting the law of Roman society to the problems of their own day. The methods of the Commentators were much influenced by the new spirit of rational inquiry and speculative dialectic that would be brought to its highest form in the work of Thomas Aquinas (d. 1274). This way of thinking liberated them from the literalism of the Glossators and led them to search for the rationale and underlying principles of various Roman legal rules. Bartolus (d. 1357) is remembered as the greatest of the Commentators.

The thousands of students who came to the Italian law faculties from every corner of Europe carried back to their own nations and universities, not only the law of the Corpus Juris Civilis but also the methods and ideas of their teachers. They and their own students became the new profession of lawyers who found places not only in universities, but in the bureaucratic administrations of princes, cities and the Church. Their work was influenced at least as much by the Bolognese method of decision-making (bringing a case within the terms of an abstractly formulated authoritative text) as by the substantive norms of Roman law. In Paris and Oxford, Prague and Heidelberg, Cracow and Copenhagen, a fusion took place between the medieval Romano–Germanic law and the new learning based on the revived Roman law. In different ways and to varying degrees this amalgam formed the base on which future variations and modifications would take place in all the civil law systems. The new learning, acquired by all those trained in Northern Italy, furnished the common methodology for the further development of national laws.

It was the shared background of these influential torch bearers of the new legal science that consolidated the civil law tradition. The Roman civil law, together with the immense literature generated by the Glossators and Commentators, came to be the *jus commune*, the common law, of Europe. As John Henry Merryman has written, "There was a common body of law and of writing about law, a common legal language and a common method of teaching and scholarship." Canon law continued to play a role in this shared tradition, but in a new, more refined and "Romanized" form, as Bolognese scholars systematically compiled and digested some 700 years of ecclesiastical enactments and decrees. Gratian in the twelfth century is generally credited with having transformed canon law into an independent "system" which then began to be taught alongside Roman civil law in universities all over Europe.

## § 6. Commercial Law

In addition to Roman civil law and canon law, commercial law furnished another universalizing element as Europe emerged from the localism and relative economic stagnation of the Middle Ages. With the rise of towns, the birth of markets, fairs and banks, the rapid expansion of maritime and overland trade, and the eventual development of large flourishing commercial centers, there appeared the need for a body of law to govern business transactions. Since Roman law did not prove readily adaptable for this purpose, guilds and merchants' associations established their own rules and their own tribunals. The merchants' courts worked out informal rules and expeditious procedures that were practical, fair, and grounded in the usages of businessmen. These rules in time came to be recognized and applied as customary law by secular and ecclesiastical authorities. Eventually the "law merchant" became international, a body of generally accepted commercial rules that transcended political boundaries. It spread even into England where the Roman law, brought back from Italy, had found favor in universities, but was stoutly resisted in the civil courts.

## § 7.   Reception of Roman Law

The Middle Ages were an era of numerous overlapping and competing jurisdictions and sources of law. In the absence of strong central states, the modern notion of law as command of the sovereign had no meaning. Ecclesiastical courts applied canon law; the courts of a guild would usually apply the law merchant; while other judges in cities and towns would tend to search for an appropriate rule, first, in local custom or statute, then, with the help of university scholars, filling the gaps with the jus commune. Aided by the expansion of economic activity, the enthusiasm of legal scholars, and by the idea of the "continued" Holy Roman Empire, the jus commune became the basic law of a great part of continental Europe. It proved capable of dealing with many of the new problems posed by a more complex economy; yet as part of a not entirely forgotten past, it had a certain familiarity. Through the process that civil law lawyers call *reception*, the revived Roman private law (including the writings of the Italian jurists and the canon law) moved from the universities into the courts. (It should be noted, however, that Roman public law (including criminal law), itself relatively undeveloped, was not similarly received. There was no real place for public law so long as no strong central governments existed.)

The formality and the extent of reception in a given country and the type of interaction that occurred between the jus commune and the medieval Romano–Germanic base varied considerably. In certain parts of Italy, the influence of Roman law had remained continuously so strong that it is perhaps not quite accurate to speak of a "reception" there. In Spain, however, the jus commune was always in tension with various vigorous local customary traditions. In the regions of France south of the Loire where Roman law influence had been strongest, the local customary law was already heavily romanized. Thus, there was a more extensive reception there than in the northern regions of France where the various local customs had always been of greater importance than Roman law.

The jus commune infiltrated the law of the various regions of the Holy Roman Empire of the German confederation to the point where it came to be regarded as the common law of the empire. In 1495, when a central imperial court was established, its judges were obliged to decide cases according to this common law, unless a conflicting local custom or statute could be proved. The difficulty of proving a controlling German rule meant in practice that the received Roman law became the basic law of all the regions of Germany. The reception of Roman law on such a large scale in Germany is usually explained by a combination of factors. Roman law met no resistance from a strong national legal profession, central court system or from the existence of a common body of "German" law. Both the weakness of the imperial power and its claim to being the successor to the Roman Empire facilitated the reception. Finally, and probably most importantly, Roman law filled the increasingly urgent need to deal with the inconvenience that the variety of local customs posed for intercourse among the many small independent territories that formed the German confederation.

The wide-scale Roman law reception in Germany was a crucial event for the later development of German legal science, producing a much more extensive systematization of law than occurred elsewhere. From the beginning, judges relied heavily on legal scholars for information and guidance concerning the local law as well as the received Roman law. Indeed, by 1600, it was a common practice for judges to send out the record of a difficult case to a university law faculty and to adopt the faculty's collective opinion on questions of law. This practice of *Aktenversendung,* which continued until the nineteenth century, resulted in the accumulation of an extensive body of common doctrine that transcended the borders of the various German political entities. Systematized in reports and essays, distillations from scholarly opinions rendered in actual controversies became a kind of case-law, located in the learned writings.

In Europe generally, the jus commune, like the Latin language and the universal Church, was an aspect of the unity of the West at a time when there were no strong centralized political administrations and no unified legal systems, but rather a continuous struggle among the competing and overlapping jurisdictions of local, manorial, ecclesiastical, mercantile and royal authorities. From the fifteenth century on, however, the relationship between the received jus commune and the diverse local and regional customary laws began to be affected, in varying degrees, by the rise of nationalism and the increasing consolidation of royal power.

## § 8.   Nation States and National Law

Gradual political unification in Europe did not immediately bring about national legal unification, but it did arouse interest in customary law as "national" law. The way for this development had been prepared, in a sense, by the fourteenth century Commentators who had turned scholarly attention from textual exegesis of the Digest to a consideration of the adaptability of Roman legal rules to contemporary conditions. In the sixteenth and seventeenth centuries, as the center of legal scholarship shifted to France and Holland, the methods of the Bolognese Commentators were replaced by those of the French Legal Humanists and the Dutch Natural Law School. The Humanists used the techniques of history and philology to study Roman law. Their view of Roman law as a historical phenomenon and of the Corpus Juris Civilis as merely an ancient text (rather than as "living law" or "written reason") marked a step toward eventual displacement of the jus commune. This indirect challenge to the authority of Roman law was continued by the seventeenth century Dutch Natural Law

School, whose members developed a systematic theory of law grounded in what they conceived to be the universal law of nature. The comprehensive legal system-building of these Dutch jurists was the prelude to modern codification, even as their search for universals laid the foundations for the law of nations, which evolved into modern international law.

The awakening of interest in national law was only one of several parallel developments that marked the end of the unity of the West and the rise of modern nation states. National literatures began to appear. The vernacular languages began to be used in universities. Schisms developed between national churches and Rome. In the legal area, so long as the state had been non-existent or minimal, there was no public, administrative or constitutional law in the modern sense. However, as political power became sufficiently centralized, at different times in different parts of Europe, public law, national law and the international law of nations developed rapidly.

## § 9.   Codification

In many parts of Europe, legal nationalism early found expression in the form of codification. The first of these national codes appeared in the Scandinavian countries in the seventeenth and eighteenth centuries. Then, a second generation of codes not only aspired to bring about legal unity within one kingdom, but also attempted to incorporate the political and philosophical thought of the eighteenth century. These codes were the product of "enlight-ened" monarchs, like Voltaire's friend Frederick II of Prussia, and Joseph II of Austria, and their bureaucratic administrators. They were founded on the belief that a rational, systematized, and compre-hensive legal system would be an improvement on traditional law. One consequence of the unification of national law in these early codes was that the jus commune was displaced as the basic source of law. To be sure, the draftsmen of the national codes drew heavily upon the jus commune as well as on national law, but the authority of the law from the codification era onward was derived more from the state than from tradition, or from the inherent reasonableness of the legal norms themselves.

Not all of the codes were successful. The Prussian General Territorial Law of 1794, for example, is chiefly remembered today as a monument of legal hubris. In its ambition to foresee all possible contin-gencies and to regulate the range of human conduct down to the most intimate details of family life, it was hampered in operation both by its excessive detail and its failure to acknowledge the limits of law.

Two national codes, however, had such wide-spread and lasting influence that they and their accompanying ideologies can be said to have become part of the contemporary civil law tradition. The French Civil Code of 1804 and the German Civil Code of 1896 have served as models for most other modern civil codes. So different from each other, yet growing out of a common tradition, they have both decisively affected the shape of civil law systems of today. French revolutionary ideas and German legal science not only gave a special stamp and flavor to their respective national codes but affected legal thought throughout and beyond the civil law world.

The consolidation of French royal power in the period from the end of the fifteenth century to the Revolution of 1789 made France the first modern continental nation, a politically unified society under strong central rule. The *ancien régime*, however, never succeeded in bringing about legal unification. A traveller in France changed laws, Voltaire famously said, as often as he changed horses. It remained for Napoleon to provide France with a nationally unified body of law. Under his rule, five basic codes were promulgated: the Civil Code, the Penal Code, the Commercial Code and the Codes of Civil and Criminal Procedure.

The French Civil Code of 1804, drafted in a remarkably short period of time by a commission of four eminent jurists, has a just claim to being the first modern code. Although, in form, it hewed rather closely to the framework of Justinian's Institutes, it was not, as Justinian's Code basically had been, a restatement of the law. Its substantive provisions incorporated the results of a profound intellectual, political and social revolution. Though it is often referred to as the "Code Napoleon", its original name was the *Code civil des Français* (the civil code of the French people). In what its title represented, as in other ways, it was unlike all earlier efforts at codification. It represented a new way of thinking about human beings, law and government.

The three ideological pillars of the French civil code were private property, freedom of contract and the patriarchal family. In the first of these areas, the Code consolidated the Revolution's rejection of the feudal past. Through such private law devices as prohibitions on restraints on alienation and limitations on freedom of testation, the Code's architects consciously sought to break up the estates of the powerful landed aristocracy. By the very fact of claiming the areas of property, contract and family for private, civil law, the Code was performing a quasi-constitutional function. In these three spheres, the primary role of the state was to be to protect private property, to enforce legally formed contracts, and to secure the autonomy of the patriarchal family.

At the same time that the French Civil Code was introducing new elements into the field of private law, French revolutionary ideas were contributing in important ways to the newly developing field of public law. The French Revolution and subsequent Napoleonic rule had furthered the processes of strengthening the central state and eliminating intermediate sources of power and allegiance. In this new political situation, there was little role for Roman or medieval law to play in the fashioning of the rules that henceforth would regulate the relationships of the branches and agencies of government with each other and with citizens. (Recall that the reception of Roman law was a reception mainly of Roman private, not public, law). In the nineteenth century, modern public law was emerging from a crucible where the ways of thinking about government associated with the American and French revolutions were transforming older, royal, bureaucratic traditions. To varying degrees, in different parts of the world, American, English and French ideas about equality, democracy, representative government, the separation of powers, and natural rights to life, liberty and property were helping to shape systems of public law.

In spite of all that was new in the French legal revolution, there was still much continuity with the past. First, and most obviously, continuity was provided by the sources drawn upon by Napoleon's draftsmen. With only a few months for the drafting process, and under much pressure from the First Consul, they could not, and did not try to, create a code out of whole cloth. Naturally they turned to the jus commune, the royal ordinances, the learned writing, and customary law—particularly the influential Custom of Paris, which had been conveniently reduced to writing in the sixteenth century. Like the draftsmen of other Enlightenment codes, they thought of themselves as putting all this prior legal material through a "sieve of reason", retaining or rejecting various elements according to rational principles. But the formal tripartite structure of their end product (Persons, Property and the Different Modes of Acquiring Property) remained virtually identical to that of the first three books of Justinian's Institutes. So far as the substantive rules of law were concerned, the draftsmen drew primarily, and in about equal measure, on both customary law and the jus commune.

A few innovations, such as divorce by mutual consent and the institution of adoption, are attributable to the influence of Napoleon. The great personal interest that Napoleon took in the Code was not so much in its substantive content, however, as in the fact of its existence. He wanted to be remembered as a great lawgiver. Because of the importance he accorded to the Code, he made its adoption a priority in France, and imposed it in his conquered territories—in Italy, Poland, the low countries and among the ruins of the Hapsburg Empire. In exile on St. Helena, Napoleon referred to the Code as a greater achievement than all his military victories: "One Waterloo wipes out their memory, but my civil code will live forever."

In form and style, the French Civil Code stands in marked contrast to the German Civil Code which appeared nearly a century later. The *Code civil des français* was meant to be read and understood by the citizen. With its clear, fertile and intentionally concise provisions, its style resembles that of the United States Constitution, more than it does the German Civil Code of 1896. The founding fathers of the French Civil Code, like the framers of the United States Constitution, recognized that a legislator cannot foresee all possible applications of basic principles. The draftsmen opted for the flexibility of general rules, rather than for detailed provisions. The words of one of the draftsmen, Portalis, are still frequently referred to in this connection: "We have avoided the dangerous ambition to regulate and foresee everything.... The function of law is to fix in broad outline the general maxims of justice, to establish principles rich in implications, and not to descend into the details of the questions that can arise in each subject."

## § 10.   German Legal Science

The German Civil Code (*Bürgerliches Gesetzbuch*) appeared at the end, and the French Civil Code at the beginning, of the turbulent century of the Industrial Revolution. The German Code emerged from an intellectual and political background that differed in many ways from the Enlightenment and revolutionary thought that informed the *Code Civil*. It is thus not surprising that Germany and France have inspired somewhat different sub-traditions in the civil law world. Unlike France, where political unification had been achieved long before legal unity, Germany had remained a loose confederation of kingdoms, duchies, principalities and independent city states until it was unified under Bismarck in 1871. Indeed, as we have seen, the lack of effective central government and the need for a common law to facilitate trade had set the stage for the large scale reception of the Romanist jus commune in fifteenth century Germany. However, as German scholars worked with the jus commune, a certain "renationalization" of German law gradually took place, especially in the seventeenth and eighteenth centuries. Like the Bolognese Commentators, these

German scholars were occupied with adapting the Romanist law to their own contemporary conditions. In the course of their work, which came to be known as the *usus modernus pandectarum* (Pandects was their name for the Justinian Digest), they increasingly introduced Germanic legal content into what remained a basically Romanist structure. This was particularly so in the areas of property and associations.

In the nineteenth century, as the French Civil Code began to be widely admired and imitated, the idea of codification aroused the interest of certain German jurists. By this time, Germany was already a leading center of legal scholarship on the continent, and codification became the subject of a famous scholarly dispute. In 1814, a Roman law professor named Thibaut advocated prompt adoption of a code as a means of furthering the process of political unification of Germany. Thibaut claimed that the Prussian, French and Austrian codes could serve as helpful models. The Prussian and French codes were in fact already in force in parts of Germany. Thibaut's view was disputed by members of the so-called Historical School, whose leading spokesman was Friedrich Carl von Savigny. Savigny maintained that law, like language, was part of the genius and culture of a people. It could not be derived by logic from abstract principles of natural law. Rather, he claimed, a nation's law would be revealed by the methods of historical research. It followed that a German code should not be adopted without extensive preliminary study of the development of German legal institutions.

The point of view of Savigny and the Historical School prevailed. Under the influence of their ideas, 19th century German legal scholars by and large abandoned the ahistorical natural law approach of the Enlightenment codes in favor of what they thought of as a science of law. They viewed Germanic, and classical and received Roman law as bodies of data, and regarded themselves as scientists formulating and systematizing concepts and principles from this data. Some put their principal energies into the historical investigation of indigenous law. Others, including Savigny himself, turned to Roman law—looking beyond the jus commune to ancient Roman law. There they rediscovered that the Roman jurists had been rather pragmatic individuals. If the Romans at times reflected on the methods and underlying structure of their legal system, they did not leave records of their ideas on these matters. So it came about that in nineteenth century Germany, legal scholars set themselves the task of investigating classical Roman law with the aim of discovering its "latent system", which they might adapt to the needs of their own society. In the process, they brought the study of the Digest to its highest and most systematic level, and thus became known as the Pandectists. Though the Pandectist School grew out of the Historical School, in the end it came to adopt a rather ahistorical stance toward law. Believing in the superiority and lasting validity of the legal institutions of the Romans, the

Pandectists tended to neglect social, ethical, economic and practical considerations. As at the time of the Reception, there was still no organized and powerful class of practicing lawyers in Germany to leaven this academic tendency. The methods and concepts developed by the Pandectists dominated legal scholarship in Germany just at the time the preparation of the German Civil Code began in 1874.

The work on a civil code for the new German nation turned out to be a massive project. The code went through two drafts and took over 20 years to complete. It was finally promulgated in 1896, to go into effect four years later—on the first day of the new century. In the end, the Code was neither Romanist nor Germanic, but Pandectist. It was constructed and worked out with a degree of precision that had never been seen before in any legislation. A special language was developed and employed consistently. Legal concepts were defined and then used in the same way throughout. Sentence construction indicated the location of the burden of proof. Through elaborate cross-references, all parts of the Code supposedly interlocked to form a logically closed system. The draftsmen avoided both the prolixity of the Prussian Code and the "epigrammatic brevity" of the French. Though they did not attempt to regulate in detail, their system was refined to the point where, in theory, the various parts of the Code could be made to articulate neatly about almost any given problem falling within its scope. At the beginning of the Code is the "General

Part", in which definitions, concepts and principles of great breadth are set forth. These apply to all the specific subject matter areas covered by the Code. Other pervasive general principles are established within and for particular areas of law. These general provisions are in turn often qualified or restricted by specific provisions within the various sections of the Code dealing with particular subjects. The result was not a handbook for the citizen, but a system to be operated by highly trained experts. Within the civil law world, German legal science and the German style of codification developed their own sphere of influence.

Though the German and French civil codes differ in form, style and mood, one should not lose sight of their similarities. In the first place, they both drew heavily on a common source, the jus commune, as well as on their respective national law. In both codes, the influence of the Romanist jus commune predominated in the law of obligations and in the general structure of the system, while indigenous sources were more influential in property and succession law. Secondly, there is an ideological correspondence between the two codes. Both were grounded in nineteenth century European-style liberalism. That is, they were infused with then current notions of individual autonomy, freedom of contract and private property. But over the course of the near-century that separated the two codes, society had been changing profoundly. Industrialization and much social unrest had intervened. Thus, while the German Civil Code still resembled the French in its solicitude for private property, freedom of contract and the traditional family, it also reflected a number of new developments that had occurred since 1804. Several important provisions of the German Civil Code, for example, recognize a social obligation inhering in certain private rights, as well as the idea that rights can be misused. In family law, the authority of husbands and fathers is less absolute than in the French Code. Women have somewhat more power with respect to their own property, and the definition of the family is more narrowly drawn. Certain aspects of contract and tort law show the effects of the increasing complexity of commercial transactions as well as the advance of industrialization.

In the years immediately following the promulgation of the German Civil Code, German scholars concentrated mainly on the task of making it applicable in practice by explaining its difficult text and developing its main principles. But gradually that process of interpreting the Code "out of itself" yielded diminishing returns, and the stage was set for a new phase of German legal science. A reaction against the extreme formalism of the *Pandektenrecht* had indeed already begun to set in the late nineteenth century when Rudolf von Jhering, a product of the Pandectist School himself, began to question its methods and assumptions. In a devastating satire of the movement, he placed its leading practitioners in a "heaven of legal concepts" to which no one could be admitted unless he gave up all memory of the real world. But it was not until the years following World War I that German legal science generally began to move beyond what had become a series of increasingly sterile exercises. Then, salvaging from the Pandects their genius for formulating generalizations, but joining this for the first time to an obsession with detailed facts and concrete applications, German legal science entered a new and dynamic phase until interrupted by the advent of National Socialism. With this new direction, born of the ability to relate powerful abstract reasoning to irreducible and stubborn facts, German scholars began to develop the methods that came to be associated with jurisprudence of interests, legal realism and the sociological schools of legal thought. These new ways of thinking about law entered the mainstream of American legal theory, too. Initially, the German influence was felt through the writings of Holmes and Pound, both of whom had been much impressed by the work of von Jhering. It continued to be strong in the work of the American legal scholar and codifier of commercial law, Karl Llewellyn, and was given further impetus by the many eminent German jurists who fled to the United States during the National Socialist period.

### § 11.   Distribution of the Civil Law

France and Germany probably have been less influenced by each other's law, legal institutions and scholarship than have other countries within the civil law world. The distinctive French and German codifications and styles of thought each had far-reaching influence, and to some extent their influences overlapped. Thus, a case can be made that the "typical" civil law systems today are not those of France or the Federal Republic of Germany, but rather those civil law systems which in modern times have undergone the combined influence of both. Nevertheless, in the post-codification era, French law and German legal science have remained the two principal tributaries to the modern civil law tradition.

Just as ancient Roman law was once introduced into the conquered territories of a vast empire, the French Civil Code was brought by Napoleon and his armies to Belgium, the Netherlands, parts of Poland, Italy and the western regions of Germany. Then, in the colonial era, France extended her legal influence far beyond continental Europe to parts of the Near East, Northern and sub-Saharan Africa, Indochina, Oceania, French Guiana and the French Caribbean islands. The influence of French law both outlived and went beyond the Napoleonic conquests and French colonialism, for the Code was widely admired for its own merits. Its clarity and elegance of style and its consolidation of the results of a Revolution which had abolished the old, unequal statuses and relations of feudalism inspired imitation in many countries, especially in Latin America. Thus, one can speak of a "reception" of the French Civil Code not only in countries which retained it after French armies and colonial governments withdrew, but also in countries that were untouched by French military or colonial power.

The French Civil Code remains in effect to this day, with revisions, in Belgium and Luxembourg; and was a major influence on the Netherlands Civil Code of 1838 (replaced in 1992), the Portuguese Civil Code of 1867 (replaced in 1967), the Spanish Civil Code of 1888, some of the Swiss cantonal codes, and on the legal institutions of nineteenth century Italy, as well as on those of some of the Eastern European countries. French law and legal theory remained important for France's former colonies and possessions even after they gained independence in the latter half of the twentieth century. Furthermore, when the Spanish and Portuguese empires in Latin America dissolved in the nineteenth century, it was mainly to the French Civil Code that the lawmakers of the new nations of Central and South America looked for inspiration. French culture and the French revolutionary heritage were widely admired in the Latin American countries. The language and concepts of the French codes were clear, and were already familiar because of their affinities with the legal ideas and institutions that had been introduced by the Spanish and the Portuguese. It seemed natural to turn to French law as a model.

It was another story in nineteenth century Germany, however. Though French law and legal ideas were influential in German procedural and administrative law, they had hardly any effect on the thinking that went into the late nineteenth century German private law codification. The German Civil Code of 1896 put before the world an entirely different model from the French and earlier codes, but one which appeared too late to be as widely imitated as the French. By the end of the nineteenth century nearly all the more developed countries had already adopted codes. Apart from those that had been influenced in varying degrees by the French Civil Code, there was the Austrian General Civil Code of 1811, the product of several decades of drafting under a modernizing but authoritarian monarchy, which had in turn influenced the law of some parts of Eastern Europe. The Nordic countries, where the earliest national civil codes had appeared, historically had been and remained relatively far removed from the composite of influences from which the civil law tradition was forged.

Even if the German Civil Code had not appeared relatively late in the codification era, its highly technical and complicated structure in all likelihood would have discouraged its direct transplantation to many foreign soils. Nevertheless, the German Civil Code did play a significant role in the preparation of the Italian Code of 1942, and was the major influence on the Greek Civil Code of 1940, effective in 1946. Although the German Code as a whole was not built to travel, the legal science that preceded and accompanied it has had an important influence on legal theory and doctrine in other countries, particularly in Austria, Czechoslovakia, Greece, Hungary, Italy, Switzerland and former Yugoslavia. It was one of many influences on the eclectic Brazilian Code of 1916, and on the Portuguese Code of 1967. The Japanese Civil Code drew heavily upon the first draft of the German Civil Code and, as a result, German civil law scholarship has remained important in Japan. Through Japan, the German civil law influence also spread to Korea. Since the end of World War II, however, American law, too, has had a substantial impact on the law of Japan and South Korea.

Switzerland, except for certain cantons, had remained aloof from the reception of the French Civil Code, and when Switzerland achieved legal unity through its Civil Code of 1907, and its Law of Obligations which went into effect together with the Civil Code in 1912, it did not follow either the French or the German model. A single scholarly draftsman, Eugen Huber, fashioned for the confederation a civil code that was inspired by Swiss traditions and adapted to Swiss circumstances. He drew upon German and, to a lesser extent, French sources but did not permit them to dominate. In 1926, the Swiss Civil Code (together with the Law of Obligations) was adopted, almost word for word, as the Civil Code of the newly formed Republic of Turkey.

After World War II, the civil law influence on the European continent subsided when the socialist countries of Eastern Europe adopted new civil codes. Though these codes retained many characteristic civil law features, the dramatically different socialist public law plus significant innovations in private law caused most comparatists to classify the East European systems as part of a new, socialist, family of laws. With the fall of Soviet-style regimes, however, most of the East European nations are once again showing strong affinities to the civil law tradition. Central and South American countries have looked increasingly to North American models, particularly in the areas of public, constitutional and business law. Still, the civil law system remains dominant there in other fields of law, as it is in many former French, Belgian, Spanish and Portuguese colonies in Africa. The Nordic legal systems, though touched by the Roman law revival and affected in important ways by their proximity to the modern civil law systems, are generally thought of as sui generis, set apart by several unique features both from the common law and the mainstream of the civil law.

Civil law survives in certain "mixed" legal systems such as the civil and common law hybrid systems of Louisiana, Quebec, the Philippines and Puerto Rico. Japan and South Korea have added so much civil, especially German, law, to their indigenous law, that some would classify them as being Romano–Germanic, rather than Far Eastern systems. However, in Japan and South Korea, as in Latin America, the law of the United States has had an important effect on public law. French-inspired civil law and legal theory remain influential in West Africa, and, in combination with Islamic law, in most North African states as well as in many Near and Middle Eastern countries. Civil law is also one of many elements in the complex legal systems of Israel and Lebanon. In Asia, civil law influence extended to, and combined with, other legal influences in Cambodia, Indonesia, Laos, Vietnam, Taiwan and Thailand. Finally, it should be noted that civil law and codification are not coextensive. A few places in the civil law world remained apart from the codification movements of the eighteenth and nineteenth centuries. Thus, for example, in the hybrid systems of Scotland and South Africa, the Roman jus commune survived in uncodified form, combined in the case of Scotland with common law, and in the Union of South Africa with common law and Dutch law.

As the civil law has spread and entered into combination with other legal elements, its influence has become attenuated. In the wake of codification and national law movements, each country tended to concentrate on the development of its own legal system. Legal actors turned less frequently for inspiration and ideas to the fund of sources once held in common all over Europe. As a result, it is difficult today to identify a single "civil law rule" on any given legal problem. Indeed, there is probably as much diversity among the responses of civil law systems to various legal issues as there is between civil law and common law countries. This makes it appropriate to ask what now remains that sets the civil law tradition apart from other legal traditions today. Law reform has become increasingly eclectic. Searching for legal approaches to new social problems common to many different countries, legislatures have been less concerned with the provenance than with the promise of new techniques and ideas. Outside the continental European cradle of the civil law, the received European law never fully penetrated the mores anyway, nor did it ever completely displace customary and religious laws.

Within the European continent, contemporary civil law systems are becoming in several important ways like the legal systems of other developed nations. Civil law, common law, and Nordic systems are associated ever more closely in the European Union, a fact certain to continue promoting legal convergence in many areas. What, then, if anything, besides history, links the civil law systems together?

The germ of an answer may lie in a closer examination of the various meanings of the term "civil law." Historically, the term *jus civile* (from *civis*: citizen) referred to the law applicable to Roman citizens, the law which was eventually compiled by Justinian's jurists into the Corpus Juris Civilis. Common law lawyers, and we in this Nutshell, use the phrase "civil law systems" to describe the legal systems of all those nations predominantly within the historical tradition described in the foregoing sections. But for lawyers within those systems, the term "civil law" has a narrower meaning, while some such term as "Romanist" or "Romano–Germanic" is used to designate the family relation among systems. Although the term "civil law" (*droit civil*, *Zivilrecht*) is sometimes used as a synonym for "private law", continental European lawyers usually understand it in a more limited sense: the civil law is the law relating to those subject matter areas covered by the civil codes and their auxiliary statutes. Thus, it not only does not include the entire legal system, it does not even take in all of private law if, as is usually the case, part of the private law is contained in a separate commercial code and other codes and statutes.

The continental terminology leads us closer to discerning what it is that still links the civil law systems as they move further and further from their common historical roots. At the same time, it reveals the extent to which these links are becoming looser. All the major civil codes deal with a body of substantive law within the same framework staked out by, and still similar in important respects to, Justinian's Institutes: law governing personal status, including family law; property; and obligations, which may either arise from contract or result from one's conduct. One of the great links among the "civil law systems" is that the "civil law" was for centuries, in fact, the most important and fundamental part of the legal system, and to a great extent still occupies that position in the continental legal mentality. The greatest legal scholars from the Bolognese Roman law revival to the German Pandectists devoted their lives to the study and refinement of the civil law. Their characteristic techniques of analysis, their ways of thinking about legal problems and formulating legal propositions were all developed within and for the civil law. This was all in marked contrast to the way the common law developed, with its obsession with facts and concrete situations, and its relative disdain for generalization and systematization.

Even today, though the law of the civil codes has become relatively less central in fact, the civil law remains the heart of the continental system of legal education, and thus occupies a special place in the continental legal imagination. In law faculties, in practice and in the work of legal scholars, there is not only a common fund of inherited concepts, a shared passion for theory and systematization, but more importantly, there are distinctive modes of thinking and communication. Still, it is well to remember that the edges of any system of classification of human activity are bound to be indistinct. This is especially so of legal categories. The civil law systems at the dawn of a new century are in the midst of a process of change in which the centrality of private civil law is being constantly reduced and through which the distinctiveness of the systems is somewhat diminished.

## § 12.  Contemporary Civil Law

The evolution of civil law systems over the twentieth century was closely tied to the transformation of liberal laissez-faire governments into modern social welfare states engaged in the never-ending quest for the optimal mix in a mixed economy, and for the sort of regulatory apparatus that furthers social welfare aspirations without undermining economic productivity. As noted, the classification of civil law systems proceeds as if the only law worth taking into account were the areas of law covered by the civil codes. In those areas, the classical codes established a large role for individual autonomy and foresaw a minimal role for governmental intervention. This scheme reflected then-prevailing views about individualism and the market economy. By the end of the nineteenth century, however, the forces that would transform the legal and social order were already at work. Over the twentieth century, it became clear that the gradual shift away from classical liberalism and the unfettered market economy meant a shift in emphasis from private or civil law to public and regulatory law. To varying degrees in different places, the legal order increasingly began to take on the characteristics of a bureaucratic, or administrative, order.

The dynamics of that legal change worked primarily through a movement away from the civil codes (via special legislation and judicial construction), and through code revision, constitutional law, harmonization of law within the European Union, and the acceptance through treaties and conventions of a variety of supranational legal norms. Over the twentieth century, legislation removed large areas from the coverage of the civil codes, and created entirely new areas of law outside the codes. These areas (for example: landlord-tenant law, employment law, insurance, contracts of carriage, competition and monopoly, agricultural holdings, urban housing, and consumer protection) are typically governed by special statutes in which the relatively unrestricted freedom of contract of the civil codes is replaced by a network of mandatory provisions, prohibitions on certain types of agreements, and requirements of controls, permits, licenses, and the like—often designed to protect the party perceived as at a bargaining disadvantage.

While the legislatures created new bodies of law outside the civil codes in traditionally private-law areas, the courts extensively transformed the codes by interpretation or supplemented them with bodies of new judge-made rules. Such judicial adaptation of code norms to new conditions brought into being a substantial corpus of "common law" in the form of a gloss on the legislative texts. In some systems, such as the French and those based on its model, this process was facilitated by the structural features (gaps, ambiguities and incompleteness) of the code. Since the lawmakers of 1804 never imagined such litigation-producing aspects of modern life as industrial and traffic accidents, photographic reproduction of images, and the mass circulation of publications, it is not surprising that modern French tort law is almost entirely judge-made. In later codes, such as the German and the Swiss, judicial adaptation to changing circumstances was facilitated by the so-called "general clauses", code provisions which deliberately leave a large measure of discretion to the judge.

Although traditional civil law dogma denied that judges "make" law and that judicial decisions can be a source of law, actors in contemporary civil law systems more and more openly acknowledge the inescapable dependence of legislation on the judges and administrators who interpret and apply it. There is, of course, a lively discussion in civil law and common law systems alike regarding the scope, limits, and legitimacy of the power of judges to apply legislative and constitutional norms to new and changing circumstances.

To some extent, the legislatures themselves have kept the civil codes up to date by amending their texts. The German Civil Code in particular has been amended frequently in recent years. But given the magnitude of social change since their original adoption, many civil codes have been revised less frequently and less extensively than might be expected. Indeed, many civil law countries have changed governments and constitutions more readily than they have amended their civil codes. (To the extent this has been the case, the codes resemble the U.S. Constitution more than they do American statutes.) Code revision has been particularly extensive in the area of family law. Many of the family law reforms were either prompted or made necessary by post World War II constitutional provisions or international conventions promoting new ideals of equality and liberty that were at variance in several respects with the traditional family law of the civil codes. In other areas, where the interests of organized economic groups are more affected, the legislatures have often found it hard to make necessary reforms within the structure of the civil codes. They have resorted instead to statutes outside the codes which are more easily amended as circumstances change.

Contemporary legislation and code revision differ in several important respects from the earlier classical codifications. In the first place, law reform has tended to be marked by more eclecticism. This often takes the form of using comparative law to investigate approaches and solutions to common social problems even if the country whose law is being studied does not happen to be a member of the civil law family.

That tendency was evident in the new civil code of the Netherlands, which went into effect in 1992. The Dutch drafters drew not only on a variety of continental European models, but on the common law and on international conventions. With the presence of non-civil law countries (England, Ireland, and the Nordic nations) in the European Union, it can be expected that the exchange of ideas among common law, civil law and Nordic systems will accelerate. This is not only because of the "harmonization of law" provisions of European treaties, but simply as a result of increased communication, mobility and cooperation. Second, modern law reform tends to take greater account of diversity in society, in contrast to the civil codes which typically upheld one model of behavior for all. Third, contemporary lawmakers are more pragmatic than the drafters of the Enlightenment codes or the highly abstract German Civil Code. This may reflect a decline in the belief in universally valid legal postulates and a greater emphasis on law as a social system. Thus, private law reform in European countries today is often preceded by considerable fact and opinion research. In this way, sociology has found a place with comparative law among the tools of the lawmaker. Finally, contemporary civil law shows an increased awareness of the limits of law, and has become more modest as well as more sophisticated in its attempts to control and regulate many kinds of behavior.

Taken together, the shift from private to public law, the influence of new ideas about fundamental rights, the legislatures' eclecticism, pragmatism, and their senses of social diversity and the limits of law, tend in the long run to blur the distinctions between civil law systems and the legal systems of other modern states. Nevertheless, significant differences remain. Often subtle, they show up as often in the area of mental processes, in styles of argumentation, and in the organization and methodology of law as in positive legal norms. Thus, the distinctive characteristics of the civil law systems will become more apparent as we take up the subjects of legal education, the role of scholars, ideas concerning the divisions of the law, the working of the codes, and the judicial process, as they exist in the contemporary civil law world.

# CHAPTER 2

# LEGAL STRUCTURES IN CIVIL LAW NATIONS

## § 1. Parliamentary Government

As we have seen, the classification "civil law systems" has no necessary connection with public law and government. Nevertheless, if one were to categorize different countries according to the structure and relations of the organs of their governments, most of the civil law nations would be found to have governments of the type known as parliamentary. But since many common law countries, England in particular, also have the parliamentary form of government, one cannot say this is a hallmark of civil law systems. Moreover, a number of civil law nations outside Europe, notably in Latin America, have adopted a presidential, rather than a parliamentary, model. France, since 1958, has gone far in this direction as well.

Parliamentary government is the form of constitutional government in which the executive authority emerges from, and is responsible to, the democratically elected legislative authority. Thus, it differs from the presidential government of countries like the United States where the members of the executive branch and the legislature are elected independently of each other. Within the essential union of the legislative and executive branches that characterizes the parliamentary form of government, the legislature is supreme. The chief executive, the prime minister, usually is appointed by the head of state (a constitutional monarch or a ceremonial president chosen by the parliament). The head of state must choose as prime minister a person whom a parliamentary majority would elect. Thus, in practice, the prime minister normally is the leader of the majority party. The prime minister chooses the executive heads of government departments, the most important of whom constitute the cabinet. Together, the prime minister and the cabinet are known in parliamentary systems as "the government."

The government holds office only so long as it commands majority support in the legislature. The importance of continuing parliamentary support for the government is evidenced by the fact that the government regularly submits its program and its record for parliamentary approval. An adverse legislative vote on an important issue indicates a lack of confidence which requires the government either to resign or to try to secure a new parliamentary majority by means of a general election. Thus, the familiar American phenomenon of stalemate between an executive of one party and a legislature of another is meant to be impossible. Technically, the decision to dissolve parliament and call for new elections, like the choice of prime minister, belongs to the head of state. But in practice the head of state exercises this power only on the advice of the prime minister.

The parliamentary system has taken different forms from country to country. Thus the foregoing description of its typical features will not apply in all respects to every country whose government is organized in this general form. France, in particular, has become a special case. There, under the 1958 constitution of the Fifth French Republic, reflecting the extraordinary personal authority of President Charles de Gaulle, the powers of the head of state were increased to the point where the power of the executive is on an equal footing with that of parliament. The French president not only possesses substantial powers under the constitution (including that of dissolving parliament), but, since 1962, is chosen by direct universal suffrage. Thus, the president may have a popular mandate independent of parliament. This has led many observers within and without France to consider that France has ceased to have a parliamentary system and has instead a hybrid system with features of both presidential and parliamentary types.

The parliamentary system became the pattern in the twentieth century for governments in many of the new nations that emerged from colonial control in Africa and Asia. Japan, too, has followed this model. The former French colonies in Africa, however, have tended to follow France in receding from the parliamentary form. After the fall of communism in Eastern Europe, the parliamentary governments of those countries were once again based on competitive elections.

The student of comparative law should keep in mind that in some civil law countries, such as Germany, the existence of a federal system introduces important local legal structures. As in the United States, federalism creates more complexity in the legal system than is present in unitary states like England and France. The German system is, however, closer to a unitary form of government than to American-style federalism in two important respects. In the first place, the bulk of German law—criminal and civil—is federal. Secondly, federal law organizes all state and federal courts into a single nationwide system, so that the characteristic legal problems of American federalism concerning internal choice of law or forum are practically nonexistent in Germany.

## § 2.  Separation of Powers

Separation of powers means something quite different in the European context from what it has come to mean in the United States. Historically, notions about the proper distribution of power among the organs of government were shaped in England and in Europe generally by the struggles of representative assemblies against the rule of monarchs. In France, the doctrine of separation of powers was further affected by the profound revolutionary reaction there against the rearguard role that the judiciary had played in the *ancien régime*. This background is in marked contrast to the United

States where neither the fear of "government by judges" nor the dogma of legislative supremacy played much of a role in the formative period. Many of the framers of the American Constitution did fear, however, the unprecedented power of relatively popular state legislatures as a threat to property and commerce. Therefore, Chief Justice Marshall in *Marbury v. Madison* did not have to contend with the sorts of deep-seated attitudes that in Europe posed powerful obstacles to the establishment of judicial review. Separation of powers to an American evokes the familiar system of checks and balances among the three coordinate branches of government—legislative, executive and judicial—each with its independent constitutional basis. To a European, separation of powers is a more rigid doctrine, inseparable from the notion of legislative supremacy.

We have already seen the significance of the doctrine of legislative supremacy for the role of the executive in parliamentary governments. So far as the judiciary is concerned, the doctrine in its extreme form not only has been thought to exclude judicial power to review the legality of legislative, executive and administrative action, but has even been invoked to deny the courts a "lawmaking" function via interpretation of legislative texts. However, these "logical" implications of legislative supremacy have not prevented modern civil law systems from moving toward various forms of judicial review nor have they diminished the growing de facto importance of case law.

The rigid European version of separation of powers had long lasting effects on the structure of the court systems in most civil law countries. The principle of legislative supremacy and, in France, traditional mistrust of the judiciary, seemed to rule out the possibility of judicial review of the legality of administrative action or of adjudication by ordinary courts of disputes between agencies of the government. Yet some institutional mechanism for dealing with these matters was clearly needed. In France this was made one of the responsibilities of the Council of State (*Conseil d'Etat*), the central organ of governmental administration. A number of nations including Belgium and Italy followed the French model. In other nations, such as Austria and Germany, such disputes are handled by the judiciary, but within a separate system of administrative courts. Thus, the typical civil law system contains at least two (and sometimes more) separate sets of courts for administrative and private law matters, each with its own supreme court, its own procedural and substantive rules, and its own jurisdiction. This is in striking contrast with the unified American system, where a single set of courts within each state and at the federal level hears both public and private law matters and even has authority to review the legality of the actions of the other branches of government.

## § 3.  Constitutions

Two countries whose civil codes exerted great influence on the development of similar codes around the world—France and Germany—demonstrate the role a national constitution can have within the structure of government. The Basic Law for the Federal Republic of Germany emerged out of the end of the Second World War and survived to embrace the reunification of west with east in 1990. France's Constitution of the Fifth Republic was adopted in 1958 under the leadership of Charles de Gaulle and continues today.

The fundamental rights guaranteed by these constitutions would inevitably come into contact with the prevailing civil codes. In some ways, the codes precede the constitutions in time *and* in substance. The French code outlasted enough governments and historical turmoil to be considered the "real" constitution of the land, while the systematic breadth and length of the German Civil Code address nearly all areas of private law. Yet the constitutions make certain claims that limit the codes in turn, empowering constitutional courts, or the specially created Constitutional Council in France, to strike down laws, even those in the code, as unconstitutional.

## § 4. Judicial Review

Despite the difficulties that traditionally stood in the way of judicial review of the constitutionality of legislative and executive action in civil law countries, there was a decisive movement after World War II toward the establishment of some form of constitutional control over governmental power. This was especially so in those countries that adopted constitutions containing guarantees of fundamental rights, and where the constitution cannot be amended by ordinary legislation.

The introduction of judicial review took different forms in different countries. As is the case with parliamentary government, classifications of legal systems in this area do not always coincide with civil law-common law lines of demarcation. Indeed, so far as judicial review is concerned, France and England fall within one group of countries where its existence is, in a technical sense, still denied, while Italy, Germany and the United States come within another group where power to review legislation for conformity to the constitution not only exists but is vigorously exercised by the courts. In between are several countries which to varying degrees have admitted the practice, but where the courts have been relatively cautious in implementing it. In recent years, however, the practice of judicial review at the national level has increased under the influence of the European Court of Justice and the European Court of Human Rights (see infra).

The peculiar history of the judiciary in France— its identification with feudal oppression, its role in retarding even moderate reforms in pre-revolutionary France, the post-revolutionary reaction against, and the vestigial distrust of, judges, plus the comparatively non-prestigious role of the modern civil-servant judge—has militated against placing the power to review the constitutionality of legislation in the judiciary. The ordinary civil courts are not even permitted to review the legality of administrative action, this task being reserved to the administrative tribunals within the executive branch. So, when France in 1958 instituted a system of constitutional review of laws passed by the National Assembly, it created a special new governmental organ, the Constitutional Council. This body is authorized to review legislation, but only at the request of the executive or a specified proportion of the legislature, only *before* promulgation, and only for the limited purpose of ascertaining whether the laws are in conformity with the constitutional division of powers between the executive and legislative branches.

Though originally meant by de Gaulle to be a mere "watchdog" of the prerogatives of the executive, the Council greatly expanded its own authority in a landmark 1971 decision. In that ruling the Council claimed for itself, and has since exercised, the power to review laws (upon proper petition and prior to their taking effect) for conformity with the Constitution generally, including the unwritten "fundamental principles" of the French republican tradition. Thus, even France is slowly moving away from the older, rigid view of legislative supremacy.

In Austria, Italy and Germany, constitutional courts were established after World War II as part of the judicial system. These constitutional courts are special separate institutions within the judiciary with their own jurisdiction and judges. In Germany, when a party raises a constitutional objection to a statute involved in any civil, criminal or administrative case, the court hearing the case will refer the question to the Constitutional Court for decision if it thinks that the statute is unconstitutional. After the decision of the Constitutional Court is issued, the original proceeding is resumed. In contrast to France, where the courts are not competent to sanction violations of individual constitutional rights, the German Constitutional Court also hears complaints filed by individuals aggrieved by allegedly unconstitutional official actions, provided they have first exhausted their other remedies. In addition, certain governmental agencies or officials can test the validity of a statute in the Constitutional Court even though the statute is not involved in an existing dispute. The decisions of the Constitutional Court, unlike those of ordinary courts, are binding on other courts in future litigation, but not on the Constitutional Court itself.

## § 5.  Public Law Courts

In a typical civil law system, the various types of disputes that are handled by courts of general jurisdiction in the United States are entrusted to two or more separate hierarchies of specialized courts, each with its own supreme court. The jurisdiction of the ordinary courts typically is limited to criminal law and private law disputes. The tribunals which adjudicate most public law matters and most disputes in which the government is a party are separate from the ordinary courts. In some countries, as in France, the administrative courts are within the executive rather than the judicial branch, although care is taken to assure their independence from regular executive functions. In other countries, Germany for example, the administrative courts are one of two main court systems within the judiciary.

In either model, it is necessary to have some mechanism for resolving disputes concerning which court system has jurisdiction over a particular case. In France, a special Tribunal of Conflicts has been created to decide whether a case falls within the administrative or the ordinary jurisdiction. In the German system, where there are a number of separate hierarchies of courts, the basic rule is that the courts have power to determine their own jurisdiction and to transfer cases over which they decline jurisdiction. A final decision refusing jurisdiction is binding in the transferee court, which may, however, transfer the case to still another court system.

Although the French model was shaped by specifically French historical circumstances, it has been more widely imitated than the German system of separate judicial jurisdictions. Because modern administrative law largely took shape in the nineteenth century, the French experience was the principal model available to other countries as they searched for mechanisms to control their rapidly growing public administrations. As noted earlier, the French revolutionary doctrine of separation of powers seemed to require that the actions of administrative bodies and disputes among or involving them should not be subject to control by the judiciary. Thus the administrative dispute-settling mechanism had to be located elsewhere. In Napoleonic times this authority was vested in the Council of

State (*Conseil d'Etat*) which began as a body of advisors to the king under the old regime and later developed into the central organ of governmental administration. The membership of the present Council of State is composed of professional public administrators, whose backgrounds and training are quite different from those of the ordinary judiciary. (In the terminology commonly used in Europe, the "administration" is the civil service, while the "government" consists of the prime minister and the cabinet).

To this day, the Council of State performs its dispute-settling function through special "sections" which are separate from its regular administrative functions. In the first instance, an administrative dispute normally is brought before one of several lower administrative courts. The Council of State functions as the highest appellate court for this system, and also as the court of first and last instance for certain types of cases, such as where the constitutional status of an administrative act is challenged. It will be recalled that constitutional review by the Constitutional Council extends only to parliamentary legislation, not to other governmental actions. But under the 1958 French Constitution, the legislature has power to legislate only in enumerated areas, leaving an extensive residuary law-making power to the executive. In a landmark decision of 1959 (*Syndicat Général des Ingenieurs– Conseils*), the Council of State boldly asserted, and has since regularly exercised, power to review this "executive legislation". The surprising result is that an institution which is, at least theoretically, part of the executive branch has the exclusive power to review the legality or constitutionality of the acts of the executive. The great independence and prestige of the Council of State, however, support it in its assumed role as an unofficial, second constitutional court in France.

Of the countries that have followed the French model, Belgium and Italy have done so rather closely, while most others have considerably varied and adapted it to suit their own circumstances over the years. Some of the developing nations which have followed French law in other respects, have adopted a unified court system for want of a sufficient number of judges to staff a dual hierarchy of courts.

Historically in Germany, unlike in France, the idea of separation of powers was not understood to require the administrative courts to be outside the judicial system. Rather they constitute one of five principal separate court systems within the judiciary. In contrast to the United States, where a single federal Supreme Court stands at the apex of a pyramid of all lower and intermediate federal courts (with considerable power over state judicial determinations), Germany has several judicial pyramids, each with its own jurisdiction and each headed by its own Supreme Court. The two main hierarchies are the ordinary (civil and criminal) courts headed by the *Bundesgerichtshof*, and the administrative courts, headed by the *Bundesverwaltungsgericht*. In addition, there are hierarchies of labor courts, tax courts and social security courts. The highest court in each system is a federal court, but the trial courts and intermediate appellate courts are state courts. The Federal Constitutional Court, with its two chambers known as "Senates", is yet another separate part of this system, not only exercising the power of judicial review, but also hearing complaints about violations of constitutional rights and deciding disputes of a constitutional nature among the various governmental organs and entities.

The German administrative courts have jurisdiction over public law disputes generally, except for constitutional issues, and except for those administrative matters which have been assigned to the specialized tax and social security courts. There are three levels of administrative jurisdiction: the administrative tribunals, intermediate appellate courts, and the *Bundesverwaltungsgericht* which is the supreme administrative court.

### § 6.   Ordinary Courts

Just as the civil law is the heart of the substantive law in civil law countries, the so-called "ordinary courts" which hear and decide the great range of civil and criminal litigation are the core of the judicial system. These courts are the modern-day successors to the various civil and criminal courts that existed in Europe during the long period of the *jus commune*, before the modern state with its panoply of public and administrative law came into being. In the post-codification era, the main concern of the ordinary courts became the interpretation and application of the basic codes, but today they deal with a great body of law that is not found within the civil, commercial and criminal codes. The ordinary courts of first instance may include a number of specialized courts, such as family courts and criminal courts ... Intermediate appellate courts, as well as the highest court, usually sit in specialized panels or chambers.

In the French system and its variants, the ordinary law courts and the administrative law courts form two separate and independent hierarchies, the public law system headed by the administrative Council of State, while the private and criminal law system is headed by the Court of Cassation (*Cour de Cassation*) on the other. Technically, only the private-law system constitutes what is known as the "judicial order." The Tribunal of Conflicts stands between the two systems as a kind of traffic officer for jurisdictional disputes. At the first level of ordinary court jurisdiction, several specialized courts co-exist with the regular civil and criminal trial courts. Matters arising under the Commercial Code, for example, are first heard in one of France's many commercial courts where the part-time judges (sitting in panels of three) are businessmen elected by their colleagues. Disputes between employers and individual employees in the first instance are brought before one of the labor courts (*Conseils de Prud'hommes*) where two elected representatives each from labor and management sit together. These labor courts attempt to settle disputes first by conciliation. If the matter proceeds to adjudication, and the judges become deadlocked, a professional judge sits with the panel. There are also special courts for agricultural leases and social security disputes. Except where minor civil or criminal matters are involved, courts of the first instance are collegial.

An appeal from a court of first instance is heard in the Court of Appeal within whose territorial jurisdiction the lower court is situated. At the highest level, the Court of Cassation has jurisdiction over the ordinary courts of the entire country. It is composed of about 125 judges who sit in varying combinations on panels in six specialized chambers (five civil and one criminal), and, in certain situations, in mixed chambers or plenary assembly.

In the German system, there are not two, but several, independent court systems, each with its own supreme court. The "ordinary jurisdiction" there includes all the criminal and civil (including commercial) cases which are handled within the regular courts, and labor cases which are handled in a separate Federal Labor Court system. Traditionally, in Germany, as in most other civil law countries, the first-instance courts of general jurisdiction have sat in panels consisting of a presiding judge and two associate judges. However, legislation in the 1970s made it possible for many types of cases to be decided by a single judge. In commercial matters, the judge of first instance sits with two lay judges who are specialists in this field. Appeals from the first instance are heard in an intermediate appellate court (*Oberlandesgericht*), with final review by the Federal Supreme Court (*Bundesgerichtshof*). In the labor court system, appeals from the lower courts are taken first to the Labor Court of the state where the lower court is located, and finally to the Federal Labor Court. At the first and second levels, the judge acts in consultation with labor and management representatives.

# CHAPTER 3

# LEGAL ACTORS IN THE CIVIL LAW TRADITION

A legal system, like any other system, needs to be understood as a dynamic process involving a group of functionally related, mutually conditioning, interdependent elements, which together give the system its special character. The formal legal structures just examined are but one set of such elements. None of these structures is a necessary feature of a civil law system. However, these institutions enter into a nation's legal culture, absorbing particular characteristics from, and imparting them to, that underlying culture. We have briefly traced the historical evolution of the common legal culture of civil law systems. Now it is time to turn to the modern-day individuals who have inherited this tradition and who will set its future course—the practicing lawyers, the judges, the attorneys in government service, the prosecutors and professors. It is they who give life and a distinctive imprint to the legal structures of their societies. The way a society defines their legal roles and the status it accords to them is as revealing of its legal culture as are the composition and the relations of the organs of government. Of equal importance are the formation and identity of the legal actors who are assigned or permitted to play these roles. Therefore, our next step into the legal culture of the civil law world takes us to law school.

## § 1.  Legal Education

What might first strike an American lawyer as a major difference between legal education in the civil law countries and in our own system is that civil law training is undergraduate university education. Like most college training everywhere, it tends to be general and interdisciplinary rather than professional. But this way of organizing legal studies is also found in England. What is really distinctive about civil law legal education grows out of its methodology, which perpetuates the tradition of scholar-made law, just as our "case method" emerged from and contributes to the maintenance of the common law tradition of judge-made law. In both cases, there is a certain discrepancy between the traditional image and the present-day reality. In fact, a good argument can be made that changes now occurring will in the long run eliminate many of the differences between the civil and common law systems of legal education. At present, however, legal education in both systems still draws its basic approach from the historical circumstances under which it developed. In England, legal education from early times was in the hands of the *bar*. On the continent, from the time of the Roman law revival, it was the province of the *universities*.

Against this background, it is not surprising that one of the greatest differences between legal education in common law and civil law systems appears in the manner in which the student is initiated into the study of law. While an American law student typically spends the first days of law school reading cases and having his or her attention directed over and over again to their precise facts, a student of the civil law is provided at the outset with a systematic overview of the framework of the entire legal system. The introductory text (a treatise, not a casebook) may even include a diagram depicting "The Law" as a tree, with its two great divisions, public and private, branching off into all their many subdivisions and categories—each of which will become, in turn, the subject of later study in a curriculum consisting mainly of required courses. The first year "introduction to law" course itself is apt to be taught by a professor of civil law and to deal mainly with the basic concepts of private law, the law of the civil codes.

While the common law student is taught to mistrust generalization and is expected to ferret out individually whatever patterns and structure are there to be found, the civil law beginner is kept at a certain distance from the facts of particular cases. He or she starts out with a ready-made version of the overall organization, methods and principles of the system. The student is introduced to a particular style of legal reasoning and learns what some civilians have called "the grammar of law": a network of precise interrelated concepts, broad principles and classificatory ideas. All this is in keeping with the tradition of legal science so firmly ingrained in the civil law culture.

The methods of civil law legal education are a natural outgrowth of its principles. Teaching materials ordinarily consist of systematic treatises and, where appropriate, an annotated code. Typically the professor lectures rather than engaging in discussion with the class. It is not uncommon for one professor to have several hundred students in traditional lecture courses. Lectures and treatises alike are relatively less concerned with practical application of legal theory and with concrete social problems than class discussion and teaching materials in a common law system would be.

Much has happened in recent years, however, to lessen these contrasts. Both common law and civil law schools are seeking a better balance between theory and practice. American law professors increasingly consider the case method only one of several useful pedagogical devices, while civil law faculties have come to recognize the importance of practical work, tutorials and small classes where discussion is possible. In Europe, where nearly all legal education is public, there has been considerable pressure to modernize the curriculum. In response, many European universities are making legal education less general and more professional.

## § 2.  Legal Professions

Undergraduate legal education of the kind just described is not meant to produce lawyers who are ready to embark immediately on the practice of law.

In fact, many students who "major" in law in civil law countries do not do so with a view toward becoming legal practitioners. By graduation, a student has acquired facility in the grammar of law and a knowledge of the basic principles of the most important fields of law, but has only a limited ability to do legal research and a nodding familiarity with the practical aspects of law. In contrast, the American law graduate is supposed to be prepared to do any kind of legal work (although some kind of informal apprenticeship is needed before a beginning lawyer in the United States is capable of handling many matters alone). If the civil law graduate wants to enter a branch of the legal profession, some further formal practical training is required.

The type and duration of such training varies from country to country and often depends in part on the kind of legal career the graduate wishes to pursue. The civil law graduate is faced upon graduation or shortly thereafter with a choice among the various branches of the profession, a choice which is likely to be final. In a fundamental way this puts the civil law graduate in a quite different position from that of a budding American lawyer. It is uncommon for a civil law lawyer to change, as American lawyers often do, from one kind of legal career to another, or to combine careers during one's professional life. Once trained to be a practicing lawyer, a judge, a civil servant or a scholar, the civil law lawyer is more apt to remain so than a common law lawyer, though the latter often experiences a gradual reduction in mobility over time through increased specialization.

In France, the crucial choice is made early since different kinds of practical training are required for different branches of the profession. The German *Referendar* system, which serves as an apprentice- ship program for several different types of legal careers, gives the law graduate more time and a better opportunity to make an informed choice of career. There, all law graduates must pass a "first state examination", somewhat similar to our bar examinations, in order to be eligible to enter a required practical training period *(Referendarzeit)*. This is a two-year internship spent in different "stations" each corresponding to a different branch of the profession. For example, one might divide the apprenticeship among a court, a legal aid bureau, a private firm, a government agency, and the public prosecutor's office. The internship is then followed by a "second state examination," after which the young lawyer generally settles upon a career path.

The European Union, in keeping with the impor- tance it places on the free movement of goods, capital and services within the EU, has issued sev- eral directives aimed at facilitating the transnation- al practice of law. Some directives regulate the recognition of foreign diplomas, others the use of professional titles, and still others the conditions that may be imposed upon lawyers from one mem- ber state wishing to practice in another member state. A 1998 directive, amended in 2001, gives any lawyer qualified to practice in his home country the right to practice in any other member state, and, after three years of such practice, to be admitted to the profession in the host state. Despite such initiatives, the integration of the legal profession has proceeded slowly in the EU, owing to significant differences in the structure of the profession from country to country, and, of course, to language differences. Accordingly, in recent years the European Commission undertaken initiatives aimed at developing a European strategy for common judicial training and at developing a common European legal culture.

## § 3. Private Practice

In order to enter private practice, the civil law graduate must ordinarily prepare for and pass a special examination and serve a practical internship in a legal setting, as under the German system just described. In France, however, there is no such multi-purpose training period. A French law student who wishes to become a practicing lawyer must first obtain the *licence en droit* (the university degree awarded after three years of law study); the *maîtrise* (the degree awarded upon successful completion of a fourth year); and then pass a bar examination. Upon passing the bar, the graduate becomes a probationary lawyer for at least three years, during which time there is further course work and practical training.

In most civil law countries, the practicing legal profession is officially divided to some extent, at least between lawyers and notaries. The *notary* occupies a special position in civil law systems. Unlike the common law figure with the same name, the civil law notary is an important legal personage. The notary has three major functions: drafting certain documents such as marriage contracts, wills, mortgages, and conveyances; certifying documents which then have a special evidentiary status in court proceedings; and serving as a an official depositary for the original copies of wills and the like. Part of the uniqueness of the notary's position comes from the fact that a notary is a public official with a state-protected monopoly over some of these functions (typically marriage contracts and mortgages) within a given region. There are a limited number of notarial offices established by law. If a law graduate wishes to be a notary, he or she must pass a special examination and then wait for a vacancy. Unlike the regular lawyer, a notary is supposed to be impartial and to instruct and advise all parties involved in the transactions he or she handles. Because of the nature of these transactions, the notary often becomes a trusted family legal advisor whose assistance is needed in connection with the property aspects of such major events as marriages, divorces and death of a family member.

Whether or not the bar is officially divided, there tends to be in most civil law countries, as in the United States, a de facto division of labor between those lawyers who advise clients and those who appear and argue before courts, as well as among the various legal sub-specialties. In recent years, especially in the more developed countries, the practice of law has been profoundly affected by the types of legal services demanded by large enterprises. It is often observed that this kind of client requires planning and drafting more than litigation services, and that a certain bureaucratization of the private bar has resulted. The increase of lawyers engaged in serving large organizations has brought about an expansion of the roles of the legal consultant and the notary, and, although small law firms have been the rule in civil law countries, a trend has emerged toward larger-sized firms. At the same time, with the expansion of government in modern times, large public bureaucracies have absorbed increasing numbers of lawyers.

## § 4.  Government Lawyers

As in common law countries, many civil law graduates enter government service after completing their training and examinations. In some places, Germany for example, lawyers dominate the higher offices in the civil service, while in others, such as France, the various official bureaus and agencies are apt to be staffed by persons who have been trained in a prestigious special school of public administration. In Italy and Spain, a central government agency serves as the "law firm of the state", providing legal advice and representation to other government departments.

The public prosecutor in civil law countries is a civil servant, too. Like a district attorney in the United States, the public prosecutor prepares and argues the government's case in criminal matters. But in this role he is much more an officer of the court than an American prosecutor normally is. In most civil law systems, the prosecutor has an additional function—that of representing the public interest in certain ordinary civil cases. On the theory that the parties to such proceedings will not always provide the judge with a full presentation of the facts and law, and will never provide an impartial view, the prosecutor is permitted, and in some cases required, to intervene in civil cases. In this role, the prosecutor is supposed to represent the interest of "society" as distinct from the interest of the state. Some civil law systems, like the German, are content to let the judge perform this function.

An interesting aspect of the position of the public prosecutor in Italy and France is that the prosecutor is a member of the judiciary. A prosecutor follows the same course of training as a judge, and they both may move from one role to the other in the course of their advancement in the civil service. In France, the judges are known as the *magistrature assise* (sitting judiciary) and the prosecutors as the *magistrature débout.* (standing judiciary). In Germany, although the prosecutor is not technically a member of the judiciary, he or she is not strictly separate from it either. There, too, prosecutors and judges move easily from one position to the other.

## § 5.  Judiciary

A law student in a common law country who gives any thought to becoming a judge one day is

apt to consider a judgeship as a far-off dream—
something one might look forward to as a recognition of outstanding performance at the bar. In some
American states, judges are chosen by popular election, rather than being appointed. In civil law systems, by contrast, a judicial career is just one of
many options open to a beginner. A new law graduate who aspires to be a judge can expect to be
sitting on the bench as soon as he or she completes
a training period and successfully passes an examination. This is because the judiciary, except at the
highest levels, is just another civil service hierarchy
in civil law countries. A young judge enters at the
lowest level and over time works up through a
regular series of promotions. Ordinarily, only positions on the highest courts are open to distinguished practitioners or professors as well as to
career civil servants. Lateral entry into the judiciary
at any level is uncommon.

In some countries, such as France, Spain and
Japan, there are special schools for training judges.
In others, such as Germany and the Nordic countries, judicial training is acquired in the post-law
school practical internship period. In Germany, for
example, a law graduate may be appointed to a
lower court after completing the *Referendar* period
and passing the Second State Examination. After
serving a three-to-four year probationary period, he
or she becomes eligible for an appointment for life.
In France, the first step to becoming a judge is to
pass an annual competitive examination for which
students prepare by taking a special program in

their last year of law studies. Successful candidates then must undergo 28 months of further training consisting of a period of formal study at the National School of the Judiciary in Bordeaux, followed by a series of short practical internships in such settings as police departments, law offices, prisons and the Ministry of Justice in Paris. This training culminates in a judicial apprenticeship, during which the future judge participates on a daily basis in all the activities of a variety of courts. Upon completion of their training period, the students are ranked on the basis of their grades and the evaluations of supervisors, and then assigned to their first positions in the judicial system. Since the administrative law courts in France technically are not part of the judiciary, but rather belong to the administration, most judges for these courts are drawn, not from the lawyers trained in the National School of the Judiciary, but from the civil servants trained in the National School of Administration.

One advantage of the civil law systems of judicial recruitment is that they make the career more accessible to members of diverse groups in society. It is striking that there are proportionately more women judges in European countries than in the United States. Another advantage is that the civil law system provides greater assurance that all judges will be able to perform in a competent manner. The likelihood of a person with no particular qualifications becoming a judge is practically ruled out. On the debit side, however, it is frequently observed that civil law judges, because of their standardized training, tend to share a common out-look. Some observers believe that the judges' concerns about advancement promote a civil-service mentality which discourages initiative and independence.

Though there are signs of change, the judge still has a relatively low profile in most civil law systems. John Merryman has described the standard image of the civil law judge as that of "a civil servant who performs important but essentially uncreative functions." While the common law tradition reveres the names of the great judges who created the system and accords prestige and power to their modern successors, the names of civil law judges of the past are hardly remembered and their present-day successors work largely in obscurity. The tendency toward judicial anonymity is reinforced by the fact that civil law judges, even at the lowest levels, usually sit in panels and their decisions are presented per curiam, rather than being signed by individual judges. Except in a few courts, such as the German Constitutional Court, any disagreement among the judges will not show, either in the form of a dissenting opinion, or in a notation of the judges' votes.

Today this area of contrast between the civil and common law systems is diminishing somewhat as lower court judgeships in the United States cease to attract the best candidates, while appointments to certain civil law high courts, such as the German Constitutional Court, tend to be made from among outstanding jurists. As with the bar, bureaucratization seems to be responsible for a certain convergence. Increased litigation and crowded dockets have made much of the work of American judges administrative in nature, at the same time that civil law judges and their societies are slowly becoming conscious of the real law-making power of the judiciary. Furthermore, the German experience shows that prestige and civil service are not mutually exclusive. Nevertheless, in contemporary reality as well as in folklore, the common law judge remains a more powerful, creative and respected figure than his or her civil law counterpart.

One need not search far for the historical roots of the difference. From the time the administration of English justice was centralized in the King's Courts at Westminster by the end of the thirteenth century, the law was developed by judges, and the practicing bar dominated legal education. Although there were moments in history when things might have gone differently, the existence of a powerful English legal profession was an important, perhaps the crucial, factor in blocking an English "reception" of the Roman law brought back by English scholars from Bologna, and in checking the influence and power of university legal scholars. In our historical survey of the civil law tradition, we have seen that the central actors were not judges, but great law-givers, like Justinian and Napoleon, together with the great scholars. Next to these towering figures, the judges are almost invisible. This was so even in the classical Roman times when the lay *judex* who decided cases and the *praetor* who gave him the formulae for decisions turned to the Juris-consult for expert advice on the law. We have also seen how medieval judges depended on University law faculties for opinions on the law. The idea of the judge as a legal actor without inherent law-making power, who applies the will of the sovereign and looks outside for advice, is thus quite deeply rooted. When French judges, in support of the social order of the *ancien régime*, began to break out of this traditional judicial role and to behave more like English judges, making new rules and dealing crea-tively with the sources of law, they became the targets of revolutionary fury and post-revolutionary reaction. Then, when French ideas, law and institu-tions spread to other countries in the nineteenth century, this reinforced the traditional civil law conception of the judicial function as a strictly limit-ed one.

The narrow conception of the judge's role is no-where so evident as in France. We have seen that the doctrine of legislative supremacy took an espe-cially rigid form there, to the point of forbidding judges to announce general rules when deciding cases, and denying that law could be made by judges. Indeed, to this day, French legal writers say that the judiciary is not really a third "branch" of government. From this proposition it seemed at first to follow, logically, that a court could not decide a case on the basis of its own or even a higher court's prior decision. The judge was merely to find and apply the law made by the legislative representatives of the people. Today, France has long since retreated from the extremes of these positions, but civil law judges in most countries still are far from exercising the kind of leadership that traditionally characterizes their American and English counterparts.

## § 6.  Legal Scholars

When the renowned sociologist Max Weber turned his attention to the study of the world's legal systems, he observed that each had been decisively shaped by a particular group of leaders to whom he gave the name *Rechtshonoratioren*, the honored men of the law. The religious legal systems of Islamic, Jewish and Hindu secular communities were fashioned by theologians. The English common law was the creation of those judges whom Blackstone called the "living oracles" of the law. And, as we have seen, European continental laws received their characteristic features through the work of learned jurists.

It is the names of scholars, not judges, that have come down to us over the centuries of the civil law tradition, as the centers of high legal learning shifted from ancient Rome, to sixth century A.D. Byzantium, to thirteenth century Bologna, to sixteenth century France and Germany, to seventeenth century Holland and back to Germany in the nineteenth century. The civil law world venerates such names as Gaius, Bartolus, Domat, Pothier, Grotius, Pufendorf, Savigny, Gény and Jhering, as the common law world does Coke, Mansfield, Marshall, Story, Holmes, Hand, and Cardozo.

In our historical introduction, we traced the ascendancy of academic jurists in the civil law world through the nineteenth century. The longstanding practice of judges to ask professors for their opinions in difficult cases was, in some places, institutionalized, so that binding decisions in lawsuits were actually rendered by university faculties. The absence, at crucial formative periods, of centralized government and unified legal systems assisted the university scholars in gaining and holding their dominant position. As the "law" in civil law systems increasingly became codified or statutory, and as the doctrine of legislative supremacy took hold, one might well wonder why the law-maker did not fully supplant the scholar as the central actor in the civil law tradition. The answer seems to be related to the fact that it was the scholars and the professors who were the architects of the doctrine of legislative supremacy and the draftsmen of the codes (or important influences on the draftsmen). After the codes appeared, reliance on pre-code authorities declined, but the need for interpretation intensified. Legal scholars became the authoritative expounders and interpreters of the codes. The law of the codes thus remained, in an important way, scholar-made law.

This is still largely the case today so far as the civil codes are concerned. When the family law provisions of the French Civil Code were extensively recast in the 1970s, the government turned the task over to the highly respected French civil law scholar and legal sociologist, Jean Carbonnier. The situation is different, however, when we depart from the domain of the civil codes.

As civil law systems, like those of the common law, have become increasingly dominated by frequently amended public and regulatory statutes outside the codes, one may expect this change in the sources of law to affect the position of the civil law scholars. John P. Dawson pointed out that it was important for the success of the nineteenth century German legal scholars (culminating in the adoption of the German Civil Code) that their activities were almost exclusively concentrated within the supposedly apolitical and relatively non-controversial area of private law. In the twentieth century, as law becomes more public and bureaucratic, the roles of university jurists are changing too.

Thus far it seems that the prestige of the academic lawyer in the civil law systems is relatively secure. In the first place, all other actors in the legal system receive their training from the scholars who transmit to them a comprehensive and highly-ordered model of the system that to a great extent controls how they organize their knowledge, pose their questions and communicate with each other. This model is not only taught in the universities but constitutes the latent framework of the treatises and articles produced by the professors. Furthermore, legal periodicals, which in civil law countries are run by professors rather than students, play a much more important role there than in common law countries in bringing new legislation and court opinions to the attention of the profession. The official reports of cases do not necessarily report all court opinions, nor do they always set forth the opinions in full. The bar tends therefore to rely on the editors of the privately published legal journals who select and print what they consider to be the most significant decisions. Typically each case is followed by an annotation written by an expert (not necessarily a professor) who may amplify the facts of the case, relate the case to other decisions, and discuss its general significance. Such legal periodicals are an indispensable tool of legal research.

Though not a formal source of law, the weight of scholarly authority, known in civil law terminology as "the doctrine," is everywhere taken into account by legislators and judges when they frame, interpret or apply law. Unlike in the United States, with its complex federal structure, the expert authors of this critical literature can concentrate on the relatively manageable output of a single legislature and, basically, of two sets of courts, public and private. The interaction between these legal institutions and the scholars who closely watch them tends to result overall in a more coherent and predictable body of national law than that generated by the legislatures and courts in the 50 states and the federal system in the United States. A critical case note by a leading author, is, in effect, like an important dissenting opinion, indicating where controversy exists and signalling the possible future direction of the law.

Given the influence and prestige of the academic branch of the profession, it is not surprising that the career of a law professor is not one that is easily accessible to law graduates in civil law countries. In order to become a law professor in France, a law graduate must first obtain the degree of *Doctorat d'état* (a process that can take several years). That degree makes him or her eligible to take a rigorous national examination called the *Agrégation*. There are separate *Agrégations* for public and private law, a circumstance that tends to reinforce the strong separation that exists in legal pedagogy between those fields. After successfully passing that examination, the candidate becomes eligible for governmental appointment to a university position.

One must not exaggerate the contrast with the role of legal academics in the United States. Especially in Germany, the status and influence of civil law judges has reached the point where their relationship with legal scholars has become a close working partnership that has greatly benefited the legal system as a whole. At the same time, in the United States, Max Rheinstein noted already in the 1970s the rise of law teachers and scholars as a "new group of co-leaders of the law," and the tendency of American law to assume some of the traits of "professorial" law, which, however, because of the active role of professors here in social reform, assumes a different character from European-style professorial law.

To summarize, then, even in bureaucratic modern states where scholar-made civil law is in decline, it is still the university scholars who supply the vocabulary, concepts, and methodology of the system.

Though the word of the legislator is accorded the supreme position among the sources of law, the word often has its origins in, and its ultimate meaning determined by, the academy. With the rising power and prestige of civil law judges and the growing influence of legal scholars in the United States, however, the traditional distinctions between these legal roles are tending to diminish.

# CHAPTER 4

# PROCEDURE IN CIVIL LAW SYSTEMS

## § 1. Civil Procedure

In civil law countries, civil procedure occupies the same central position in procedural law that the civil law occupies within substantive law. The basic source of law in this area is typically a code of civil procedure. Modern procedural codes stress that judicial proceedings must be public and that, in principle, the control of the allegations and proof belongs to the parties. This latter principle, however, tends to be tempered in practice by the civil law judge's extensive power to supervise and exercise initiative in the proceedings as well as by the role that the public prosecutor can play in private actions.

In a typical civil action, after the pleadings are filed, a period of evidence taking begins. From the outset, several differences from common law civil procedure appear. These differences can be summed up by noting that on the one hand, there is no real counterpart to our pre-trial discovery and motion practice, while on the other hand there is no genuine "trial" in our sense of a single culminating event. Rather, a civil law action is a continuous process of meetings, hearings, and written communications during which evidence is introduced, testimony is taken, and motions are made and decided. A primary goal of the system is to facilitate settlements.

During this process, the judge plays an active role in questioning witnesses, and in framing or reformulating the issues. Although the questioning is typically done by the judge, the questions are often submitted by the parties' counsel who sometimes are permitted to question a witness directly. As the action proceeds, the judge may inject new theories, and new legal and factual issues, thus reducing the disadvantage of the party with the less competent lawyer. In addition, the court may obtain certain types of evidence, such as expert opinions, on its own motion. There are no requirements that documents be formally admitted into evidence, nor are there any rules against hearsay and opinion evidence. Rather, the parties informally introduce documents after providing the other side with notice and an opportunity to inspect. The weight to be accorded the evidence is for the free evaluation of the court.

Except for minor matters which do not concern us here, the bench is usually collegial, but as a rule only one judge will preside over the evidence-taking stage of the proceedings. In some countries, it may happen that the case is decided by an entirely different judge or panel from the one or ones who heard the parties and took the evidence. The better practice, as exemplified by Germany, requires the judge who conducted the proceedings to render the decision in the case. A money judgment on the merits is generally executed out of the defeated party's property. As civil law courts traditionally had no contempt power, it is said that their decrees are in rem rather than in personam. However, today some civil law judges are authorized to hold persons in contempt of court and, in other jurisdictions, the judge may impose financial sanctions (the French *astreinte*) on persons who refuse to comply with a court order. Costs of litigation are taxed in such a way as to discourage hopeless or frivolous causes: as a rule, the defeated party bears the cost of litigation, including attorney's fees. If each party wins and loses in part, costs are allocated proportionately.

Many of the differences between the foregoing model and the usual American trial seem attributable to the absence of the civil jury in civil law countries. The civil law countries have never felt the need to bring the parties, their witnesses, their lawyers and the judge all together on one occasion because they have not had to convene a group of ordinary citizens to hear all the evidence, to resolve factual issues, and to apply the law to the facts. The factor of the civil jury also helps to explain the relatively great number of exclusionary rules in the common law of evidence and the relatively few restrictions on admissibility in the civil law systems. However, recent developments in both systems tend here, as in some other areas, in the direction of a certain convergence. American discovery practice and pre-trial hearings bring us close to a situation where, as in the civil law, there are few surprises at trial. Meanwhile, civil law desire for efficiency and economy has led, notably in Germany, to experiments with a single comprehensive hearing model that is said to work well for the relatively simple cases that form the great bulk of civil litigation.

Pointing out that the usual distinction between our adversarial procedure and the civil law's supposedly nonadversarial procedure is often overdrawn, John Langbein, a leading specialist in comparative procedure, has noted that, "Apart from fact-gathering, ... the lawyers for the parties play major and broadly comparable roles in both the German and American systems. Both are adversary systems of civil procedure. There as here, the lawyers advance partisan positions from first pleadings to final arguments. German litigators suggest legal theories and lines of factual inquiry, they superintend and supplement judicial examination of witnesses, they urge inferences from fact, they discuss and distinguish precedent, they interpret statutes, and they formulate views of the law that further the interests of their clients."

The main difference, Langbein suggests, between continental and American litigators is that the former are mostly "law-adversaries", while the latter are "law-and-fact adversaries." The key difference between the two systems, in his view, is that the American system leaves to partisans the work of gathering and producing the factual material upon which adjudication depends, while the civil law systems place greater responsibility upon the judge for investigating the facts alleged by the parties.

## § 2.  Criminal Procedure

There are three common misconceptions in the common law world about criminal procedure in the civil law countries: that the accused is presumed guilty until proved innocent, that there is no jury trial, and that the trial is conducted in an "inquisitorial" fashion (with pejorative connotations of unfairness to the accused). The first of these notions is simply false. The second is incorrect as to some systems, and, in the case of other systems, overlooks the fact that lay judges who participate on mixed courts with professional judges are functionally analogous to the jury. The third misapprehension has resulted from the fact that the usual mode of proceeding in criminal cases in civil law systems is quite different from that which evolved in the common law. The epithet "inquisitorial" apparently derives from the active role played by the judge in the conduct of the trial, and, often, in investigating the facts. A better word to describe this process would be nonadversarial.

The first phase of a criminal proceeding is an extensive pre-trial investigation, conducted in some countries by a judge, in others by the public prosecutor. This official decides whether there is sufficient evidence to warrant formal charges, after interrogating the witnesses, collecting the other evidence, and questioning the suspect. Under modern codes of criminal procedure, the accused has the right to be represented by counsel during the interrogation and to remain silent.

If the examining magistrate or prosecutor determines that there is what we would call probable cause, the dossier compiled during the preliminary investigative phase is forwarded to the criminal court. In Germany and some other countries, the prosecutor has no discretion not to prosecute (and therefore no power to plea bargain) if there is reasonable cause to believe that the defendant has committed a serious offense.

There is considerable variation among systems as to the composition of lower criminal courts. Typically, one or three professional judges sit with a number of lay judges. Both the professional and lay judges participate in the decision of all factual and legal issues relating to the determination of guilt, and also in the sentencing decision. Verdicts need not be unanimous.

In contrast to the accused in an American criminal prosecution, the defendant in a civil law country has an unlimited right to discovery of all the evidence assembled by the prosecution. During the trial, the presiding judge takes the lead in examining the witnesses and the defendant. Two major differences from the common law adversary model are that the judge is less a passive arbiter between the parties, while the prosecutor is less partisan. The system seems to elicit no such dissatisfaction and controversy in the major European democracies as have plagued the American criminal justice system. "Except for political cases, which no system handles well, ... the task of detecting and punishing crime is generally perceived to be handled effectively and fairly," according to Langbein.

A peculiarity of criminal procedure in the civil law systems is the role accorded to the victim. In some countries, if the same wrongful act gives rise to both criminal and civil liability, the injured person is permitted to intervene directly in the criminal action rather than bring a separate civil suit. If the victim chooses to become a party to the criminal suit, and is successful, the court may order civil damages to be paid to the victim at the termination of the proceedings. In France, this *action civile* is not uncommon. But in Germany, procedural and practical difficulties have discouraged its use. However, Germany, like many other civil law countries, has another way of permitting the victim to join the prosecution. In recognition of the victim's interest in seeing justice done, a victim who does not seek damages may sometimes be allowed to intervene on the side of the prosecution. A guilty finding in such a case will then play an important role in any subsequent civil action by the victim. Also, in certain types of cases, if the prosecutor declines to bring charges, an injured person may be permitted to bring a criminal proceeding individually.

## § 3.  Appellate Review

Decisions of the ordinary civil and criminal courts of first instance may as a rule be appealed to an intermediate appellate court. In criminal cases, the prosecution as well as the defense has the right on appeal. Unlike a common law appeal of a trial court's decision, the proceedings in this intermediate court may involve a full review de novo of the facts as well as the law of the case. The panel of appellate judges initially will make its independent determination of the facts on the basis of the original record. In addition, however, the appellate court may question the witnesses again, or even take new evidence or send out for expert opinions. A party dissatisfied with the results of the appeal may seek review by the highest court which, like a common law appellate court, in theory considers only questions of law. (It may be noted in passing that civil law high courts have not been more successful than common law appellate courts in distinguishing factual from legal issues.) Some of these high courts follow the French system of "cassation", while others follow the German system of "revision." (In some civil law countries, appellate procedure in *criminal* cases does not follow the above pattern of review *de novo* of both law and facts. In Germany, for example, decisions of the courts which have first instance jurisdiction in cases of serious crime are subject to appeal only on points of law, and such appeals are heard, not by intermediate courts, but by a court of last resort. The right to appeal *de novo* does exist, however, for minor criminal offenses which are first heard before a single judge or a local court.)

The French Court of Cassation has several peculiar features which can only be explained historically. The Court, as originally conceived, was to act on behalf of the legislature to supply authoritative interpretations of the law and to guarantee the obedience of the judicial system as a whole to the norms of legislatively-given law. Article 5 of the French Civil Code specifically forbids judges to decide cases submitted to them by way of pronouncing a general rule. They were supposed only to find and apply the law of the Code or other legislation. The Court of Cassation was supposed to see that lower courts did not exceed this role. Its own functions were narrowly drawn. When a case is appealed to it, the Court can decide only the question of law referred to it, not the case itself. This means that it has only the option to affirm, or to quash the decision and remand the case for reconsideration by a lower court in the light of the Court's opinion on the legal questions (hence its name, Court of Cassation, from *casser*: to break or quash). It may not substitute its own decision for that of the lower court. If it disagrees with the original lower court's decision, it sends the case, with its own interpretation of the law, to a different lower court. In France, the court to which the case is remanded theoretically is free to decide the case the same way as the previous lower court. If this happens, a second appeal may be made to the Court of Cassation, which will sit this time in a plenary session. If the lower court decision is again set aside, the case must still normally be remanded to a third lower court which, by an 1837 statute, is then required to give judgment as directed by the Court of Cassation.

Legislation in 1967, and again in 1979, has expedited this archaic procedure somewhat, and has permitted the Court of Cassation to dispose of some cases without remand after the second appeal. The cassation system as practiced in Italy is much simpler. There, the first time the Court of Cassation remands a case, the lower court is bound to follow the high court's views.

Under the system of revision as practiced in Austria, Switzerland and Germany, the high court may, if it finds reversible error, either reverse and remand, or it may modify the decision and enter final judgment itself.

It will be recalled that the administrative courts in most civil law countries are in a separate hierarchy from the ordinary courts. The procedure in lower administrative courts, by comparison with civil procedure, from which it is to a certain extent derived, tends to be more informal, less expensive and more controlled by the administrative law judge. In France, as we have seen, the decisions of these lower courts are reviewed by the Council of State. The procedure of the Council of State differs in material respects from that of the Court of Cassation. In the first place, decisions of the Council of State are final. Second, the statutory rules of administrative procedure are supplemented by a number of judge-made rules. The bulk of substantive French administrative law, which is uncodified, consists mainly of the case law which has been built up by the Council of State. A number of civil law countries, including Belgium, Italy and several developing countries formerly with in the French sphere of influence, have followed the French model.

In countries, such as Austria and Germany, where the administrative courts are part of the judiciary, the procedure for appellate review is essentially similar to that for civil cases in the ordinary courts. The lower court decision is reviewed de novo in an intermediate level administrative court, and the supreme administrative court hears appeals only on questions of law.

# CHAPTER 5

# FIELDS OF SUBSTANTIVE LAW IN CIVIL LAW SYSTEMS

## § 1. Divisions of Law

Comparative legal analysis can be a relatively simple matter when the jurisdictions being compared share common legal structures, procedural rules and similar ideas about how legal problems ought to be classified. An American lawyer in one state, for example, need hardly reflect on the everyday process of consulting the law of sister states for guidance on a difficult or controverted question. Legal comparisons may be dangerously misleading, however, when they take place between systems with different legal institutions, different procedural settings and different methods for classification of legal phenomena. Varying rules of procedure, for example, may produce substantially different outcomes in legal systems where identical substantive rules govern a given case. Apparent contrasts in substantive law, by the same token, often diminish when the rules are seen in their institutional and procedural contexts.

In particular, the distinctive ways in which different legal systems identify and deal with legal problems, may pose obstacles for the comparatist. Consider, for example, the difficulties that our historic distinction between "legal" and "equitable" rules and remedies must pose for comparatists from civil law countries where the division between law and equity is unknown. The categories according to which civil law lawyers are accustomed to arrange their legal norms are similar enough from country to country to greatly aid transnational communication within the civil law orbit. But they are sufficiently different from common law categories to constitute a stumbling block to civil law-common law comparisons.

A fundamental distinction is made in all civil law systems between public and private law. That classification, which is only latent or implicit in the common law, is basic to an understanding of the civil law. For one thing, as we have seen, it produced the distinctive patterns of organization of the court systems of civil law countries. As public law disputes became justiciable in the nineteenth century, separate tribunals were created to handle them. The jurisdiction of ordinary courts today remains limited to disputes governed by private law, with the one major exception of criminal matters. Besides these jurisdictional consequences, the public-private distinction has produced a characteristic division of labor within the legal profession. The members of law faculties tend to identify themselves as either "publicists" or "privatists." Courses and treatises tend to focus on one or the other area, despite the fact that today any given subject matter is likely to have at least some public law aspects.

Though a distinction between public and private law is universally recognized within the civil law world, there is no agreement among civil law lawyers on its theoretical basis or justification, and no uniformity among countries as to its scope and effects. Generally speaking, however, public law concerns relations among organs of the state and between citizens and the state. It includes at least constitutional law, administrative law and criminal law. Private law, dealing with relations among citizens or private groups, includes at least civil law and commercial law. The classification of several other areas is the subject of dispute. Civil procedure, for example, is included by some systems within the private group of subjects, and treated by others as belonging to the field of public law. Labor law, agricultural law, social security, as well as a number of other modern regulated areas, are sometimes said to be "mixed" public and private areas, and sometimes described as sui generis.

## § 2.  Public Law

Although the public-private law distinction has roots in Roman law, public law remained a relatively undeveloped category until modern times. It was the preserve of the sovereign, prudently left aside by jurists. As we noted in our historical introduction to the civil law tradition, nearly all the Roman legal literature that has come down to us is concerned with private law, and continental legal science traditionally concentrated on private law. We observed too, that in the localism and legal diversity of the Middle Ages, there was little place for public law. But when the centralized state and its administrative organs began to emerge on the continent (coinciding with the growing influence of legally trained professionals), conditions were favorable to the development of administrative law. In the nineteenth century, as administrative law began to flourish, it seemed to civil law lawyers that the ordinary private law rules that applied to disputes involving private individuals or associations could not simply be carried over to relationships in which the state was a party. In France it seemed, too, that the ordinary courts could not be entrusted with the task of resolving disputes involving the state. The French view of the separation of powers led, as we have seen, to the establishment of a separate set of public law courts within the administration.

In Germany, it was otherwise. There, concern about administrative oppression was more prevalent than mistrust of the judiciary. So, to avoid having disputes between citizen and administration adjudicated by the latter, Germany created a separate system of administrative law courts within the judiciary.

Today, as the French Council of State has established its independence from the administration proper, advanced the protection of individual rights, and extended its own control over the administrative process, the fact that it is technically not a court is of diminished importance. In modern civil law states, whether on the French or German model, the tendency has been toward increasingly effective review of the legality of administrative action.

Today, when one speaks of public law in the civil law systems, what is meant is often merely administrative law. Constitutional law, as it pertains to the form and structure of the state and its organs, is still thought of as being akin to political science. As we have seen, it is only in relatively recent times that courts or other institutions have acquired the power to review the constitutionality of the acts of government. As for criminal law, though technically classified as public law, it has traditionally been the concern of the "privatists" and everywhere falls within the jurisdiction of the ordinary courts. Thus, the bulk of public law in civil law countries in fact consists of administrative law.

It is hard to specify precisely what is included within the concept of administrative law, even within a single country. Generally speaking, it consists of the norms which regulate the organization, functions, and interrelations of public authorities other than the political and judicial authorities, and the norms which govern the relationships between the administrative authorities and citizens. Tax law has become a major specialty within this field. Administrative law does not completely coincide with the jurisdiction of the administrative courts, because, in all civil law countries, certain administrative matters are relegated by special legislation to the jurisdiction of the ordinary courts.

It is primarily in the field of administrative law that the distinctive characteristics have developed which are thought to set public law apart from private law in the civil law systems. The most striking of these is the uncodified state of administrative law. The fact that the great codifications left public law (except for penal law) untouched accentuated the division between private and public law. The separation deepened as the courts assumed a large role in establishing the general principles and rules of administrative law, a role formally denied them in the area of the civil law. At the present time, administrative law in civil law systems tends to be scattered among various statutes, with case law playing a major role. The relative importance of the case law is greater in France; that of enacted law is greater in Germany and Austria.

As might be expected, public and private law often arrive at similar solutions to similar legal problems. Nevertheless, the student of comparative law must always be aware of the possibility that the classification of a dispute as private or public will bring into play a quite different substantive rule or a different method of interpretation. For example, in France during the severe inflations after World War I, the private law courts refused to grant relief to creditors whose fixed contractual claims had become practically worthless, while the Council of State developed a doctrine of unforeseeability to come to the aid of obligees in contracts governed by public law. Administrative law is said, too, to be set apart from private law by its susceptibility to frequent change; by the wider scope it allows for official discretion and the little room it leaves to the discretion of the parties; and by its more vague and fluid legal concepts. However, it should be noted that the general principles of private law are often carried over to supplement or to fill gaps in administrative law.

## § 3.  Private Law

Just as the term "public law" is commonly used to designate administrative law, "private law" is often used interchangeably with civil law. In civil law systems, however, private law comprises two grand divisions of its own: civil law and commercial law. Civil law, in principle, applies to everyone and its basic provisions are found in the civil codes, supplemented by auxiliary statutes. Commercial law, which concerns specific groups of persons and/or specific types of activities, is in most civil law countries contained in a separate commercial code. In Italy and Switzerland, there are no commercial codes, but commercial law nevertheless is considered and taught as a separate private law subject. Besides commercial law, there are a number of other fields which are usually classified as separate from civil law, but within the domain of private law: literary and artistic property, maritime law, insurance and industrial property. Labor law developed from the civil law of the individual employment contract. However, today it is variously classified as a special category of private law; as mixed public and private law; or as being a field unto itself, neither public nor private.

## A. *Civil Law*

Civil law (*droit civil, Bürgerliches Recht*—or *Zivilrecht*) is traditionally arranged in treatises and for teaching purposes under the following major headings: the law of persons; family law; marital property law; property law; succession law and the law of obligations. These categories are not exhaustive, nor do they precisely correspond with the way the subjects are distributed within the civil codes of various countries. In Switzerland, for example, there is a separate Code of Obligations, and in France, family law is included within the law of persons.

The *law of persons* consists of all the norms concerning the status of the individuals and legal entities which are the subjects of the law. It includes the legal rules relating to such matters as names, domicile, civil status, capacity and protection of persons under legal incapacities of various sorts. Most legal entities have long been subjected to special regulation by administrative, commercial and labor law, so that only a few associations are now left within the domain of the civil codes.

*Family law* covers marriage formation; the legal effects of marriage; marriage termination by divorce, separation, and annulment; filiation; and family support obligations. In the first of these areas, which has remained quite stable, the civil law systems have taken from the French the requirement of a civil ceremony for the formation of a valid marriage. In all the other parts of family law, extensive code revision has taken place under the influence of three major trends: the liberalization of the grounds for divorce; the equalization of the positions of women and men in the areas of family decision-making and property rights; and the assimilation of the status of children born outside legal marriage to that of children born to parents who are married to each other.

*Marital property law*, with close links to family law, property law and succession law, is traditionally treated as a separate area of civil law. The civil codes establish and regulate a "legal marital property regime," the system that governs the property relations of all spouses who do not choose an alternative regime by marriage contract. The legal regime is typically a form of community property, usually with pre-marital property and property acquired through gift or inheritance kept separate if it can be identified as such. The modern trend favors forms of the so-called "deferred community" in which the spouses are treated as separate owners of whatever they respectively acquire during the marriage, but property acquired during the marriage is divided equally upon termination of the marriage by divorce or death. In addition to establishing the legal regime, the marital property provisions of the civil codes typically establish and regulate a number of alternative regimes which may be chosen by contract, as well as the procedures for making and altering marriage contracts.

*Property law* in civil law systems makes a distinction between movable and immovable property, which roughly corresponds to the common law distinction between personal and real property. Historically, as in the common law, land was of greater importance than chattels, and the law of the older codes, especially, reflects that state of affairs. In the liberal tradition, the right of ownership was considered virtually absolute, and the protection of private property was regarded as an important function of the state. In practice, the absoluteness of property right as described in the civil codes has long since been extensively limited by public law legislation, by new constitutions and by judicial interpretation.

Another traditional attribute of civil law ownership, not found in the common law, is its unitary character. Although the civil law recognizes certain forms of co-ownership, it is hard for a civil law lawyer to conceive of ownership as a "bundle of rights" that can be parcelled out in various ways, or divided over time (as is the case with common law present and future interests). The distinction between legal and equitable title is unknown. Thus it is difficult for civil law nations to develop institutions which perform all of the useful social functions of the flexible common law trust. Property is thought of as having one owner (or one set of concurrent owners) and other interests affecting it are generally thought of as restrictions or encumbrances on the title of the owner. Leases of real estate are not considered property at all, but fall within the contractual area of the law of obligations. In modern civil law, however, the idea of unitary ownership seems to be eroding somewhat as new forms of shared ownership gain in popularity.

*Succession law* covers the disposition of property upon death by will or by intestate inheritance. Freedom of testation in civil law systems is typically limited in favor of the testator's children who are entitled to a "reserved share" of their parent's estate. Unlike American law, civil law systems do not traditionally accord such a forced share to the surviving spouse, whose economic interests are thought to be sufficiently protected by the division of marital property upon death. The modern trend everywhere, however, has been to improve gradually the successoral position of the surviving spouse, and in some countries, Germany for example, this has brought about a reserved share in his or her favor.

Two typical aspects of civil law succession have attracted considerable interest in the United States. The first is the practice of having a will authenticated before a notary during the lifetime of the testator, a procedure which dispenses with the need for probate. The second is the fact that, in the normal situation, there is nothing corresponding to our period of administration of a decedent's estate. An inheritance simply vests upon death in the persons designated by the will or the laws of intestate succession, subject to their right of renunciation. Another idea from the civil law of succession has already been widely incorporated into American probate law reforms. This is the inclusion of certain types of inter vivos transfers within the decedent's estate for purposes of calculating the forced share.

*The law of obligations* is the most technical, abstract and (at first sight) stable part of the civil law. It covers all acts or transactions which can give rise to rights or claims and is customarily divided into three parts: the law of contracts, the law of tort (delict), and the law of unjust enrichment. The contract law sections of the codes typically begin with a few general rules which are applicable to all contracts, and then set forth special rules for particular sorts of contracts: sales, leases, agency, loans, etc. The civil law conception of tort liability is a unified one: in contrast to the common law which developed separate pigeonholes for different kinds of harms, it is a law of *tort* rather than torts. The civil law of unjust enrichment has been built up from general principles with a heavy component of case law.

The distinction between contractual and delictual (tort) responsibility has been treated as fundamental in civil law theory, even though both contract and delict are regarded as parts of the single field of obligations. As with other legal classifications, however, a great deal of literature has been devoted to the distinction without successfully clarifying its precise nature. And, as with other legal categories, there is no uniformity among systems as to which acts fall within which domain. French scholar André Tunc has stated, in a comparative survey, that there is a trend in modern practice toward the decline, but not the disappearance, of the distinction, as contractual and tort liability become increasingly intertwined and as the underlying unified principles of the law of obligations (including unjust enrichment) come more prominently into view.

Chief among the convergence factors within the law of obligations are the expanded range of facts that modern courts everywhere consider legally relevant, the movement away from formalism, and trends toward protecting reasonable reliance and expectations. However, at the very time that contractual and delictual responsibility appear to be converging, the scope of the field of obligations appears to be diminishing. At the outset of this section we stated that the law of obligations is at first sight the most stable area of the civil law. If one looks only at the civil codes, the parts containing the law of obligations have been little changed, and they are recognizably related to the oldest parts of the civil law tradition. Legislation outside the codes, however, has altered both the substance and the underlying philosophy of the law of obligations.

## B. Commercial Law

Commercial law (*droit commercial, Handelsrecht*) generally includes corporations and other business associations, securities, banking, and negotiable instruments, as well as other commercial transactions. We noted in our historical introduction that commercial law had developed from mercantile customs and the practice of merchants' courts into a well-established separate branch of private law even before the codification period. The dichotomy between civil and commercial law survived both codification and the centralization of justice, thanks mainly to France which adopted the *Code de Commerce* in 1807 and established separate commercial courts within the first level of jurisdiction. Most other civil law countries followed suit.

The division between civil and commercial law is not, however, absolute or clear-cut. First, all systems have found the concepts of "merchant" or "commercial act" difficult to define for purposes of determining whether a transaction is governed by civil or commercial law. Second, the commercial codes lack the general principles and internal coherence of the civil codes. Thus, civil law is frequently brought in to fill the gaps in the commercial codes and their supplementary laws. This is so much the case that some writers speak of the "civilization of commercial law", by which they mean that commercial law is becoming a special field within the civil law. Third, the differences are further diminished by a countertrend toward "commercialization of the civil law." The commercial law influence on the civil law has manifested itself in a reduction of unnecessary formality, increased protection of reliance by third parties, and a tendency to view transactions as parts of on-going relationships, rather than as isolated legal events. Finally, in Switzerland, Italy, and The Netherlands, the decision has been made to dispense with a separate commercial code, a development which may represent the wave of the future.

However, at the same time that civil and commercial law, through mutual enrichment, are coming to resemble parts of a unified field within private law, another legal trend is operating to remove much of commercial law from private law altogether. Originally based on custom, then codified on the liberal principle of individual freedom of contract, commercial law has increasingly been shaped by a body of legislation regulating commercial and corporate activity. One aspect of this movement has been the development in civil law countries, as in common law nations, of a separate body of consumer law in which the distinction between merchant and nonmerchant is significant. Another aspect is the subjection of commercial activity generally to requirements for official licenses, permits, and so on. Where state economic planning is extensive, it is hard to distinguish some parts of commercial law from administrative law. To take account of the role of public regulation of the market, French and German writers have renamed the classification. Instead of "commercial law", they refer to the field of "commercial and economic law," economic law being the regulatory law of the state.

## C.  Labor Law

If commercial law now lies somewhere along the border between public and private law, it is clear that labor law, for most practical purposes, has escaped the private law domain entirely. The employment contract, once a civil law relation, is heavily regulated by rules which are of a public law nature. The "labor codes" which exist in some countries are not codes of the classical variety, but rather collections of diverse statutes pertaining to employment relationships. With general statutory protection against discharge without cause in most civil law countries, and with mandatory employee participation in shop-floor decision-making as well as in the actual control of the enterprise, the role of private autonomy is reduced mainly to the decision whether or not to enter into an employment relationship. The question arises whether labor law is, as is sometimes said, a special field unto itself, or whether it is in fact increasingly typical of law in modern states where the public-private distinction is increasingly difficult to maintain.

## § 4.   Merger or Desuetude of Divisions

Legal classifications can never completely contain the fluctuating variety of human activity upon which they are imposed. However, it does not necessarily diminish their utility that there will always be definitional problems about where they begin and end, about what is included or excluded. The distinctions between public and private law, civil and commercial law, contractual and delictual responsibility, need not be shown to be impermeable or to have an inherent logic in order to be functional for various purposes, not the least of which is pedagogical. Thus, it is likely that, however much some parts of contract may merge with certain area of delict, there will still be, as the English scholar, Anthony Weir has put it, reasons to distinguish between "transactions and collisions." Similarly, though civil and commercial law have fused in many ways, it is probable that commercial law will continue to be studied as a separate subject and that it will tend to be practiced mainly by specialists. The civil law classification that is most eroded by time and events is the "fundamental dichotomy" between public and private law, but that too survives, in the court systems and in the minds of civil law lawyers.

As we have observed throughout this section, intervention by the state in areas once reserved to private activity increasingly blurs the public-private law distinction. Yet the French comparatist René David wrote in the 1970s that, in contrast to public law, which he described as especially subject to the vicissitudes of change and political crises, the Civil Code still seemed to French private lawyers to be "the most lasting and the only true constitution of France." There is indeed a sense in which the Civil Code is constitutional: the law of the Civil Code is the area of the law in which the function of government is limited in principle to the recognition and enforcement of private rights. Especially in the field of contracts, the civil codes impose few rules in the name of public policy. Most of the law of contracts is of the type that civilians call dispositive, suppletive or directory, as opposed to compulsory. Dispositive rules apply only if they have not been expressly or impliedly excluded by the parties. However, one can maintain this "constitutional" view of the civil codes only if one ignores the effect that statutory law has had upon them. Special legislation has been an institutional bypass through which the codes have been left intact but drained of much important content.

Legislation outside the civil codes has, first and foremost, undermined the constitutional function of the codes by establishing a new and competing set of premises. While freedom of contract still appears to be a fundamental principle of the civil codes, a variety of mandatory (non-waivable) provisions and prohibitions have been introduced by statutes in the name of public policy—which in some cases means protection of the weaker party; in other cases, the effectuation of economic planning; and in still others the promotion of the interests of organized groups. In the area of property, the codes still promote the notion that the role of government is to protect private property, while special legislation qualifies the property right by subtracting elements in the public interest, or modifies it by adding social obligations. With the development of public and private insurance schemes, delictual liability is no longer the main source of compensation for personal injuries; there is now a wide overlap between private tort law and public social security law. The stability which is so characteristically associated with the civil codes appears as an illusion when one considers how frequently all this legislation is amended. Indeed, the volatility of the special legislation is often cited as a reason why the civil law cannot be re-integrated into the codes.

The contraction of the area which is left for regulation by the civil codes is not the only manifestation of the expansion of public law. Administrative law, the child of the nineteenth century, came into its own in the twentieth century. Not only did new areas come under regulation, but government's role in providing social services increased. The public agencies that were created to perform these services have often appropriated private law means and institutions to do so. In the process, the distinction between public and private is further blurred. Also, the state's increased role in the economy not only modified the civil law of contract, tort and property, but has led to new kinds of "economic law" regulating competition, the structure and activities of enterprises, and employer-employee relations. As more areas of public concern are identified, such as protection of the environment, or protection of health and safety in the workplace, the scope of administrative law continues to expand.

Still, the idea of a distinction between public and private law has a strong hold in the habits, attitudes, and practices of civil law lawyers. For that reason, even if it is vague or dissolving, it remains important to the understanding of the civil law tradition. René David once wrote: "[W]hen one says public law, a Frenchman knows that it is not and cannot be law in the strict sense.... Law in the strict sense can only develop in the area of relations between individuals, where the state is an impartial arbiter."

# CHAPTER 6

# SOURCES OF LAW AND THE JUDICIAL PROCESS IN CIVIL LAW SYSTEMS

## § 1. In General

Civil law theorists make a fundamental distinction between primary sources of law, which can give rise directly to binding legal norms, and secondary sources, sometimes called *authorities*. The primary sources in all civil law systems are enacted law and custom, with the former overwhelmingly more important. Sometimes "general principles of law" are also considered a primary source. Authorities may have weight when primary sources are absent, unclear or incomplete, but they are never binding, and they are neither necessary nor sufficient as the basis for a judicial decision. Case law and the writings of legal scholars are such secondary sources, and in The Netherlands, the draft of the current civil code was treated as an authority for many years prior to its enactment.

In theory, enacted law is the pre-eminent source of law, and court decisions are not binding in subsequent cases, either on the courts that issue them or on lower courts in the same hierarchy. A study of the process of *interpretation* of enacted law, however, reveals a considerable discrepancy between theory and practice. For purposes of comparison, it is essential to supplement formal sources of law theory, not only with an examination of what happens to the primary sources through interpretation, but also with a functional analysis of the mechanisms which promote the values of certainty and predictability while permitting growth and adaptation within the system. Finally, it must be cautioned that the significance of the sources of law within civil law systems, and the range of judicial behavior with respect to them, varies from country to country, and, even within a country, from time to time and from subject matter to subject matter.

## § 2.  Primary Sources

### A.  *Enacted Law*

The concept of enacted law includes not only those legal rules adopted by legislatures, but those issued by executives and by administrative agencies, or adopted by popular referendum. The various types of enacted law form a hierarchy with the constitution at the pinnacle, followed by legislation (which, in France, may emanate from the executive as well as from the parliament), then by executive decrees pursuant to delegated legislative power, then by administrative regulations, and finally by local ordinances. In federal states, this hierarchy must be supplemented by the rules concerning the relationship of state to federal law. Account must also be taken of the increasing importance of international treaties and conventions and the effect given to them under local law. Within the European Union, for example, community law may take primacy over internal law.

In general it can be said that parliamentary legislation is today the principal source of law in civil law countries. Within this category, the various codes, though still of great importance, now constitute only a small part of the total volume of existing legislation. The ever-growing body of separate statutes reinforces the traditional pre-eminence of enacted law within civil law systems, but draws attention away from the codes.

Special mention should be made here of the role played in France since 1958 by executive legislation. Recall that a cardinal tenet of the French Revolution was that all law-making power was to be vested in a representative assembly. However, it soon became apparent in France, as elsewhere, that the complexity of modern government requires the legislature to delegate substantial power to the executive to implement legislation and to issue administrative regulations. Such delegated power was not thought to derogate from the principle of separation of powers.

But the 1958 Constitution of General Charles de Gaulle's Fifth Republic went a step further, by putting the law-making power of the executive on an autonomous non-delegated basis. In Article 34 of the Constitution, those matters falling within the parliamentary law-making domain are enumerated. Then, in Article 37, the Constitution states that matters other than those reserved for the legislative domain by Article 34 are of an executive character. Thus, the legislative law making power, though it covers the most important matters, has become the exception and the executive-administrative jurisdiction the rule—a direct repudiation of the traditional French doctrine of legislative supremacy. This grant of autonomous law-making power to the executive is in addition to the executive's delegated power to issue regulations in the course of executing parliamentary laws.

Two further aspects of the modern French development of the law-making power of the executive are noteworthy. The first is the treatment of the problem of the constitutionality of executive legislation. The Constitutional Council, it will be recalled, has power to review only parliamentary legislation for conformity to the Constitution. The concern that executive legislation might escape review altogether was allayed by the Council of State which promptly claimed and has continuously exercised constitutional control over it. The second aspect of the 1958 changes in the distribution of power between the executive and legislative branches is that these changes conferred upon the executive a privileged position in the parliamentary law-making process. As a leading civil law scholar has put it: "Legislation has become to a great extent the work of the Ministry of Justice and other departments. It is something of a return, if not to the Justinian style, at least to that of the Jurisconsults."

## B.  Custom

In the civil law theory of sources of law, custom is regularly listed as a primary source, but routinely dismissed as of slight practical importance, except in Spain and some of the other Spanish-speaking countries. In certain provinces of Spain, notably Catalonia, the national Civil Code does not apply to matters covered by local customary laws (*fueros*). In other civil law countries, where custom is less important but still considered to have binding force, there is an apparent difference between systems, such as the German, which permit custom in certain cases to prevail over written law, and those systems which, like the French, permit custom to supplement, but not to abrogate, the written law. The real extent of this difference may be questioned, though, in view of the rigorous insistence of the former system on the establishment of a "true custom", and the relaxed attitude of the latter concerning the nicety of the distinction between "supplementation" and "abrogation." As might be expected, custom (in the form of trade usage) plays a greater role in commercial and labor law than it does in civil law generally. Some treatise writers have characterized settled case law as custom, but it is not officially recognized as such.

## C.  General Principles

It is sometimes said that "general principles," derived either from norms of positive law or from the existence of the legal order itself, are a primary source of law. They are so characterized by some

French writers, especially in connection with discussions of French administrative law, but also in discussions of the judicial doctrine of abuse of rights and the expansion of the notion of unjust enrichment. Such a characterization raises the question whether the source of law is really the general principle or the judge, a problem which will be discussed below in connection with interpretation.

## § 3.  Authorities

### A.  Case Law

Case law (*jurisprudence, Rechtsprechung*) plays an enormous role in the everyday operation of civil law systems, because of the necessity to interpret and apply the "written" law. An important area of convergence with the common law systems emerges here when we consider the extent to which the law of England and the United States became statutory over the course of the twentieth century. Nevertheless, unlike the common law, the civil law tradition from ancient times has regarded the judicial function as limited to deciding particular cases.

The notion goes back to Justinian that only the sovereign can make a generally applicable rule. In modern nation states, that notion developed into the idea that only a representative legislature should be able to "make" law. However, modern civil law systems have retreated from that principle to a significant degree.

As it became generally recognized that judges frequently do in fact make law, the question arose whether and to what extent judicial decisions were a source of law. Civil law theory does not recognize the existence of a formal doctrine of *stare decisis*. Thus, judicial pronouncements are not binding on lower courts in subsequent cases, nor are they binding on the same or coordinate courts. In the extreme French situation, as we have seen in our discussion of procedure, the decision of the highest civil court is not even binding on a lower court in the same case until the second remand, and then only by statute.

This formal civil law theory of the role of case law is, however, subject to a number of qualifications. Initially, it is not a simple matter for a high court to decide a particular case one way and later to decide a similar case another way. If a division of the high court wishes to deviate from a prior decision, the legal question involved will usually have to be referred to a super-panel of the court. This procedure has the purpose of assuring consistency in the output of the court charged with the ultimate responsibility for the uniformity of the application of the law within its own hierarchy. Second, in bureaucratic judicial systems, the de facto influence of higher court decisions upon lower court judges (whose promotions may be affected by too many reversals) is considerable. Third, the decisions of the Constitutional Courts of Germany and Italy on the compatibility of statutes with the constitution do have the force of law. Fourth, a settled line of cases (*Jurisprudence constante, ständige Rechtsprechung*) has great authority everywhere. In some parts of the Spanish-speaking world this settled case law is made binding by legislation. Some legal theorists consider that, in rare instances, a line of cases can create a rule of customary law which is then binding as such. Fifth, it is observable that entire bodies of law in civil law systems have been built up by judicial decisions in a manner closely resembling the growth of anglo-American common law. This is notably so, for example, in the case of French tort law, and also in French substantive administrative law which is largely uncodified.

As a practical matter it is generally recognized in civil law systems that judges do and should take heed of prior decisions, especially when the settled case law shows that a line of cases has developed. Where the case law has not become "settled", prior decisions of high courts have some weight. Even in France, where the force of precedent is weaker than in Germany, the decisions of the Council of State are considered reliable precedent, and writers say that a single decision of the Court of Cassation can be important in settling the case law. Court decisions, then, are de facto sources of legal norms whose authority varies according to the number of similar decisions, the importance of the court issuing them, and the intrinsic persuasiveness of the opinion. The fact that few civil law courts (with the notable exception of the German Constitutional Court) disclose or publish dissents further complicates the task of discerning the strength of a precedent. The extent to which a court has relied on prior decisions, however, is not always easy to determine in a given case. In this respect, judicial opinions in German-speaking countries bear a certain resemblance to American decisions with their relatively full presentation of facts, reasoning and authorities. But the cryptic opinions of the French Court of Cassation summarize the facts only briefly and do not refer to prior cases. Lower court opinions in France sometimes do cite cases and provide more ample fact statements, but they are less informative than a typical German or American opinion. When the courts are not forthcoming about their reasoning processes and the sources they have relied upon, it is only by reading a line of cases that one can make inferences about the influence of precedent.

Civil law decisions have de facto weight for the same reasons that underlie the common law doctrine of *stare decisis*. The most important of these reasons go to the very heart of the legal system: the requirements of reasonable certainty and predictability; the elementary demand of fair ness that like cases be treated alike; and the related, but distinct, consideration that justice should not only be done, but should appear to have been done. In addition to serving the values of predictability, fairness and legitimacy, continuity in the case law is itself in no small way promoted by such homely considerations as the conservation of mental energy and the fear of reversal.

In view of the de facto importance of case law as a civil law authority, one might expect the differences between the common law and civil law systems in this area to diminish over time. Certainly, the presence or absence of a formal doctrine of stare decisis is not of crucial significance. As a "rule", stare decisis applies in the United States only to require a lower court to follow the decision of a higher court in the same jurisdiction in cases that are "on all fours" with each other. The stricter English rule, by which courts purported to be bound by their own prior decisions, was abandoned by the House of Lords in 1966. Whether bound to or not, though, judges in all legal systems acknowledge an obligation to treat like cases alike. With computerized access to prior decisions, it seems likely that civil law systems will eventually develop flexible systems of precedent that will resemble the anglo-American systems. Thus far, however, the traditional conception that a single case has no binding effect seems to have led civil law systems to experienced considerable difficulty in developing theories and techniques for dealing with case law. According to some scholars, these methodological shortcomings can entail serious practical consequences in terms of unequal treatment for similarly situated parties, a relative lack of predictability, and difficulty in integrating case law into the legal system as a whole.

## B.  *Doctrine*

The writings of legal scholars (*la doctrine*, *die Rechtslehre*), like the decisions of courts, are considered authorities in civil law systems. The role of doctrine is, however, quite different from that of the case law. As we have just seen, case law authority operates to settle the law and to assure a degree of consistency within a judicial hierarchy. The learned writing, on the other hand, exerts its greatest direct influence when the law is unsettled or when there is no established law on a point. But the two types of authorities are related, in that civil law systems have left the task of organizing and analyzing the case law mainly to the learned writers. Thus, the doctrine indirectly controls, to a great extent, the judges' understanding of the case law.

The weight attached by judges to doctrinal writing varies according to a number of circumstances, including the reputation of the author and whether the view expressed is an isolated one or represents the consensus of the most respected writers. In general, it can be said that civil law judges pay close attention to scholarly opinions, as expressed in general and specialized treatises, commentaries on the codes, monographs (including the best doctoral theses), law review articles and case notes, and expert opinions rendered in connection with litigation. Persistent doctrinal criticism will often prompt re-examination of a holding, and will sometimes even lead to the abandonment of an established judicial position.

As we noted earlier in our discussion of the role of legal scholars in civil law systems, the importance of the academics' function in presenting analyses of cases and statutes to judges and lawyers is hard to overestimate. There is a circular chain of reinforcement among the civil law theory on the force of case law, the mechanics of law-finding, and the influence of legal writers. Since case law (theoretically) is not binding, civil law systems long lacked sophisticated and comprehensive citators for direct access to cases and for the coordination of cases with each other and with statutes. The absence of such tools in turn, made it very difficult for a reliable sense of precedent to develop. Periodicals and treatises which collect and analyze the most important cases became the main sources relied upon in research. But this means that one set of authorities is pre-selected and filtered by another. Civil law practice and adjudication are bound to be profoundly affected by the introduction of computerized law-finding devices.

Once again, however, the apparent differences between the civil and common law systems should not be exaggerated. In the latter, certain kinds of legal writing and certain writers have become highly influential, as evidenced by the measurable increase in citations to law review articles in contemporary judicial opinions. Judges and lawyers in common law systems also rely to some extent on treatises and articles to find, organize and analyze the case law. On the other hand, the introduction of computerized law-finding devices in civil law systems will probably liberate civil law practitioners and judges somewhat from their traditional reliance on the academics. Nevertheless, differences are likely to persist in the degree of deference accorded to scholarly opinion, and, perhaps, in the degree to which the care and responsibility exercised by the

respective academic professions merit such deference.

## § 4.  Interpretation

One of the many ways in which the classic codifications represented a break with the immediate
past was in their transformation of the idea of
sources of law. The *jus commune*, local customs,
and previous authorities of all sorts were displaced
by systematic legislation that was supposed to be
comprehensive within the areas it covered. Then, in
the post-codification era, scholarly attention and the
judicial process focused on the codes—their language, their structure, the relations among their
parts, and their animating spirit. An enormous volume of literature on interpretation was generated.
Indeed, one may say that the technique of interpretation of enacted law became as much of an art in
civil law systems, as did the techniques for dealing
with case law in common law systems. Since it is in
connection with the civil codes that these techniques were refined, the discussion here will be
concerned primarily with code interpretation. But it
must be remembered that in modern civil law systems, a judge's everyday work is as much concerned
with ordinary statutes, decrees and regulations as it
is with the language of the codes, and that the
theory and techniques of interpretation vary, depending on the source of the legal norm involved.

Since the time of the codifications, there has
been a considerable evolution in the way the relation of the judicial process to the written law has

been perceived, an evolution which has taken somewhat different courses in different countries. We may begin our consideration by distinguishing four different types of intellectual operations that are often grouped together under the general heading of "interpretation." First, there is the kind of interpretation involved in every use of language: the ascertainment of the linguistically most plausible meaning to be ascribed to the words used. If one meaning is much more plausible than others, and it covers the case before the court, the judge applies that version. This process of ascertaining meaning may be so automatic and unconscious that judges and commentators sometimes think of it as "law finding". The dream of the draftsmen of the Prussian Civil Code that *all* law could be so "found" and "applied" has long since been recognized as just that—a dream. But the fact remains that many everyday legal questions can be and are resolved in just this way.

A second type of interpretation occurs when there is an ambiguous or unclear provision, or an apparent inconsistency among provisions in the text. A third type occurs when there is a gap in a legislative text. In these second and third situations, the process of interpretation becomes a conscious one. Here, as we shall see, all civil law systems are characterized by the presence of a number of methods devised to elucidate unclear or ambiguous texts and to help fill the gaps in legal rules. All of these methods have in common the ultimate aim of applying the legal rule as clarified or completed.

A fourth, and quite different set of intellectual operations is involved when the usual gap-filling or ambiguity-resolving methods fail to yield a solution; when the law is completely silent on a matter that is arguably within its scope; or when an old law, because of changed circumstances, has become completely unsuitable to current conditions. Though the judge's activity in these situations is often disguised or characterized as interpretation, it is clear that whatever process he or she engages in is no longer simply a search for the meaning of a legislative text. In this fourth group of situations, judges develop the law on their own, but there is great variation in the extent to which this is openly acknowledged, in the manner in which the judges proceed, and in the degree of freedom they consider themselves to possess. In France, for reasons which are largely historical, the process of judicial development is still largely hidden from view, in contrast to the more open development of the law in Germany.

In the early years after the adoption of the French and German codes, the codes were treated, not as complete, but as self-sufficient, in the sense that they were presumed to contain a comprehensive body of rules and principles, and (the German more than the French) to embody a system for applying these norms to all cases arising within the areas they purported to cover. Interpretation was thought of as the process of "enlarging the code out of itself". No matter what type of problem arose, if the text failed to supply an answer, the judge was supposed to endeavor to derive its solution from the code, from the relation of its parts, from its structure, or from its general principles. To be sure, this process resulted in the creation of new judge-made norms, but the activity of judges was almost universally disguised as the finding and application of legal rules consistent with legislative intent or purpose.

So long as interpretation was viewed as the process of discovering the express or implied will of the legislature, its principal techniques were exegetical. They involved grammatical analysis, and such logical operations as reasoning by analogy or *e contrario* from code provisions, or deriving an inclusive principle from a set of related sections. In this type of interpretation, legislative history, particularly of the type known in civil law terminology as "the preparatory work" on a statute or code, is an important aid to determining legislative purposes so as to choose between conflicting or competing views of the meaning of the text. In many cases, grammatical or logical interpretation, or the search for legislative intent on a specific problem will be fruitful and will lead to the assignment of a plausible meaning to the text. But when these procedures led to a dead end, the pretense that the judge was doing no more than carrying out the will of the legislature was facilitated by the so-called "general clauses", provisions of such breadth that, somewhat like common law equitable principles, they can be used to modify the effect of more rigid code provisions or to set the course of a new development.

General clauses may range in their application over the entire subject matter of the code. For example, Article 6 of the French Civil Code forbids individuals to derogate in their private arrangements from laws concerning public order and good morals (*bonnes moeurs*), and Article 138 of the German Civil Code provides that a transaction that offends good morals (*guten Sitten*) is void. Other general clauses are confined to specific subject matter areas, as for example, Article 242 of the German Civil Code and Article 1134 of the French Civil Code, both of which require good faith in the performance of obligations.

Gradually, it has become widely recognized and accepted in both France and Germany, as well as in other systems, that the courts, at least when they are dealing with situations of the fourth type mentioned above, are engaged in a modest law-making function. The response to this recognition has varied significantly in different civil law systems. Let us consider, for example, approaches to the process of interpretation in France, Germany and in those civil law countries whose codes contain specific directions on what the judge is to do when the law is silent.

In France, a number of factors contributed to the firm establishment and long predominance of the exegetical school of interpretation. Not the least of these was the Civil Code itself. Recall that the revolutionary reaction against the royal courts found expression in Article 5 of the French Civil Code of 1804, forbidding judges to lay down general rules in deciding cases, and that mistrust of judges importantly affected the organization of the court system. Article 4 of the Code forbids a judge, on pain of misdemeanor, to refuse to decide a case "on the pretext that the law is silent, unclear, or incomplete." Nevertheless, the draftsmen of the Civil Code of 1804 had a sophisticated conception of the judge's role. The chief drafter Portalis knew full well that the law in its generality required the cooperation of the judge to fill its gaps and adapt it to change. Portalis acknowledged that the legislature could not and should not try to foresee everything: "How can one hold back the action of time? How can the course of events be opposed, or the gradual improvement of mores?" Conceding that a great many things are necessarily left to be determined by the judges, he wrote: "[T]he science of the judge is to put the principles [of the law] into action, to develop them, to extend them, by a wise and reasoned application, to private relations; to study the spirit of the law when the letter killeth, and not to expose himself to the risk of being alternately slave and rebel. . . ."

The judges under the Napoleonic regime, however, were not eager to test the limits of their power. They were more concerned to show their submissiveness to the new order. The Court of Cassation led the way by developing a cryptic opinion style which usually consists of a single long paragraph containing a recital of the applicable legal provisions, a brief description of the facts, and a series of "whereas" clauses through which the decision is made to appear to emerge as though from a mechanical process of application of the enacted law to the facts. This style, an outward sign of deference to the legislature through strictly literal obedience to Articles 4 and 5 of the Civil Code, has persisted to the present time in the Court of Cassation, while the opinions of lower courts are only somewhat more ample. Within this form however, the judges have in fact been quite creative: the lower court judges through their power to find the facts, and the Court of Cassation aided by the very conciseness and generality of the French Civil Code. In recent years, the uninformative nature of the opinions issued by the highest court has not escaped attention and criticism, and intermediate appellate courts, led by the Paris Court of Appeals, have begun to set forth their reasoning more fully.

In legal scholarship, the school of literal interpretation held sway until nearly the end of the nineteenth century when François Gény, in a celebrated work on methods of interpretation and sources of law, pointed out that the judges had in fact been making law all along. Gény argued that, when the text is unclear or silent, the judge *should* be freed from the limitations inherent in the traditional methods of textual exegesis. The new technique of *libre recherche scientifique* which Gény expounded was supposed to liberate judges in difficult cases to look to whatever materials were available to resolve the problem—not only to case law, custom, and learned writing, but to the entire social and economic context. Gény's views transformed French legal science, but were not welcomed—at least not visibly—into the practice of the courts. The stylized form of most French judicial opinions continues to this day to mask what Jean Carbonnier called "a tactical eclecticism in methods of interpretation." It is implicit in the outcomes of the cases that French judges interpret legislative texts so as to adapt them to current social and economic conditions. But their actual reasoning process is rarely discernible in their brief and uninformative decisions.

Unlike the French Civil Code, but in consonance with the views of Portalis, some of the other nineteenth century codes openly acknowledged and dealt with the relation between legislation and interpretation. The Austrian Civil Code of 1811, which had been in preparation over the latter part of the eighteenth century and was strongly influenced by natural law ideas, directs the judge to look to the "principles of natural justice". The Spanish Civil Code of 1888 provides that deficiencies in the law shall be supplied by reference to "general principles of the law", understood as those principles which can be derived from the rules of positive law. The draftsmen of the German Civil Code considered including some such explicit interpretive directions, but eventually rejected the idea. Their position was that their carefully constructed Code implicitly contained its own methods of interpretation. If the ordinary methods of exegesis inherent in the structure and system of the code yielded no answer, it was anticipated that the judge would resort to general principles, not limited to those discoverable in the positive law, however, but including those principles which arise from the spirit of the legal order. This concept was later made an explicit direction in Article 12 of the Italian law on interpretation of legislative texts.

The most famous of all such interpretive directions is contained in Article 1 of the Swiss Civil Code of 1907, which provides that if the judge can find no rule in the enacted law, he must decide in accordance with customary law, and failing that, according to the rule which he as a legislator would adopt, having regard to "approved legal doctrine and judicial tradition." This provision, with its unprecedented grant of authority to the judge, was regarded at the time by continental legal theorists as revolutionary. In fact, however, in the years since the Swiss Civil Code has been in force, Article 1 has been rarely invoked, Swiss judges almost always preferring to couch their decisions in the language of more traditional methods of interpretation.

In Germany, after an initial period of conventional exegesis, the judges began to exercise their authority to adapt and develop the law openly. They developed an opinion style which resembles the American in its attention to the facts and its exposition of the reasoning process through which the court arrives at its decision. As anticipated by the draftsmen of the German Civil Code, the courts have not considered themselves to be tightly confined within the limits of statutory authority. They have, however, taken seriously the idea that they are bound by the legal order, the idea of law as a whole. Their care, when exercising what may be called their creative function, to incorporate new institutions into the framework of the legal order and to conform them to the basic principles of the legal order has been admired by many foreign observers. In general, the courts' authority to develop the law in this fashion is undisputed in present-day Germany, although there is there, as elsewhere, disagreement as to the limits of such power.

In summary, it can be said that while modern theory of interpretation generally acknowledges that principles are hard to identify and that judges dealing with legislative texts are often making law, the extent to which the behavior of the courts reflects this perception varies. It varies, not so much in the results achieved (which lead one to suspect that most courts are doing the same thing most of the time), as it does in the degree to which the process is open or concealed. In France, where the process tends to be hidden, the absence of the reasoned opinion deprives the system of a valuable tool and an important mechanism for controlling the discretion of judges. In Germany, where the process is more open, criticism tends to focus on the democratic problem: what limits should there be on the legal and political decision-making power of officials who are neither representative nor politically accountable?

## § 5.  Stability and Growth

Every legal system, for optimal functioning, needs mechanisms to promote certain important aims which are always in tension, if not in conflict, with each other: predictability and flexibility, stability and growth. Traditionally, in the common law, predictability and stability were provided by legal rules developed in cases and by the doctrine of *stare decisis*, while flexibility and growth were furnished by the rules of equity and the techniques for limiting and distinguishing precedent. In the code systems of the civil law tradition, predictability and stability were assured by the "written law" of the codes, while flexibility and growth were permitted, internally, by general clauses tempering rigid rules, and externally by interpretation, made more supple by the absence of a formal rule of *stare decisis*.

In both of these traditional systems, the present-day predominance of statutory law has diminished the role of the traditional mechanisms for maintaining equilibrium. Legislation and regulations, general or fragmentary in scope, have made case law less central to the common law and the codes less central to the civil law. In this new situation, it would seem at first that the civil law systems have an advantage, in that highly developed techniques for statutory interpretation are now of more utility than are case law techniques. But in both systems, relative certainty and predictability are adversely affected by the fact that modern statutory law, unlike the civil codes, generally is neither stable nor particularly rational (in the sense of being systematically organized). Its susceptibility to frequent amendment does not introduce much flexibility in the traditional sense either, since it is not in the nature of the political process to develop legal rules on a reasoned or principled basis. The courts, for their part, are increasingly called upon to rule not only on particular disputes, but also on problems of social conflict which often cannot be resolved by the reasoned elaboration of principle. Thus, both the civil and the common law, still living on their Roman inheritance of legalism and administration, share common problems of legitimation in modern states.

## SELECTED BIBLIOGRAPHY
## AND SUGGESTIONS FOR
## FURTHER READING

Franz Wieacker, "Foundations Of European Legal Culture", 38 *American Journal of Comparative Law* 1, 4B29 (1990).

Konrad Zweigert & Hein Kötz, *An Introduction to Comparative Law*, 3rd rev. ed., trans. Tony Weir (Oxford University Press, 1998).

James Gordley & Arthur Taylor von Mehren, *An Introduction to the Comparative Study of Private Law* (Cambridge University Press, 2006).

John Henry Merryman & Rogelio Pérez–Perdomo, *The Civil Law Tradition : An Introduction to the Legal Systems of Europe and Latin America* (Stanford University Press, 2007).

Otto Kahn–Freund, Claudine Lévy, and Bernard Rudden, *A Source–Book on French Law,* 3rd rev. ed. (Oxford University Press, 1991).

John Bell, Sophie Boyron, and Simon Whittaker, *Principles of French Law* (1998).

Gerhard Robbers, *An Introduction to German Law*, 4th ed. (Nomos, 2006).

Nigel G. Foster, *German Legal System & Laws*, 2nd ed. (1996).

John Bell, *Judiciaries Within Europe : A Comparative Review* (Cambridge University Press, 2006).

\*

# PART 2

# THE COMMON LAW TRADITION

---

## CHAPTER 7

## HISTORY, CULTURE AND DISTRIBUTION

### § 1. Introduction

English common law evolved from necessity, rooted in the centralized administration of William, conqueror at Hastings. A single event, the 1066 Norman Conquest, was the progenitor of this tradition. Its foundation was a unique, "unwritten" constitution and the orally rendered, and ultimately recorded, decisions of an extraordinarily gifted and respected judiciary. The harmony of a homogeneous society, tested by internal stresses but free of successful foreign invasions for nearly a millennium, aided an orderly development of legal institutions. Focusing on the pragmatic resolution of specific, current issues, English law developed insulated from the continental reception of Roman law, and the later emphasis on codification. As Pollock said,

English laws "grew in rugged exclusiveness, disdaining fellowship with the more polished learning of the civilians."

Comprehension of the rule of law in England today, and its litmus role in other common law systems, calls for an understanding of the cardinal incidents in English history which were generative of the slow but persistent development of institutions and concepts which comprise the common law tradition. The contemporary face of English law has numerous lines which compose a road map of the legal system reaching back nearly a millennium.

## § 2.  Roman Occupation

Legal institutions before the Norman Conquest made few lasting contributions to the common law. Pre–Conquest law was mostly unwritten, passing through generations by oral tradition. Over centuries the tribal laws changed to accord with the times, although little is known with exactitude of when the changes occurred or the precise forces impelling those changes.

Julius Caesar led exploratory expeditions to the Southeast of the island in 55 and 54 B.C. Disparate Celtic tribes, about whose legal structures Maine has commented, "One rude folk are much like another," supported periodic revolts in Britain against the Roman dominion. A century later Claudius, timidly seeking status as a conquering caesar, chose weak Britain to subdue. Romans ruled parts of the island for nearly four centuries. England was marked indelibly with Roman culture—the rose,

road system, Latin language and central heating—
but the Romans did not bestow upon the inhabit-
ants the Roman legal system. England had not been
developed, it had been occupied. Roman law was an
incident of occupation. It governed relations between Romans, but it began a decline in 410 A.D.
when the legions departed to protect Rome. What
Rome contributed to the English legal system was
indirect, occurring through the survival of remnants of institutional structures of a civilized society.

## § 3.  Roman–Norman Hiatus: The Anglo–Saxon Period

The Romans departure left the Britons with little
more than a few Christian missionaries to face
Angles, Danes, Jutes and Saxons—again society became dominated by diverse tribal communities, with
law predominantly unwritten local custom. There
was sufficient cohesion for Pope Gregory's mission-
ary, St. Augustine, to establish Christianity in the
late sixth century, giving English kings the impri-
matur of the supreme source of justice, but less
than the divine right of kings, the latter an important reservation in later centuries.

Anglo–Saxon law possessed elements of Teutonic
tribal traditions and customs, but personal wealth
began to replace "blood and kin" as the measure of
political power. England developed feudal attitudes,
but not in the continental sense. Landowners rather
than the community or state provided protection to
and drew loyalty from the dependent classes. Lords

administered justice for their tenants and villani, and their lands provided the source of taxes to defend the nation.

## § 4.  The Norman Conquest

The victory near Hastings by William was more a succession than a conquest. William's claim to the English throne was no less tenuous than Harold's. The law of England, an aggregate of disparate local customs, was left largely intact by the conqueror. But he confiscated all of the land and apportioned possession among his most trustworthy followers, extracting pledges of loyalty and service. William allocated the land in a manner to prevent his barons from concentrating their power and challenging his central authority.

William achieved his goal of kingly investiture at Westminster, but duties in Normandy demanded his attention. Establishing centralized rule at Westminster permitted the governance of a large number of Saxons by comparatively few Normans. William's administrative efficiency produced the Domesday survey in 1086, an inventory of all property throughout England, which facilitated a much larger revenue collection.

William resolved conflicts of royal concern at Westminster; local issues remained in the courts of the shires and hundreds. Only judicial disputes of an extraordinary nature were brought before the king as chief justiciar. Administrative necessity rather than legislative design played the central role in fashioning the early structures of the common law. William's legacy was the creation of a highly centralized legal system.

## § 5.  Royal Courts

No separation of government functions existed in early Norman England. The king, acting with close advisors in council, the *Curia Regis,* exercised judicial as well as executive and legislative powers. The council was as mobile as the king. But some functions of the *Curia Regis* later were delegated to newly created institutions. Judicial powers were assumed by the royal courts, beginning an important unification, the development of a law common throughout England. The three courts which were to develop over the ensuing two and a half centuries affirmed centralized judicial authority. They sat at Westminster even in the absence of the king.

The Court of Exchequer, a judicial offspring of the financial side of the *Curia Regis,* was the first common law court. It reflected the king's paramount interest in efficiently settling tax disputes. The Court of Common Pleas resolved issues between subjects which did not involve a direct interest of the king, thus the name *common pleas.* The disputes usually dealt with title to land, or personal actions of debt, covenant or detinue. The third central court was King's Bench, established to hear issues with a direct royal interest, pleas of the Crown. It issued writs of mandamus, prohibition, certiorari and habeas corpus, to control questioned actions of public officials. King's Bench later became an important check on the abuse of prerogative powers of the king. Its civil jurisdiction expanded, encroaching upon the Court of Common Pleas, encompassing most torts through the broadly interpreted writ of trespass and elaborate fictions, and later extending to contracts by the writ of assumpsit.

The English barons were on the verge of rebellion by the evolution of these common law courts. Although the king's courts did not replace directly the old local shire and hundred courts, if overlapping jurisdiction existed, litigants usually preferred the common law courts. Procedure was perceived as fairer in the latter, and participants avoided the harsh proof by ordeal or oath of the local courts. This preference eroded the role of local courts and reduced court fees revenue which was intensely coveted by both the king and the barons.

## § 6.　Writ System

Jurisdiction of the common law courts was limited severely by a writ system. A civil action lay before one of the courts only where a specific writ was available from a high official ("where there is no writ, there is no right"). Issued in the name of and constituting a command from the king, writs were addressed to an official authorizing commencement of specific suits, later known as "forms of action." The system was rigid; selection of the wrong writ resulted in dismissal. Early writs included debt, detinue, covenant, replevin and account. The writ of trespass was added and expanded to encompass ejectment, trover and assumpsit, important to the development of contract and tort. These writs were limited in scope, and neither the judges nor the Chancellor could freely create new writs. The Statute of Westminster 1285, limited the invention of new writs to circumstances similar to those then affording protection.

To increase further the jurisdiction of the common law courts, fictions were invented to extend the circumscribed writs. An example was ejectment. It originated as an action available only to a wrongfully ejected leasehold tenant, and was unavailable to a freeholder. But a fiction was created. The freeholder alleged a fictitious lease to a fictitious person, usually John Doe. Doe then alleged that he had been wrongfully ejected by Richard Roe, an equally fictitious character. Doe, the nominal lessee, next sued the ejector. The court had to determine the origin of the alleged lease, raising the issue of who owned the freehold. Thus, the common law court would rule on the title, an issue otherwise reserved to the local courts. This early common law emphasis on procedure was not unlike the early Roman law concentration on forms of actions, on the facts of a case rather than the origination of substantive, abstract legal rules.

## § 7.  Magna Carta

The progressive loss of jurisdiction of the rural courts, among other things, induced revolt among the English barons. Joined by a similarly aggrieved clergy the barons in 1215 extracted a charter from King John, later to become venerated as the Magna

Carta. It was a self-serving document for the barons, who viewed the charter as a contract to halt their losses of feudal privileges. But the charter also included a very few stipulations protecting ordinary citizens—provisions which much later endowed it with stature as a constitutional document of exceptional magnitude.

The Magna Carta contributed to the evolutionary demise of the rural courts, a process which continued for three centuries after the Conquest. The common law courts and the writ system were central to this demise, supported by the Crown assuming ownership of all land, and the diminished power of local sheriffs. The Magna Carta denied sheriffs the right to hear pleas of the Crown, and the Statute of Gloucester 1278, was interpreted to severely restrain civil jurisdiction of rural courts.

## § 8. Ecclesiastical Courts

Ecclesiastical courts persisted as rivals to the Royal Courts longer than the rural courts. The ecclesiastical courts applied canon law, the roots of which were firmly in the Roman law. The church vigorously defended its right to try "religious" offenses, including adultery, incest and less distinct offenses against morality. It also assumed civil jurisdiction over family issues, principally marriage and succession, as well as criminal jurisdiction over clergy. "Benefit of Clergy" allowed a convicted cleric to transfer the case from a temporal to an ecclesiastical court for sentencing. This unique doctrine persisted for several centuries, protecting persons with the most transient connection with the church, and ultimately even anyone who could prove literacy. The jurisdictional clash of church and state reached violent dimensions during the Plantagenet period, provoking the murder of Thomas à Becket in 1170 in Canterbury Cathedral. Although the church largely forfeited its judicial role, ecclesiastical jurisdiction over family and succession issues persisted until the mid–19th century, when it merged with other civil matters before the Royal Courts. But the imprint of canon law remains to this day on English family and inheritance law.

## § 9.  Equity

Forms of actions developed a rigid inflexibility by the early 15th century. A plaintiff unable to obtain a proper writ was left with no remedy. John Austin said that English equity "arose from the sulkiness and obstinacy of the common law courts, which refused to suit themselves to the changes which took place in opinion, and in the circumstances of society." However obstinate it may have been, the common law was not so rigid; it accepted new and competing institutions. To counter the severity of the writ system and provide relief other than money damages, the king and later his Chancellor, the "keeper of the king's conscience," accepted petitions for equitable relief. Heard in an inquisitorial fashion modeled on canon and Roman law, these equitable proceedings focused on avoiding the strictures of the common law. It was successful, and a formal Court of Chancery soon assumed jurisdiction of pleas in equity.

If the addition of such equitable concepts as injunctive relief and specific performance to supplement the common law was equity's paramount general contribution, the origin of the trust was its most important conceptual addition. The common law did not recognize an interest in a party who was not the titleholder to land. The transfer of property to a party to hold either for benefit of the grantor, who may have been trying to avoid feudal obligations, or a third party, did not create legal rights enforceable by beneficiaries. The Court of Chancery, acting to fill this acknowledged void in the common law by using its powers to demand good conscience, would rule that the holder of the property must administer it for the benefit of the donor or third party, as specified in the initial grant. From this concept arose an equitable interest held by the beneficiary, the person in possession assuming the status of a trustee obligated to deal with the property considering the nature of the equitable interest of the third party.

The discretion exercised by early Chancellors—John Seldon remarked that equity varied "according to the length of the Chancellor's foot"—had by the 18th century evolved its own procedural rules, paradoxically as rigid as those which equity had been created to avoid.

## § 10.  Justices of the Peace

The Crusades of the 12th century disrupted rural English life. Returning soldiers had tasted the fruits of conquest. Concern over the maintenance of order in England moved Richard I to name Keepers of the Peace, knights commissioned to maintain rural order. Their authority was expanded by the Justices of the Peace Act 1361, granting to "knights, esquires or gentlemen" of the area authority to "pursue, arrest, take and chastise" those breaching the peace. Lesser offenses were tried directly by these lay Justices of the Peace; more serious crimes were referred to the king's judges who conducted County Quarter Sessions four times annually. For 600 years the judicial process for keeping the peace has been lodged principally in the hands of ordinary citizens, rather than a professional judiciary. These J.P.s now comprise the magistrates' courts.

## § 11.   Wars of the Roses

The Wars of the Roses (1455–1471) tested English constitutionalism with civil disturbance, inept domestic rule and factionalism. Englishmen tended to prefer public order over freedom, accepting a firm rule which would have been unacceptable in the absence of the domestic disturbances. Common law institutions were strained, and later subordinated to sovereign decree during the Tudor and Stuart reigns, but they survived this single serious challenge to the common law in English history.

## § 12.   The Tudors

Henry VII (1485–1509), the first of the Tudor kings, created the Court of Star Chamber. Evolving from the judicial remnants of the King's Council, the Star Chamber was vested with extensive criminal jurisdiction, including conspiracies, forgeries and perjury. Its history of coercion to extract confessions and the names of accomplices has identified it with unreasoned judicial harshness, but it was not at the time considered particularly repressive. Its fines and punishments were not unduly severe, nor did it impose the death penalty.

The inquisitorial procedure of the Star Chamber was canon and Roman law in origin. It was staffed by persons with a civil law education at Oxford and Cambridge, who showed disdain for what they viewed as an overly formal common law system, preferring anything touched by the Renaissance, including the allegedly more understandable civil law. But there was to be no reception of civil law in England, its influences limited mainly to aspects of commerce affected by international trade, particularly mercantile and maritime law.

The establishment of Parliament as a legislative chamber separate from the monarch and his or her council, although still closely controlled by the monarch, was a more positive contribution of the Tudor period than the new judicial institutions. The strengthening of Parliament was backed by the proponents of the common law, who feared the gathering power being exercised by the monarch. A populace benefiting from an improving quality of life and concerned with the unsettling consequences of the abuse of royal power, began to limit the use of the royal prerogative; feudalism was on its deathbed. By the end of the Tudor period Parliament achieved status as the supreme law-making body; only its laws, not sovereign decrees, were binding on the courts.

## § 13.  The Stuarts

The sovereign-parliamentary conflict again surfaced under James I (1603–1625), first of the Stuarts in England. The Star Chamber became an oppressive institution of royal power, giving credibility to its reputation of unjustness undeserved at its formation. James would not admit to the philosophy of common law lawyers that ancient royal prerogative powers were divisible, vesting foreign policy and the declaration of war with the king, but assigning other issues to Parliament.

English judges, unlike the common law lawyers, were divided on the issue of sovereign power. Judicial loyalty to the Stuart conception of royal power was attributable to the historical control by the king over the appointment and removal of judges. Edward Coke led the opposition from his position as Chief Justice, ruling persistently to preserve the autonomy of the common law courts.

This divisiveness swelled under Charles I (1625–1649). He convened and dismissed Parliament with a frequency measured by its loyalty to the Crown. Parliament responded with the Petition of Right 1628, an impermanent attempt to reestablish due process concepts of the Magna Carta, and thus restrict sovereign power. Charles' response was eleven years of rule without a Parliament (1629–1640). When Parliament reconvened, it was hardly repentant. It purged the nation of the Star Chamber and made government ministers accountable to Parliament as well as to the king. The ensuing civil war was the final test of the separation of powers, a conflict which brought to Charles defeat and execution (1649), followed by several years of ineffectual rule and then Oliver Cromwell's self-appointment as Lord Protector of the Commonwealth. In 1660, eleven years after its demise, the monarchy was restored as the lesser evil.

The House of Lords, abolished after Charles' defeat, was reestablished, with the House of Commons reinforced as vested with greater initiation and authority. The king conceded to the grievances of Parliament, confirming its power over the process of legislation and control of taxation. A bloodless revolution in 1688 established an enduring Protestant royal succession and constitutional government. The Bill of Rights 1689, joined the Magna Carta as foundations of English constitutionalism. The Bill mandated parliamentary consent for a peacetime standing army, free election of Parliament, parliamentary approval of the suspension of law or levying of taxes, regular parliamentary sessions and limitations on bail, fines and cruel and unusual punishment. The Act of Settlement 1700, created an independent judiciary, with judges removable only by Parliament. The Act confirmed what Coke had said decades earlier, the sovereign may not dismiss judges.

The common law had survived the tumultuous Stuart era. English political and legal institutions had been altered, but the challenge to the Stuarts did not spring forth from opposition of the same nature as that in France in 1789, where a radical overhaul of the legal system was a consequence of the political revolution. The common law lawyers in England had successfully protected their turf, Coke even once suggesting that common law precepts could not be amended by statute. The threat of civil law notions imposed on English soil, of codification of the very heart of the common law, was for the time dormant.

Nearly as influential within England as Coke, William Blackstone, the Vinerian Professor of English Law at Oxford, wrote his Commentaries on the Laws of England in a readable style and concise form, which allowed them to be easily carried to outlying areas of the colonies. His 1771–72 American edition was the first general law book printed in America. Had Blackstone's work not been available, American lawyers would have been left to Coke's confusing Institutes or the inaccessible and complex case reports, or they even might have turned to civil law codes. Blackstone's impact in America is immeasurable; no other legal book so affected American legal practice as these published lectures of this once obscure lawyer.

## § 14.   19th Century Reforms

English law in the 19th century was altered by structural and social legislative reform. Jeremy Bentham and others who had little respect for tradition and the sanctity of precedent, viewed the common law as inordinately slow in responding to social needs. They urged codification to provide certainty and comprehension to the law, and to avoid a social revolution. The conservative judiciary and bar neither desired reform nor believed that legislation should be its source. Parliament became the progenitor of social change, however, enacting laws extending education, creating a competitive civil service exam, broadening House of Commons representation, reforming child labor laws and the Poor Law system, centralizing such government activities as road construction and adopting a freer trade policy by reducing protective tariffs. It did not codify rules, but adopted laws directed to more narrow issues which supplemented rather than replaced English precedent. Although Bentham's influence was apparent in the vast amount of new legislation, he found little support for codification of English law in the tradition of the civil law.

Parliament next turned to make some order out of the fragmented judicial structures. Overlapping jurisdiction and prolonged delays, ridiculed in prose by such authors as Dickens in his Bleak House, were reduced by the Judicature Acts 1873–75. These acts created a Supreme Court of Judicature consisting of the High Court of Justice and the Court of Appeal. The High Court brought together as its new divisions the former courts of Chancery, Queen's Bench, Common Pleas, Exchequer and Exchequer Chamber and Probate, Divorce and Admiralty (the last—"wills, wives and wrecks"—included subjects with influences of Roman law). Less than a decade later Common Pleas and Exchequer were merged into the Queen's Bench Division.

At first abolished as an appellate court, the House of Lords soon was restored to its judicial role by the Appellate Jurisdiction Act 1876, restricting its appellate jurisdiction and professionalizing the chamber by limiting members sitting on appeal to the Lord Chancellor, peers who had held high judicial office and newly created judicial peers, named Lords of Appeal in Ordinary. No longer could lay members of the House of Lords sit on legal appeals.

The Judicature Acts hastened the fusion of law and equity. Each division of the High Court was required to apply rules both of law and equity. But equity, that historically infant sibling of law, was to prevail in the event of a conflict. Despite the fusion, the Chancery Division has retained much of its original character as the equity court, and matters involving complex equity questions generally are there directed.

The rigid forms of action were abolished by the reforms; civil trials henceforth commenced with a general writ of summons. With the addition of a more unified procedure, the contemporary English trial presents far fewer technical obstacles to reaching the substantive issues than earlier existed.

## § 15.  The Modern Period

The election victories of the Labor and Liberal parties in the early years of the 20th century markedly altered the structure of British society. The Victorian era was in its finale. Working class dominance in the House of Commons aroused new conflicts with the House of Lords. When the Lords persisted in questioning proposed legislation which its members considered radical, the Commons responded by reducing the legislative power of the Lords, effectively limiting it to a right of delay, permitting neither amendment nor rejection of laws passed in the Commons.

The Supreme Court of Judicature was further refined in the Courts Act 1971. Courts of Assize and Quarter Sessions were abolished. The Crown Court assumed criminal jurisdiction, technically but not geographically joining the High Court and Court of Appeal as part of the Supreme Court. The Courts and Legal Services Act 1990 along with subsequent reforms, provided increased access to solicitors both to act as advocates before, and be appointed as judges to, the higher courts, both positions previously the prerogative of barristers.

English legal institutions have survived centuries of stresses and constitutional crises. The system has shown a remarkable resiliency in adversity. Current issues, including the adoption of a Human Rights Act, a Supreme Court, Seperation of Powers, Devolution (perhaps even as a form of federalism), the role of the House of Lords, the progressive fusion of barristers and solicitors, an increasingly multicultural society and many other significant and ongoing developments in Britain will continue to generate stresses on the common law. But its adaptability is illustrated by the distribution of the common law throughout the world. Although some of the strength of English law must be attributable to the homogeneous population in which the law developed, it is a system of justice which has been received in heterogeneous societies with as much success as the civil law.

## § 16.   "English" Law

There is some definitional confusion with the term *English law,* additionally blurred by references to Great Britain, the United Kingdom, or the Commonwealth. From its origins in Southern England, the common law became the principal basis of the procedure and/or substance of the legal systems for nearly a third of the world's population. It is inappropriate, nonetheless, to suggest that it is *English* law which exists in the United States or Australia or India or South Africa, or that there is a Commonwealth law applied in the Commonwealth, or a British law of Great Britain. English law applies only in England and in increasingly modified form in Wales.

Great Britain, the political geographic term for England, Wales and Scotland, has no common legal system. While many "English" statutes are applicable in Scotland, Scotland has its own and different legal system. For example, the Scottish private law is based primarily on the civil law derived from Roman law, the result of an alliance with the Continent in the 14th and 15th centuries intended to inhibit recurrent English expansion. After union with England in the Treaty of 1707, the development of Scottish law was influenced in large part by the English common law. Parliamentary enactments in many areas of private law were often applicable in both England and Scotland, but with the creation of the new Scottish Parliament, one can expect diminished congruency between the two systems. Furthermore, Scottish law remains a curious mix of civil and common law, a "Mixed Jurisdiction", an appropriate focus for the study of the potential for interrelation between these two legal traditions.

Northern Ireland and Great Britain comprise the United Kingdom, the principal geographic area to which most parliamentary expressions apply, the latter referred to as UK law. As in the case of Great Britain, the United Kingdom is a larger area than one associates with English law.

English substantive law is not directly applicable outside of England and Wales; however, English legal institutions retain some authority in many independent nations which were formerly part of the British Empire. The remnant of authority of the House of Lords Judicial Committee of the Privy Council continues a slender connection between England and some former colonies, a role diminished by the independence of former Commonwealth nations and by the Statute of Westminster 1931, the latter granting to Commonwealth legislatures the right to abolish appeals to the Privy Council.

## § 17. Devolution

Nationalism in Scotland and Wales engendered a demand in the 1970s for a transfer of some law-making power from London to national assemblies. Devolution was promoted more strongly in Scotland than in Wales, the former possessing more distinct government institutions and its unique civil law based legal system. A 1978 devolution bill requiring a referendum vote was rejected by Welsh electors. The Scottish voters narrowly approved it, but not by the required forty percent of all registered electors. Although devolution in a large measure was placed on hold with the referendum, occasional transfers of government power to local authorities in Scotland and Wales continued to occur. Visited again in 1997, devolution for Scotland, Wales and Northern Ireland succeeded. While each has different levels of devolved power, discussed in more detail later in this Book, they all continue to remain a part of the United Kingdom.

## § 18.   Distribution

The distribution of the common law throughout the British Empire was not due always to a voluntary reception of English law; it often was an imposition of the law as part of British territorial expansion. Dicey has divided the distribution into those nations "seeded," (i.e., India, Hong Kong), those "settled" (e.g., United States) and those "conquered" (e.g., South Africa). In Calvin's Case in 1608 it was ruled that English law was effective when England colonized an area where there was no "civilized" local law. Common law distribution differs from that of the civil law. There was a direct linkage to England with each of the principal nations in which the common law developed—Australia, Canada, Eire, India, New Zealand and with the thirteen original colonies that would become the United States. Although generally a direct linkage with Rome existed in the reception of the civil law *within* Europe, expansion outside of Europe and the areas of the Eastern Roman Empire lacked any direct contact with Roman law. Distribution was a result of territorial expansions of European nations with civil law systems rooted in Roman law, but with specific national characteristics.

Civil law is also the more easily received tradition. The convenience of codes rather than a matrix of case law and statutes, the more complex language of the common law and the ability to accept a Roman based civil law which is private and little threat to a political system, tend to favor the civil law system in a voluntary adoption process.

The world is not easily divided into an orderly pattern of countries which received a single legal tradition. Changes in territorial dominion by colonial powers created some systems possessing elements of more than one of the principal legal traditions—called "Mixed Jurisdictions". One of the most notable example is South Africa, where a civil law system (in the Transvaal) based on Roman–Dutch law partially acquiesced to the common law upon England's succession to power. Other Mixed Jurisdictions include, among others, Israel, Sri Lanka, Quebec, Louisianna, Botswana, Puerto Rico, and the Philippines.

The distribution of English common law in the three largest areas where the English did not recognize a well-established system of justice beyond tribal law, occurred in Australia, Canada and the United States.

England confronted only a small, indigenous population in Australia, and colonized the continent without expansionist competition from other European nations. Parliament decreed in 1828 that the Australian colony's legal system was the common law, including English statutes. Australia evolved from part of a constitutional monarchy with a sovereign parliament to a constitution based on popular sovereignty. It has become a federation of six states and several territories, each with a constitution and local government, including a parliament. The Australian Constitution was influenced by the American, but federal power in Australia is more limited than in the United States. United States federalism has evolved over two centuries, its broadly stated Constitution the foundation of a continued and significant growth of central government over previously state controlled activities. In contrast, Australia has been a federal system for just over a century.

The English did not recognize any advanced cultural development within the indigenous Australian population, such as they conceded existed in India. Nor was any Australian territory acquired from other European nations, as in the case of South Africa, parts of Canada and the United States. Both procedure and substantive private law in the several states of Australia are relatively uniform. English appellate decisions, although not binding authority, have remained the foundation for the development of Australian law, an emphasis which diminishes as the quantity of Australian precedent increases. The relatively small population of Australia has meant a longer period for the development of a substantial body of Australian precedent, however, and the attention to English decisions has accordingly endured longer than in other former British colonies and possessions. Respect for English decisions further is understandable by the peaceful growth of Australia as an independent nation; separation occurred from England without the adversity of a revolution. Australian law remains the most closely identified to English law of all the major nations which trace their legal systems to England.

Acquisition by Britain in 1763 of the French settled area of Canada did not lead to a fusion of the legal systems. The British Parliament divided Canada into English and French speaking sections, each with a parliament. It was an unsuccessful experiment terminated in 1840 by the establishment of a common parliament with equal representation. The British North American Act 1867, created the Dominion of Canada, composed of Nova Scotia, Ontario, Quebec and New Brunswick. The relative equality in number of French and English speaking persons was altered by the incorporation of the Northwest Territories acquired from the Hudson Bay Company in 1869, and the joining in the Union in 1871 by British Columbia. Canada thereafter was influenced largely by British government, economic and social structures, although Quebec preserved its civil law system, particularly its private law. Unlike later federal constitutions granted by the British Parliament to Commonwealth countries, the 1867 Act gave the British Parliament authority to approve any constitutional amendments in Canada. Over a century later, even this residual British authority caused concern which led to further constitutional reform in the 1980s, with most linkages with Britain severed.

The Supreme Court of Canada, functioning as an appellate court for the provincial tribunals, must occasionally apply the Civil Code of Quebec. Even though Quebec has a disproportionate participation on the Court, it is still a minority and there is no weighted voting for cases from Quebec provincial courts. Supreme Court decisions applying Quebec law are thus influenced by common law methodology.

Important changes in the development of Canadian law have occurred since the 1949 termination of allowing appeals to the Judicial Committee of the Privy Council in England. Additionally, decisions of English appellate courts are no longer binding, although they are treated with respect. A Canadian jurisprudence has developed which includes influences external to the historical affiliation to English law; particular notice is given to legal developments in neighboring United States.

The contiguity of common and civil law systems in Canada and its Province of Quebec, and to a lesser degree in the United States and Louisiana, contrast with the more complex common-civil law relationships in the legal system in South Africa. South African law initially possessed a strong Roman law base, resulting from Dutch governance. Shortly before Napoleon abolished Roman–Dutch law in the Netherlands and replaced it with his famous Code in 1809, Britain took possession of the Cape and incorporated it into the Empire. English procedure was first imposed on the Roman–Dutch law of the Cape, followed by the adoption of numerous English statutes, principally affecting commerce. Where this mixture of English and Roman–Dutch law was unclear, South African jurists, nearly all of them English trained lawyers, tended to look for guidance to English case law. Political independence for the Union of South Africa in 1910 generated a restoration of Dutch culture, including a resurgence of legal scholarship which concentrated notably on Dutch law. South African law thus is a hybrid system; it possesses Roman–Dutch law substantive elements and aspects of English law procedural methodology and structure. The end of white minority rule is already further transforming the system, but these early influences will endure for some time yet.

British settlers in North America, Australia, New Zealand and South Africa did not, in their opinion, encounter the highly developed indigenous culture and religion which existed in India. The common law distribution in India illustrates that the expansion of English common law did not require a perceived weak, indigenous population; it was still able to contribute to the administration of justice in such a diverse social system.

Expansion to India was not by unchallenged settlement, but by permission of the Grand Mogul of India and local leaders. The penetration first consisted of establishing coastal, commercial centers. Internal disorder beset India in the 19th century. The British took advantage of this weakness, extending their influence through, among other mechanisms, transactions with Indian princes, and finally dominating all of India.

Initial attempts to apply the common law in the early 18th century in Madras, Bombay and Calcutta, to both English and Indian parties, were unsuccessful. Hindu and Islamic law were substituted for common law in land, family and succession matters, a practice which continued in the interior as English governance coalesced. But, except in matters of family and succession law, and religious issues, English trained judges considered the best justice to require the application of English law.

Reform concepts promoted by Bentham found greater reception in India in the early 19th century than in England. Uncertainty existed in Indian law; little truly Indian precedent had developed, and there was insubstantial consistency among Indian courts in determining sources of law. A Law Commission began to codify Indian law, influenced by

European codes and by the British acceptance of reforms in India after the Great Mutiny in 1857. A civil procedure code was adopted in 1859, a criminal code in 1861, and the Indian Succession Act in 1865. The private law of India thus was codified at an early date. As in most common law nations outside England, India adopted a written constitution and judicial review. Withdrawal of British rule in 1947 did not mean withdrawal of the common law. The legal hierarchy remains much like that in England.

English law influence extends far beyond the major nations noted above. It has had substantial impact in former British controlled territories in Africa and in the Middle East, in some smaller colonies in Asia and in the Caribbean basin. In many of these locations, nevertheless, particularly in Africa, the English law affected a comparatively small percentage of the population. This is not an incident attributable to the nature of English law, but to the structure of the host societies. Such an impact is witnessed also in many areas where the civil law tradition has been received, particularly in nations of Latin America with widely dispersed native communities. Reception of a legal system depends upon the fusion of the local culture with that of the settling nation. Where a cultural assimilation has occurred, the English common law has shown remarkable capacity for adaptation.

# CHAPTER 8

## LEGAL STRUCTURES

### § 1.  The British Government

In the two centuries prior to the Revolution of 1688, the English monarch exercised extensive use of the royal prerogative, the powers incident to the throne. The very existence of Parliament was challenged by the king. But after the Revolution, the Act of Settlement 1700 confirmed Parliament as the central lawmaking authority, and the royal prerogative was forever much diminished.

Contemporary parliamentary authority includes direct enactment of legislation and delegation of power to ministers to adopt provisional orders and regulations. There is little separation of legislative and executive institutions. The two are so closely identified that the Prime Minister survives only while retaining the favor of Parliament. Convention dictates that a vote of censure by Parliament of a Prime Minister's actions, or the failure of the government to promote successfully a major bill, will precipitate a call for the dissolution of Parliament and new elections. The system does not support an executive and House of Commons majority from opposing parties.

The mutual dependency of the Prime Minister and the Commons should not suggest a fusion of the two. A philosophical policy schism often evolves after the Prime Minister is appointed. Additionally, the Prime Minister possesses considerable power in directing the executive branch free from direct parliamentary control.

However interrelated may be the executive and the House of Commons, there is a clear separation between the judiciary and the executive-Parliament linkage—despite the almost overpowering concept of parliamentary sovereignty. Judicial appointments illustrate an absence of political patronage. The immutable requirement for judicial appointment, a long and successful career as an advocate (or a rare advocate/politician, and now perhaps as a solicitor), has resulted in a judiciary nearly devoid of politicians—though the future character is less certain in light of recent changes in the methods of judicial selection. The English judiciary has evolved from its own highly sectarian source, preserving a clear detachment from the executive and Parliament, however parochial are the internal constraints within the institution of the bar itself. Furthermore, that independence has been further strengthened by the radical reduction in the judicial roles of the 1400–year old position of the political Lord Chancellor.

## § 2. Parliament—House of Commons

Legislation is adopted in the House of Commons, considered by the House of Lords, and given royal assent by the sovereign. But the legislative role of the House of Lords has significantly diminished, and the sovereign by convention since 1640 must grant royal assent. Legislative power thus is lodged in the House of Commons, although effectively the cabinet is the real power base. Lack of a more balanced bicameral legislature has generated discussion of parliamentary reform for several decades, with most of the focus on the reformation of the role and composition of the House of Lords—with some limited success.

House of Commons members are elected by a plurality rather than a majority vote, referred to as the "first-past-the-post" process. Consequently, quite minor changes in voting patterns of the principal parties in the electoral districts can result in meaningful changes of power in Commons. The system also provides a close tie between members of the House and the member's constituents.

Party organization and loyalty are essential to the survival of the parliamentary party (the party in power is the parliamentary party, the major party not currently in power generally is known as the opposition party). Any serious breach in loyalty may result in a House of Commons vote contrary to the interests of the government, although obviously to the wishful expectations of the opposition party, ever prepared to confront the parliamentary party in a new election at a time of the latter's weakness.

An elected House of Commons may endure for up to five years; an extension is allowed only in an emergency, such as occurred during the Second

World War, and requires the concurrence of the House of Lords. The Prime Minister may, however, dissolve Parliament and call new elections before the five year limit expires. Dissolution of Parliament may follow adversity to the government, reflected by opinion polls, a vote of censure or the government's failure to obtain an affirmative vote on a major proposal. Moreover, the Prime Minister may call for new elections in a time of popularity, predicting voter affirmation of the government's success and granting it a new five year period.

Major legislation is initiated in the Commons. If successful in the Commons, the bill proceeds to the Lords. Any rejection by the Lords only delays the bill, a second passage in the next session will negate further action by the House of Lords. But on the second attempt the Commons might not again pass the bill, with the Lords prior delay thus being not unlike a United States presidential veto. The delaying role of the House of Lords therefore can be significant. The only authority of Lords to reject bills absolutely involves a bill to extend the duration of Parliament beyond five years, and they have initiation authority for private bills dealing with local matters or issues affecting individuals.

Public participation by approval or disapproval of actions of the House of Commons has become more common and has to a degree limited the power of the Commons. Public referenda have been used for important issues to obtain public support or input for parliamentary acts. For example, referenda were used both in confirming membership in the European Communities by a significant majority in 1975, and recently in seeking pre-approval for devolution from the electorate in Northern Ireland, Scotland and Wales. Further use of a referendum following important parliamentary acts may well develop into a form of restraint on the House of Commons. Indeed, the former Blair government was only saved from a possible significant defeat at the hands of the electorate, as a consequence of a rejection by referendum on the proposed European constitution when the constitution was withdrawn following negative votes in other European countries.

## § 3. Parliament—House of Lords

The composition of the House of Lords partially explains its decline in power. Composed of Lords Spiritual (certain bishops), Lords Temporal (peers and peeresses), and the Law Lords, this aristocratic body is largely conservative, but often also quite adventuresome. It has been criticized by the public and challenged by the House of Commons. Until recently, there were few change in its composition over the centuries, although the Life Peerages Act 1958, which allows peerages to be limited to the grantee's life, has resulted in the granting of very few hereditary peerages.

Other serious incursions on the power of the House of Lords resulted from two parliamentary acts, in 1911 and 1949, which limited the role of the House of Lords to its present delaying power. That delaying power has been used primarily against major and usually controversial proposals of Labour governments seeking social reform, often not to defeat the bills, but to obtain amendments. That happened in 1997 with a Police Bill, Lords approved it only after the Labour Party agreed to a significant amendment. In some cases, when the bills are presented in the next session of Parliament, they include amendments which may be viewed either as coerced by the House of Lords delay, or as simply reflecting new thinking due to the additional time for consideration. But some delaying actions by the Lords have led to challenges to the very existence of the upper chamber, including proposals for total abolition, though recent reforms do not go so far. The present reform of the House of Lords began almost immediately after the Labour party returned to power in the late 1990s. They then enacted the House of Lords Act of 1999—what was to be the first of a series of reforms to the Lords.

The House of Lords Act, while removing the vast majority of hereditary peers (removing over 600, and leaving around 100), left the life peers (around 600), the law lords (around 25—both retired and active), and bishops (around 25) thus providing a total of around 750 members of the House of Lords. It is expected that further substantial reform will take place. That final reform, however, has proven to be more difficult to formulate than the initial reform in 1999, though will assuredly be completed in the near future. The question is really of the future composition, methods of selection, geographic representation, and most importantly the powers such a body would exercise—whether as an equal second house, or simply as a weak reviewing body, or something in between.

## § 4.　The Prime Minister and the Sovereign

The power of a serving Prime Minister is considerable. The Prime Minister is the head of the party which is in power in Parliament and is also in charge of the executive branch of the government—from civil servants to the armed forces. The Prime Minister, however, is in an uncertain position. The importance of the position is acknowledged, but the duration is most impermanent. The office expires at the next general election, within five years or earlier in cases of the loss of confidence of the Parliament or her party. Or—if the election is successful the position is renewed. Though it should be noted that the Prime Minister is not elected directly by the public. An aspiring candidate must succeed in being chosen from among the leaders of the successful party in the national election for House of Commons seats, not from a public constituency. That choice must be confirmed by the sovereign, whose role is limited to granting approval, not participating in the selection.

The sovereign is a ceremonial figure who undertakes state visits, signs documents, receives foreign ambassadors, bestows recommended honors and performs other similar acts. England functions in the name of the sovereign, but the latter acts only upon the advice of ministers. A strong sovereign nevertheless may be influential. The survival of the English monarchy is due principally to its nature as a constitutional monarchy in which the sovereign assumes essentially a symbolic role. By convention the Prime Minister visits frequently with the sovereign to comment on actions taken at Cabinet meetings, offering an interested and astute sovereign an opportunity for discussion of developing policy and legislation, sometimes referred to as the power to advise, encourage and warn.

The structure of the monarchy and activities of the sovereign are governed by legislation and conventions. The sovereign does exercise the royal prerogative as the historical fountain of justice, but there is no effective remaining *independent* sovereign power. There are rare rumblings from Labour to abolish the monarchy, but they are not as threatening as the challenges to the other remnant of vested privilege, the House of Lords. Criticism of the monarchy usually is directed to its financial burden to the nation, or to the minor transgressions of subordinate members of the royal family. But on the whole the monarchy seems quite secure, providing the sovereign does not allow use of the royal prerogative to stray beyond the limits of symbolism.

## § 5.  Devolution

The history of government power in Great Britain since the Norman conquest has largely been one of ever increasing centralization. The conquests by England of Wales and then Ireland, as well as the attempted conquest of Scotland and its eventual absorption through political union, all reflected the growth of a strong central government. The governmental apparatus was thus largely unitary, with one central government in Westminster, despite the existence of separate legal systems within Britain.

In the twentieth century, however, that centralization movement has undergone a reversal, starting with the initial independence, after much violence, of the southern and central part of Ireland. Later, largely in the second half of the twentieth century, rising nationalism in Scotland and Wales, as well as the unsettled conditions between Catholics and Protestants in Northern Ireland, eventually led the government in Westminster to devolve power to those regions—though in different ways and to different degrees depending on the unique circumstances present in each region. Although the precise nature of that devolution is still in flux, it too, like so much else since the end of the 1990s represents a radical departure from previous British constitutional structures. It has even been argued that Britain now has a form of federalism—though one quite different to that employed in the United States.

Specifically, each of the devolved regions has their own parliament or assembly. Furthermore, the competence of each is different depending on the unique historical circumstances of each of the regions. Thus Northern Ireland's National Assembly has unique power sharing rules designed to resolve the decades, perhaps even centuries long, sectarian conflict between the protestant and catholic communities. Wales, on the other hand, as a consequence of its significantly longer relationship with Westminster, was initially accorded rather limited devolution with competence only to enact secondary legislation, like regulations in American terminology. But with the success of the Assembly and the nationalism that it fed, the Welsh National Assembly was accorded greater powers in later legislation. Scotland, as a result of its merger with England as a theoretically equal partner in the eighteenth century, had perhaps the greatest claim to self government, and was correspondingly given significant primary legislative competence as well as limited revenue raising capabilities.

This experiment in local government, in historically centralized Britain, is in its very early days, and so one should expect that there will be many years of development within the institutions as well as with the underlying relationship with Westminster. At a minimum, each of these devolved governments must now be taken into account when one considers the legal system in Britain.

## § 6.   The Judicial Structure

The English court system has been refined in the past century and a quarter principally by the Supreme Court of Judicature Acts 1873–1875, and by several acts since the early 1970s. The courts nevertheless retain characteristics associated with their structure as formed in the three centuries following the 1066 Norman Conquest. It remains essentially a unitary system; all courts, both civil and criminal, lead to the Court of Appeal and House of Lords, and from 2009 to a Supreme Court. The principal exception, the division of equity under the jurisdiction of the Court of Chancery, was transitory. The fusion of law and equity unified this one errant vestige, although many traces of equity persist in the organization and practice of law.

Ordinary courts in England most generally are classified as superior or inferior. Inferior court jurisdiction is limited both geographically and according to the nature of subject matter, and includes those civil and criminal courts which decide the vast majority of disputes, the county and magistrates' courts, respectively. Superior court jurisdiction is country-wide, and exists in the Crown Court, High Court, Court of Appeal and House of Lords (and soon the Supreme Court). The most important special courts include the Judicial Committee of the Privy Council and Restrictive Practices Court.

Although the axial courts in the English system remain the ordinary courts, in the last half century administrative tribunals of special jurisdiction have proliferated. Vested with judicial and quasi-judicial authority, these institutions are evidence of an increasing government involvement in the lives of citizens. The special tribunals provide a small measure of duality to the system, but England has no separate administrative hierarchy of courts as exists in many civil law systems.

The structures and jurisdiction of the English court system are less surprising to an American observer than several particular characteristics, such as the extensive use of lay judges for minor criminal matters in magistrates' courts, the more active participation of judges in proceedings, the comparatively minor and officially rare use of juries in civil trials, the less adversary nature of proceedings, and the colorful ceremonial trappings of court dress. But there is one interesting structural and jurisdictional character—the role two European courts play in the English system.

The unified English court system has been altered in part by participation in the European Union, and the European Convention on Human Rights. The European Court of Justice in Luxembourg is the final authority on issues of Community law, because the European Communities Act 1972, incorporated Community law into the law of England (and Scotland, Wales and Northern Ireland). Similarly, although Britain enacted the Human Rights Act of 1998 implementing most of the European Convention on Human Rights, cases can still be taken by English persons to the European Court of Human Rights in Strasbourg. That court and its decision have played and continue to play a role in the development of English principles of human rights, even though the decisions of the ECHR do not constitute English law.

## § 7.  County Courts

The county court, sometimes called the small claims court, is a familiar court to an American observer. With its comparative informality, its single professional judge, and its broad jurisdiction over less complex civil disputes involving modest

sums, the county court serves as the most important adjudicatory body for private, civil matters
throughout England and Wales.

The shire and hundreds courts, which developed
before the Conquest and which largely had declined
or perished for lack of use by the Middle Ages, were
the historical predecessors of the county courts. The
modern county court notably differs from the London based superior courts by dispersions into every
corner of England and Wales, thus providing a local
forum for civil disputes. They are cauldrons of jurisdiction, dealing with simple matters of contract and
tort, probations of small estates, equity jurisdiction
and, in some courts, limited admiralty and family
law matters. The county courts are also assigned
jurisdiction of some social legislation, but a large
amount is confined to special tribunals.

Traditionally, procedure in the county courts was
simplified in contrast to the High Court, and costs
were lower. But with the introduction in 1999 of
the new Civil Procedure Rules, discussed later in
this Book, some of the differences have been eliminated. The county court judges are professional
judges. Assisting these courts is a District Judge,
formerly called a "Registrar", who serves as administrative chief of the court, who has authority to
hear and decide both pre-trial motions and small
claims and actually is a second judge for minor
cases. Even before the recent extensions of the
rights of audience, solicitors as well as barristers
had been able to appear as advocates before the

county courts, an early intrusion by the former into the historically well preserved barristers' domain.

## § 8. Magistrates' Courts

If the organization and jurisdiction of the county courts appear to differ little from methods of resolving comparatively minor civil matters in many other common law systems, the structure of the magistrates' courts may seem most unique. Magistrates' courts primarily are staffed by ordinary but carefully chosen lay persons sitting part-time in collegiate fashion to deal in summary form mostly with minor criminal and some minor civil matters. Three magistrates usually sit, choosing their own chairperson. In front of them sits the magistrates' law trained clerk.

Typically, when there is an issue of law the magistrates ordinarily will ask the clerk for an opinion, which is to be given in open court. Furthermore, when certain issues are involved, such as the new Human Rights Act, the clerks are to provide the legal advise sua sponte. Additionally, clerks can ask questions of witnesses and are under a duty to assist parties that have no lawyer present. Recently the legally trained clerks are exercising more power pursuant to some specific laws. For example, the Crimes and Disorders Act 1998 has allowed the clerks, if delegated, the ability to exercise certain of the pre-trial powers of a magistrate sitting alone.

If one placed the clerk where a judge would normally sit, with the three lay magistrates in a box to the side to answer questions of fact, the court will have been rearranged to an image of how many common law nation minor criminal issue courts function. But in fact the magistrates participate much more than a silent jury—they are often far more inquisitorial than professional judges.

The use of lay as opposed to professional judges for less serious criminal matters has strong historical roots. The return of English soldiers nourished with plundering from the continental wars and the Crusades, and the loss of as much as one-half of the population from the Black Death (plague), encouraged government control of both wages and the free movement of persons. A few of the most influential persons in each community were appointed to keep the peace under the Justices of the Peace Act 1361. Now some thirty thousand justices, or magistrates, serve throughout England and Wales. An essential feature is that they sit near where they live, though since the Courts Act of 2003, the magistrate courts have been administered centrally, largely replacing the previous strong local control of the administration of those courts.

With the exception of a few historic locations, magistrates are appointed by the Lord Chancellor (whose Department governs the magistrate system) from local nominations. The magistrates accept office as a public duty, for the prestige of being a part of the judicial system and to be permitted to append to their names the initials J.P. They were compensated in earlier years, but the remuneration has been abolished. They are thus often referred to as "the great unpaid"—and by critics as "the great unlearned," an opprobrium which applies only to the lay magistrates. In the larger cities, there are full-time, salaried, law trained magistrates, called "district judge (magistrates courts)". These judges, who are usually solicitors, sit not in collegiate form, but alone.

Criminal jurisdiction is the paramount role of the magistrates' courts in the system of English justice. Magistrates hear applications for bail from prisoners and for arrest and search warrants from the police and as such can influence the course of an investigation. Summary offenses, such as criminal damages costing less than the equivalent of roughly $9000 or assaults on police officers or those generally of a minor character, are tried to the magistrate without a jury. The benefit is speed and the low cost of appearance, in contrast to a proceeding before the Crown Court. The disadvantage to the accused is a highly probable conviction, offset by a more lenient sanction than likely to come from conviction in a Crown Court. A large percentage of magistrates' cases are traffic offenses, although most persons so charged plead guilty and submit by mail (plea by post) specified fines, avoiding a personal court appearance. Certain indictable offenses may be tried before a magistrates' court or a Crown Court, but the more serious are tried only before a Crown Court. Ordinary appeals of these magistrate decisions also go to the Crown Court.

The magistrates' court plays an important role involving domestic affairs. Concurrent jurisdiction exists among the magistrates' courts (e.g., carrying out divorce decrees), the county courts (e.g., granting undefended divorces) and the High Court (e.g., deciding defended divorces), a compromise to having a single family court. A magistrates' court hearing a juvenile case assumes a status separate from the criminal environment of a magistrates' court proceedings. The juvenile proceeding is closed to the public and press coverage is limited. Detention of a convicted juvenile usually must be in a community home, rather than confinement with adult offenders.

Jurisdiction of the magistrates' courts extends beyond its principal criminal law responsibility to include minor civil issues involving statutory debts, such as national insurance contributions and utility charges, and licensing matters (such as licensing pubs). There is also jurisdiction over numerous domestic relations matters. Both of these areas of civil jurisdiction overlap with the jurisdiction of the county courts.

The magistrate system involves an extraordinary use of lay persons to adjudicate the vast majority of criminal offenses (97%) committed within a community. It has no parallel in the United States; but rather is more closely identified with various former comrades' courts that used to exist in socialist law systems, although it lacks the former political function of such tribunals. It possesses problems due to the number of magistrates, their geographical dispersing, and their lack of significant legal training.

## § 9.  High Court

The Royal Courts of Justice refers to the highly centralized High Court and Court of Appeal, housed in an imposing building on the Strand in London. The Supreme Court of Judicature Acts 1873–75, created the High Court by bringing together the courts of civil jurisdiction which had been formed shortly after the Conquest. The High Court was constituted in five divisions in the 1875 Act—Chancery; Probate, Divorce and Admiralty ("wills, wives and wrecks"); Queen's Bench; Common Pleas and Exchequer. Common Pleas and Exchequer were merged into the Queen's Bench Division in 1880. The Courts Act 1971, abolished the Probate, Divorce and Admiralty Division, dividing its responsibilities among Queen's Bench, Chancery and a newly created Family Division.

This divisional structure is partially illusory. Each of the three divisions theoretically has equal jurisdictional competency, although the Rules of the Supreme Court express an allocation of matters to separate divisions. Matrimonial cases in the High Court are heard in the Family Division, and Chancery is assigned numerous matters which have a traditional equity nature. A High Court judge assigned to any division, nevertheless, may exercise jurisdiction over an issue which under the Rules of the Supreme Court technically is allocated to another division.

If this divisional structure for jurisdiction is confusing, so is the geographical division. The Courts

Act 1971 allows any division of the High Court to sit anywhere in England or Wales. For centuries cases were carried to the High Court in London, and there is still a trend to bring cases there, in part due to the high concentration of barristers found in London. But, with the more recent dispersal of barristers throughout the country, pressure on the Royal Courts to hold hearings in the provinces increases. Additionally, since High Court judges have routinely travelled to other cities to hear criminal matters in the local Crown Courts, it is difficult to argue that they ought not stay and hear some civil cases. Accordingly, the Queen's Bench and Family Divisions increasingly sit in about two-dozen locations throughout the country, though the Chancery Division leaves home comparatively infrequently.

The Chancery Division originally was presided over by the Lord Chancellor, but since the Constitutional Reform Act of 2005 removed the judicial functions from the Lord Chancellor, it is now presided over by the "Chancellor of the High Court". The Chancery Division tends to concentrate on issues of an equitable nature earlier assigned to its predecessor, the Court of Chancery, including estate administration, trusts, mortgages, certain interests in land, partnership dissolution and bankruptcy of companies and some revenue matters. The Family Division—its chief judge is called President—has original jurisdiction of important matrimony, legitimacy, adoption, guardianship and certain disputes between spouses.

The broadest civil jurisdiction, original and appellate, is assigned to the Queen's Bench Division. The Queen's Bench broader jurisdiction, encompassing many contract and tort actions, is attributable to its being the successor to three of the original divisions of the early High Court—Queen's Bench, Common Pleas and Exchequer. Additionally, Queen's Bench is charged with admiralty jurisdiction, a unique function evolving from the transfer of admiralty issues from the former Probate, Divorce and Admiralty Division in the 1971 reform. The Queen's Bench Division is the only division of the High Court with any criminal jurisdiction. Two or three judges may sit as an appellate court in limited appeals from the magistrates' courts or Crown Courts.

Originally, the appellate jurisdiction of the High Court was quite limited, in part due to many cases being able to bypass the High Court and go directly to the Court of Appeal. Now, in an effort to make the whole system more efficient and to have only the most important cases heard in the Court of Appeal, recent reforms have limited such direct appeals from lower courts to the Court of Appeals, thus expanding the appellate jurisdiction of the different divisions of the High Court. The recent reforms, despite tackling these and other criticisms of the High Court, particularly in the procedural context, did not end the confusing divisions and jurisdictional competences of the different parts of the High Court.

## § 10. Crown Courts

The modern Crown Court is a superior court of criminal jurisdiction on a level comparable to the civil jurisdiction of the High Court. While the divisions of the High Court have evolved over centuries, the Crown Court was created by the Courts Acts 1971. It is, nevertheless, part of the evolutionary process of development of the criminal courts over the centuries.

Historically, the more serious of the indictable offenses were handled by the Quarter Sessions and Assizes. These were local courts, their organization and administration varying throughout the country, with special criminal courts convened in several of the larger cities. The geographic distribution of the English population, however, was altered when urbanization accelerated in the late 18th century, and the very different characteristics of local criminal courts became apparent. Uniformity was thought desirable and best achieved through a national system of criminal courts with some consistency in structure and administration. It was nonetheless very slow to develop. Only with the Courts Act 1971 was the old system replaced with a single superior criminal court, made part of the Supreme Court of Judicature and designated the Crown Court. But although part of the Supreme Court, Crown Courts do not sit in the Royal Courts building on the Strand in London, they have their own court buildings in every corner of the nation. Indeed, one Crown Court retains its historic name—the "Old Bailey" in London (originally the Assize Court for

Greater London, created by the Central Criminal Court Act 1834).

Despite the significant consolidation of the criminal court system in 1971, there was no unification of judicial qualification when the court structure was changed; the Crown Court cannot be said to have its own judges. The judges rather consist of all the judges of the High Court, plus Circuit judges, recorders (part time judges that can hear the least serious Crown Court cases) and the district court judges in the magistrates' courts. They sit alone. It is possible for a collegiate form to convene, but it does not tend to happen. A Justice of the Peace may serve if there is also a judge of the High Court present, but the former sit principally when there is a hearing on an appeal or an issue of committal for sentence.

Supplementary to the jurisdiction of the Crown Court over the principal indictable offenses, are its roles for appeals from the magistrates' courts and as a sentencing tribunal after conviction in a magistrates' court. A magistrates' court may transfer sentencing to the Crown Court if the magistrates believe that their own sentencing powers are inadequate considering the severity of the crime. Recent suggestions that the Crown Court and magistrates' courts should be merged into one criminal court was rejected, even as the government accepted the idea that the two court systems should operate more closely together. One consequence was the enactment of the Courts Act 2003 which did provide some rationalization and tighter and more coordinated administration for the two courts.

## § 11.  Court of Appeal

The Court of Appeal is part of the Supreme Court of Judicature, and is exclusively a court of appellate jurisdiction. Civil Division jurisdiction involves appeals from the High Court, county courts and certain administrative courts and tribunals. While earlier it accepted appeals more by leave than by right, thus mirroring the House of Lords, by the 1990s there was concern that the Court of Appeals was being swamped by too many appeals in civil cases, particularly too many insignificant cases from a legal standpoint. This was thought to be especially inefficient in that many of those cases had already been appealed through the High Court itself. As a result, the Access to Justice Act of 1999 introduced reforms in the way in which appeals in civil cases were to be handled. Among other reforms was the introduction of the concept that normally only one level of appeal will be allowed without permission of the court, absent exceptional circumstances such as the raising of novel issues of law.

The Court of Appeal remains very centralized, and sits nearly always in London. The Criminal Division primarily hears appeals from the Crown Courts, and sometimes sits outside London. The court is thus the point at which nearly all disputes merge if further proceedings are intended, a feature characteristic of most common law systems, in contrast to having parallel levels of appeal for several judicial hierarchies.

Appellate decisions are rendered in collegiate form, by three judges, although in some limited circumstances two judges may appear, usually to determine application for leave to appeal. If a particularly important issue of law is before the court, five judges may sit, although the resulting decision possesses no greater authority than one emanating from the more common three judge court.

The Lords and Ladies Justices of Appeal are the principal judges of the Court of Appeals, the Master of the Rolls and the President of the Courts of England and Wales Lord Chief Justice are the administrative heads of civil and criminal matters, respectively. In addition to many ex-officio judges, and the occasional borrowing of a High Court judge, there are usually around forty judges that sit in the Court of Appeals. During times of substantial caseload, a judge of the High Court may be temporarily added, illustrative of the absence of absolutes in the identification of certain judicial positions with a single, specific court.

## § 12.  The House of Lords & the Supreme Court of the United Kingdom

The term "House of Lords" has historically referred to that chamber in either its judicial or legislative function. The judicial role of the House of Lords antedates its legislative role. But few of its early judicial functions as part of the Curia Regis survive. Indeed, in 2008 this final court of appeal will be replaced by a Supreme Court, physically and legally separate from the Parliament. Because it is anticipated that the new Supreme Court will retain much of the character of the judicial committee of the House of Lords, there is value in understanding the history and present-day practices of the House of Lords. Indeed, the first justices will simply be the then existing law lords as well as any new appointed justices if there are then less than twelve law lords.

Decisions of the House of Lords prior to the 19th century did not command considerable respect. They often were rendered by House of Lords members who were not lawyers. Following the Appellate Jurisdiction Act of 1876 which established paid life-peers to hear appeals, the convention was that these Lords of Appeal in ordinary (Law Lords) would hear the appeals. These law lords constitute the Appellate Committee of the House of Lords. Until 2006 the Lord Chancellor was also a member of the Appellate Committee. The Law Lords were chosen either by direct appointment from among the most eminent barristers or by elevating a judge from a lower court. Almost always the appointments were made from the Court of Appeal. A benefit of such appointment was a life peerage, to a degree offsetting the rather modest salary. The appointment process has now been reformed to include an independent judicial appointments committee. Furthermore, in the future the justices of the supreme court will not be members of the House of Lords, though those judges already possessing a peerage will be allowed to continue to sit in the Lords. Traditionally, one or two of the Law Lords are from Scotland and are assigned to appeals from the highest Scottish court of appeal, the Court of Session, and one law Lord is from Northern Ireland and is assigned to sit in on appeals from the Court of Appeal of Northern Ireland. Indeed, the jurisdiction of the House of Lords has been predominantly appellate, and almost exclusively related to matters from the Court of Appeal in England, although as noted it is also a final court of appeal for Scotland and Northern Ireland.

Unlike most other English courts, the House of Lords as a judicial body sits quite informally. The Law Lords hear appeals in a committee room rather than the chamber of the House, and they dispense with the formality of wigs and robes. Opinions of the Lords are actually separate speeches by each individual judge, currently written down rather than read aloud, as was the early practice. The judgments are rendered in the legislative chamber. Each judge votes by standing and stating that he would allow or dismiss the appeal, as stated in his written speech. One must count up and aggregate the different opinions in order to determine the disposition of the case and whether there is an agreed legal theory to support the result.

The House of Lords while discussed here in its judicial capacity in the end cannot be divorced from the fact that it is also a legislative body. The person designated a Law Lord, or Lord of Appeal in Ordinary, is a member of the House of Lords and secondly a judge in that chamber. But she was appointed to be a judge rather than a legislator. If she did participate in the legislative sessions, and many did do so, she was not to speak on matters which involved party politics. She was supposed to limit her activities to legal issues and to voting on social questions. This role contrasts with the participation of members of the House of Lords who are not Law Lords, but who might wish to sit when the Law Lords hear appeals. As noted above, they may not. In any event, the fact that there was some overlap of the functions of its members was perhaps one of the primary reasons for the transfer of the judicial functions of the House of Lords to an independent court. Indeed, that overlap presented serious problems under certain due process and fairness provisions (Article 6) of the European Convention on Human Rights.

Sensitivity to such human rights issues and to transparency concerns were among some of the factors that eventually led the government in 2003 to announce its intention to reform major parts of the judiciary—from the elimination of the judicial positions of the Lord Chancellor to the way judges were appointed and even to eliminating the Judicial Committee of the House of Lords. Among other things, the government announced that it was going to create a new court, a Supreme Court, that would take over the appellate role of the Judicial Committee. The final details were contained in the Constitutional Reform Bill of 2005. The Supreme Court will be housed outside of the Parliament, and will consist of twelve "justices of the supreme court". The most senior member will be the "President" and the next most senior the "Deputy President" of the court. A minimum of three justices will be needed to constitute the court. The President will be able to ask other senior judges to sit on an ad hoc basis, especially if they have a relevant substantive competence for a particular case. Former Justices and former Law Lords will also be able hear cases. New justices of the court will be appointed through the use of special impartial selection committees. The Supreme Court's powers will largely be the same as the present Appellate Committee of the House of Lords.

## § 13.  Judicial Committee of the Privy Council

The Privy Council is also a judicial evolution of the Curia Regis. Gaining its authority from the royal prerogative, it assumed the role as the final court of appeals for courts throughout the Empire, and may properly be considered to be a Commonwealth court. Later known as the Privy Council, it assumed the role as the final court of appeals for courts from throughout the Empire. The Privy Council later refined its unique role as a judicial body by the creation of the Judicial Committee in the nineteenth century. Today it is primarily known for the fact that it hears appeals from the Commonwealth. The Commonwealth consists mainly of former British colonies, with the Queen as its symbolic or titular head.

In its current diminished role, its judges are mainly the Law Lords, but with the addition of a few who have held high judicial office in other parts of the Commonwealth. Sitting in five member panels in Downing Street, the cases often offer challenges not present under English law. Many of the cases involve judicial review in nations with a written constitution and bill of rights. Most recently the Privy Council was enlisted to hear matters involving the Scottish, Welsh, and Northern Ireland devolution, though those cases will soon be transferred to the new Supreme Court. Additionally, the Privy Council will hear: admiralty cases concerning "prizes" (a rare occurrence today!); appeals from certain professional bodies (such as the General Medical Council and those bodies dealing with veterinary surgeons and dentists); certain ecclesiastic matters; and occasionally the Council is called on to provide advice to the sovereign (in the past this has included advice on such issues as eligibility to sit in the Commons, certain issues in the island of Jersey, and so on).

Because there were so few judges appointed from the Commonwealth, as Commonwealth nations acquired independence they found little use for the Privy Council, preferring to establish their own national appellate courts. While such larger members of the Commonwealth as Australia, Canada, India and South Africa have abolished appeals to the Judicial Committee, a few continue its use, including such nations as the Bahamas, Antigua and Barbuda, Jamaica, Belize, Grenada, and Barbados. Had Commonwealth representation been increased significantly prior to the independence movement, the Judicial Committee might have survived as a far more consequential institution. But it never altered its status as a central court sitting in London, requiring Commonwealth Judicial Committee members to travel considerable distances to participate in deliberations. The relative inactivity of the Committee did not demand the full time presence of its members, and Commonwealth participants usually did not terminate service on their national courts. Once prestigious, this judicial vestige is now of minor stature; its future is bound securely to the fortunes of the Commonwealth.

## § 14.  Special Courts

Several special courts with limited jurisdiction supplement the court structure described above. Perhaps the most visible is the Restrictive Practices Court, a superior court but not part of the High Court. It hears a broad range of issues related to monopolies and restrictive practices, but in fact hears few cases. It is the most important court in England to use an aldermanry composition of judges. Professional judges share the bench with lay persons who possess special knowledge of industry, commerce or public affairs.

Beyond the specialist courts are the numerous tribunals which exist in England with legislative authority to dispense administrative justice. Their procedures are less formal, more rapid and less expensive than proceedings in the regular courts, but they are criticized for denying individuals their right to appear before the ordinary courts, an argument similar to that which made arbitration slow to gain acceptance. Lay participation on tribunals is far more extensive than in the regular courts. Solicitors may appear as advocates, but even they are not required in many tribunals.

No formal, recognized separate court hierarchy has developed for private and public law issues, as exists in many civil law nations. The development of special tribunals with lay "judges" (and a chair with some legal knowledge) may, however, prevent social legislation from being excessively strictly construed by the conservative English judiciary. Furthermore, the tribunals, often thought to be more policy oriented than the courts, hear some six times as many cases as the courts. But, encroachments on the role of the ordinary courts by administrative tribunals is generally viewed with suspicion by the judiciary. The Tribunals and Inquiries Acts of 1958 and 1992 increased professional judicial control over the tribunals, partly by governing their composition and partly by governing their product (by channeling appeals from tribunals to various parts of the Supreme Court). This influence of the established legal institutions has had an effect, administrative tribunals have become less flexible and accused of excessive legalism. Furthermore, in 2006 the government formally launched the new Tribunal Service as the first stage in implementing far reaching reform of the organization of the many different tribunals. An initial twenty-one different tribunals were brought under one organization framework. Thus, administrative justice in England continues to increase in scope and structure, and will continue to have an increasing impact on the lives of all English citizens.

## § 15.   The European Court of Justice

The entry of England into the European Communities by enactment of the European Communities Act 1972, added a judicial institution of then uncertain scope, but of obvious substantial importance, to the administration of justice in England. The 1957 Treaty of Rome, by the 1972 Act, became part of the law of the United Kingdom, as did those various Community laws which become directly enforceable upon their promulgation.

Because the final authority for the interpretation of Community law is the European Court of Justice in Luxembourg, an important part of English law is being developed by a judicial institution not only with a composition which differs from the ordinary English superior courts, but with a strong balance in favor of judges from civil law systems. One should not identify the court as a civil law court, however, but it does possess a structure tending to create a Community law with strong influences from civil law jurisprudence. Decisions of the European Court would thus be expected to bear a resemblance to decisions of civil law courts. If such decisions disclose a more abstract nature, it would render them less usable as precedent than decisions from common law systems. This nevertheless presupposes that decisions of the Court have some precedential value. Nothing in the organizational structure of the Court suggests such an intention, nor do the decisions give support for the creation of a European Union stare decisis. One may expect, however, that judges of the Court trained in the common law may place greater emphasis on past decisions of the Court, particularly where they contain substantive analysis rather than abstract statements. Indeed, it is the case that many decisions of the European Court place great emphasis on earlier decisions. Whether judges consider earlier decisions instructional or mandatory, numerous European Court decisions have a value which seems more distinct than decisions of many European national domestic courts.

The addition of the European Court of Justice to English judicial institutions is one of the most important changes in English common law in several centuries. The lack of an enforcement procedure for the European Court of Justice, however, may mean that its decisions will have less impact in England than decisions of domestic courts. There is evidence of this, some decisions of the European Court have been ignored by nations against whose interests they have been rendered. Fortunately that has been the exception.

## § 16.   The European Court of Human Rights

There is a second court on the European Continent that has become important to England, and at the time of this writing appears likely to become an

"English" court in much the same manner as the European Court noted above. The European Court of Human Rights, often referred to as the Strasbourg Court or the ECHR, became available to aggrieved English persons when England signed the European Convention for the Protection of Human Rights and Fundamental Freedoms in 1950, it entered into force in 1953, and England recognized the European Commission's competence to receive individual applications in 1966. Concerned with the lack of a bill of rights in England, numerous citizens have taken their grievances to Strasbourg. And to the consternation of many Conservative Eurosceptics and Government ministers, many of these citizens have won. They have not always won because they have been the beneficiaries of uniform Convention standards, the Court uses a doctrine called the "margin of appreciation" to acknowledge that each Member State ought to be able to implement Convention standards with some measure of discretion, taking into consideration specific national circumstances and traditions. Until recently, their victories have not constituted judgments enforceable in English courts, because Parliament has not enacted a law making the Convention English law. It used to be the case that success in those suits might result in offers of compensation from the Government, and Parliament would then have been encouraged, if not intimidated, into changing some laws.

With the enactment of the Human Rights Act 1998, however, those decisions of the ECHR as well as certain parts of the convention itself are now brought into English law, and may be applied by the courts. As such, the decisions of that court in Strasbourg may now directly influence English law. As such, one may say that the European Court of Human Rights has become an "English" court in the same sense as the European Court of Justice. Accordingly, there are now two exceptionally important "English" courts on the Continent, with a majority of the judges trained in the civil law. Their decisions increasingly are playing an extremely important role in the evolution of substantive English law. Of course, a significant consequence of making the Convention English law is that individuals can now take their grievances to an English court rather than the Strasbourg Court. This may result in different interpretations than would be rendered in Strasbourg, parallel to the same consequence of England entering the European Community and having Community law applicable in English courts.

# CHAPTER 9

# ROLES AND ACTORS

## § 1. Legal Education

The separation of solicitors and barristers in England evolved during the first two centuries after the Norman Conquest. Persons appearing before the new common law courts were often assisted by one of a number of attorneys or advocates who spent their days milling about the courts. The persons initially were associated with the church, which held a dominant role in many areas of law. But as church power waned, laymen assumed the advisory roles. Sergeants and barristers carved out their niche as courtroom advocates, and were assisted in preparing litigation by persons called attorneys or, in the Court of Chancery, solicitors. The distinction between attorneys and solicitors, and the position of sergeant, were later abolished, leaving only barristers and solicitors. The separate roles for barristers and solicitors has, as a practical matter, been preserved, though as a formal matter the differences separating the two are in the process of successive elimination, discussed in greater detail later in this chapter. The role of legal education in England is playing an increasingly prominent role in this radical change.

The present character of legal education in England, and correspondingly of the legal profession it creates, is like so much else in the English legal system a product of historical circumstances. Irnerius was giving his first lectures on Justinian's Digest at Bologna in the 11th century even as legal studies on the continent were becoming both systematic and scientific. But by the time the Justinian legacy reached England, having been firmly established on the continent, a practical legal system had begun in the English courts, and Irnerius's disciples' influence was confined to the universities, and not the courts. Courses in the civil law, principally Roman law, became part of the general, university educational offerings in England; they were academic and theoretical rather than professional courses. Their students studied law as preparation for a career as members of the clergy, or of parliament, or to run large estates, but not to practice law. In contrast, the education of practicing lawyers, both barristers and solicitors, began as on-the-job training, not through the university offerings. Qualification to practice law in England has never required a university legal education. Nonetheless, after many centuries a symbiosis evolved between law as taught in the universities and law as practiced in the courts, and today a baccalaureate degree, and especially a law baccalaureate, is increasingly the path selected by those intending a legal career.

More specifically, in contrast to the teaching of Roman law, common law as an academic study was introduced to universities quite late. Blackstone lectured on common law at Oxford in the mid–18th century, as the first Vinerian Professor. A chair also was established at Cambridge, and English law courses were soon introduced in University College and King's College in London. But there was no rush to enroll. The number of students studying law in universities only increased slowly. Training for legal practice, contrary to the continental custom, remained under the governance of the profession, not the universities. A modest impetus to the evolution of university law teaching was generated by a critical study on legal education in 1846 and the subsequent establishment of law degrees at Oxford and Cambridge in the 1850s, followed twenty years later by the creation of law faculties. By the mid–1900s there were some fifty university law programs, and after the conversion of polytechnics into universities in the 1980s, the number of law programs has today almost doubled in that half century. But, these are **undergraduate** programs in law, rather than the post-graduate programs as in the United States. Thus, the English student and aspiring lawyer first entering university must consequently have made the decision to study law—with most making that decision not yet being twenty years old, and sometimes quite a bit younger as a result of the specialization that takes place in the final two years of English secondary education. In contrast, the decision to pursue an education in the law is not made in the United States until, at the earliest, the final year of the non-law undergraduate degree, and often not made until after graduation, sometimes not even made until many years after graduation.

The English university student has several paths to law practice, whether that practice will be as a barrister or solicitor. The student may choose to spend three years reading something other than law (many do so to gain some breadth of knowledge, law is often viewed as anti-intellectual and dull), or decide to include law as the partial or exclusive focus of study. If the degree received is **in** law, or has included certain core law subjects, the graduate moves directly into separate barrister or solicitor vocational training. Whatever the subject of university education, it emphasizes reading and tutorials over lectures, although the stress of additional students has diminished the emphasis on small tutorial sessions. Typically, English law faculty teach a heavier load than their U.S. counterparts, but U.S. law students have more required in-class time than English students. The English law curriculum may also appear sparse to a U.S. student that is used to a wide variety of elective courses and clinics.

If the core law subjects have not been taken at university as part of a "qualifying law degree", the graduate must spend a year in an approved course leading to the Common Professional Exam (CPE) or the Graduate Diploma in Law (GDL), the last stage at which the barristers' and solicitors' governing bodies have agreed to harmonized education. The lingering division between barristers and solicitors, and their governance by different organizations, the Bar Standards Board and the Solicitors Regulation

Authority, respectively, remain reflected in the vocational educational process for each role. The choice between becoming a barrister or a solicitor—one may not be both—ought to depend on the nature of intended work, but for some it may actually depend upon personal financial resources, and generally more difficult obstacles facing aspiring barristers.

A university student with barrister expectations earlier had to maintain required "dining terms" in one of the Inns of Court in London. Those reading the law once lived in their Inns, but pressures of space ultimately forced them out. Taking a number of meals at the chosen Inn of Court was substituted for residence to retain some measure of collegiality. But the concept of mingling with senior barristers over an evening meal unfortunately became little more than being witness to the presence (at another table) of one's seniors. Concerned that the dining tradition was one element contributing to the Inns becoming legal theme parks, this anachronism was replaced with lecture evenings with dinner, residential weekends, or one-day lectures, all considerably easier for the student still at university or in a vocational program at some distance from London.

Law has become a post-university profession. Once the choice of becoming a barrister or solicitor is made upon finishing university or passing the CPE, the educational process shifts from academic to vocational, and from governance by the universities to that of the Bar Standards Board (formerly run by the Bar Council) for future barristers, and the Solicitors Regulation Authority (formerly the Law Society) for solicitors. A common vocational educational program has been debated, but rejected mostly by the Bar. While this century has not yet been witness to a total fusion of the education of the barrister and the solicitor, earning a university law degree, or passing the Common Professional Examination by those with insufficient law courses in their university program, fulfills the academic stage for both prospective barristers and solicitors. The remaining distinction in the legal education of barristers and solicitors occurs now exclusively at the vocational stage. While fusion of the professions was rejected by a Royal Commission study in 1979, and loss of an independent Bar continues to be too drastic a move to adopt outright, the changes in the two professions during the past few decades, including the adoption of the Common Professional Exam, suggest at the very minimum the presence of a rapidly accelerating but creeping fusion of more and more aspects of the legal profession. Education is one of those aspects.

## § 2.   Solicitors

Becoming a solicitor is longer but somewhat easier than the path to the Bar. Completing the academic stage, a would-be solicitor enrolls in the Solicitors Regulation Authority vocational training focused Legal Practice Course (LPC). There is some parallel to the vocational training of a prospective barrister in the Bar Vocational Course (BVC), but the LPC emphasis is on the special work of the solicitor. At the end of the academic year long course, and before being called a solicitor, the candidate must obtain a training contract as a "trainee solicitor", formerly called an "articled clerk" to a solicitor or a governmental unit. The trainee solicitor is poorly compensated. When the two year period of articles is over, the new solicitor's name is added to the list maintained by the Master of the Rolls.

The origin of the solicitor is less elitist than that of the barrister, and the solicitor's work has been less romanticized than the trial advocacy of the wigged and robed barrister. The origin of the solicitor lies with those attorneys who worked directly with clients preparing litigation for disputes before the King's Bench and Common Pleas courts, and who usually did not possess the educational level of barristers. Nor did they present the actual cases in court. The role of advocate was carefully protected by the barristers. The term solicitor initially applied to an attorney appearing in the Chancery Court; that same role was called a proctor before the admiralty and ecclesiastical courts. These attorneys, solicitors and proctors—all later called solicitors—were first jointly housed with barristers in the Inns of Court, but the solicitors were ejected in the late 16th century and organized their own association.

Solicitors vastly outnumber barristers. The 100,-000 or so practicing and employed solicitors in the United Kingdom are not as concentrated in London as are the barristers. Solicitors practicing in London do not have their offices within monastic chambers like the barristers. Solicitors have contact with the public and office locations reflect this contact, while barristers, who do not work directly with the public but only with solicitors, may work in a location less accessible to the public.

The life of the solicitor is on the whole more relaxed than the barrister, though the solicitor is less apt to achieve the fame accessible to a successful barrister, which may more easily culminate in appointment to the bench. A solicitor may reach the heights of compensation of the most successful barrister, however, and an average solicitor is more likely to achieve a comfortable financial position than her counterpart at the bar. Some new solicitors choose to accept a salaried position with a government authority or in industry, but the majority seek employment with a private firm. Entry to a solicitors' firm begins as a trainee solicitor to a solicitor, one's "principal," consisting of a two year apprenticeship. It is ostensibly to provide the trainee solicitor with experience by sitting in with the solicitor on sessions with clients and in court. The more conscientious firms provide their trainee solicitors with a variety of experiences, including moving them from one department to another where the size of the firm allows specialization. The less fortunate trainee solicitors, perhaps as many as one-third of them, receive no instruction at all, but pass their days much on their own doing minor, routine tasks, and biding their time until the "training" is over and they qualify as solicitors. Expectation of partnership after some years as a salaried associate parallels the participation in a law firm in the United States. The solicitor is expected to buy in to the partnership and, unless she has sufficient resources, she may have to remain a salaried employee. A solicitor who is a partner in a large and well known firm may expect sizable financial rewards, and also will benefit from the work of her trainee solicitors, assistant solicitors and junior partners. Large firms nevertheless are the exception; most solicitors practice alone or in a small group.

The solicitor traditionally has been primarily a law office practitioner, advising clients on legal, and often personal and business, matters. A solicitor whose practice includes litigation may today follow one of two paths with respect to litigation. The first is the traditional role of the solicitor—to accompany a barrister to court, where the solicitor may assist in the trial, but leaving the in-court advocacy to the barrister—a specialist in the rhetorical and trial skills. The more recent path is one where the solicitor may lead the in-court litigation. Solicitors have long had authority to act as advocates in the lower courts—appearing in magistrates' courts and in county courts as advocates with full rights of audience. But rights of audience for the higher courts are of more recent vintage. Several developments in the 1980s helped to create the environment that would eventually lead to solicitors having a general right of audience in the courts—subject to additional training. As an initial matter, solicitors lost their monopoly on property conveyancing and were forced to share that market with estate agents. It had been the largest contributor to the income of many solicitors. This loss spurred the solicitors' interest in acquiring new markets, especially increased rights of audience in the courts. At that time it was hoped that such a market would be provided after the creation of the Crown Prosecution Service (CPS) in 1985, a new, independent prosecution service which would employ some 1,500 barristers and solicitors as full time prosecutors. Solicitors hoped that they would have a right to appear in all criminal cases, including matters before the Crown Courts. But the plan was condemned by Bar members, who viewed it as an encroachment on the barristers' exclusive domain. The issue of such increased rights was accordingly deferred to then ongoing consideration of the reformation of legal services, that ultimately lead to the Courts and Legal Services Act of 1990 supposedly opening the courts to solicitors.

The hoped for opportunities for solicitors as a result of the Courts and Legal Services Act proved ephemeral. They gained more rights in theory than rights in actuality. Though, as it turned out, other developments increased their opportunities to exercise those rights. For example, the Courts and Legal Services Act transferred considerable business from the High Court to the County Courts. This essentially meant much more advocacy work for solicitors as they were already present in some numbers before the County Courts. The same resulted and continues from the on-going transfer of business from the Crown Court to the magistrates' courts.

Nonetheless, these reforms proved insufficient and continuing pressure to allow solicitors full and effective rights of audience before all the courts eventually paid off by the end of the 1990s with the Access to Justice Act 1999. That Act allowed solicitors, subject to completing additional training, to have all the same rights of audience as barristers. The number of solicitors appearing before the higher courts has been slowly increasing, but it will take many years before this element of fusion is complete. For many, however, the liberalization of the profession has not gone far enough. Many, including the Office of Fair trading and many consumer groups believe that the profession should remove all of its restrictive practices and open the profession to competition and allow new business structures within which legal services may be offered.

Mostly, however, the work of the solicitor is concentrated in the areas of conveyancing and estate law, in advising on business matters, and for some, litigation preparation and some advocacy. In the major cities large firms of solicitors often concentrate on advice to industry. They are quite similar to large firms in the United States, with the exception of having only a few solicitor-advocates, generally continuing to advise barristers on court appearances. There have been significant changes as international commercial work has expanded, many solicitors firms have raided American firms seeking members to do U.S. law related work, and a number of American firms have set up offices in London and raided solicitors' firms for their UK law expertise. This internationalization of legal practice is certain to influence the structure of the profession in the years to come.

The forms of fees most debated at this point are contingent and conditional fees. Both long rejected as creating too close a relationship between the lawyer and the client's case, perhaps even corrupting the lawyer, a conditional fee is now allowed in some civil cases (personal injury, human rights, insolvency) in a modest form called an "uplift", being up to 100 percent of the normal fee. The detriments of such a scheme were silenced by the perceived ability to increase access to justice without spending more money. But there are always problems of adjustment, such as how to assimilate conditional fee arrangements with the mandate that the loser pays all costs. Who is to pay the defendant's costs when the plaintiff loses, the plaintiff or perhaps the plaintiff's lawyers? With conditional fees thus established in England, U.S. style contingent fees may be the next step, with the fee a percentage of the judgment rather than an uplift from the normal fee. Contingent fee opponents suggest that would shift the focus from access to justice for the poor to access to higher fees for the lawyers.

## § 3.  Barristers

There are few institutions in England that remain more tradition bound than the practicing barristers, and the four remaining Inns of Court in London—Gray's Inn, Lincoln's Inn, Inner Temple and Middle Temple. The Inns originated in the medieval guild form of association of practitioners, fully established by the 14th century. They brought together in their cloistered lodgings in London aspiring advocates, both to live and work. Members of the bar held practice court sessions or moots, and closely counseled the professional, spiritual and personal development of the fledgling barristers. The result was an unusual personal closeness and professional unity, which, through the process of judicial selection, also characterized the bench. Pressures of space ultimately reduced the Inns to barristers' (and other professionals') offices, or "chambers", dining halls, and some limited residences for benchers, the senior members of the Inns. Until recently, most of the barristers outside government service practiced in chambers in one of the Inns in London. But as a result of a dramatic growth in the number of barristers, about a third now practice in provincial chambers outside London, and a significant number of those in London have chambers outside the Inns. Furthermore, those in the Inns are not representative of the face of the Bar's rising numbers of women and ethnic minorities. The increasing ability to undertake all of one's education, and to practice as a barrister, outside not only the Inns but outside London, suggest that time is not on the side of the Inns of Court.

The recent rapid growth of the Bar has partly been due to increasing openings in the vocational training year. Now called the Bar Vocational Course (BVC), this year was once the exclusive prerogative of the Inns of Court own School of Law, but lack of space to meet the demand, and the high cost of a year living in London, forced an end to this bottle-neck to admission to the profession. Today the Bar Standards Board is responsible for the BVC and the year course is now taught in several locations throughout England and Wales, either as a one-year full time course, or as a two-year part time course.

Passing the BVC examination leads to a call to the Bar (performed by the Inns) and a search for a one year pupilage with a junior barrister, intended to entail additional, supervised, practical instruction. The fortunate pupil may divide her time between two chambers, gaining experience in different areas of concentration. The workload and cramped space of barristers often limits the pupilage to mostly self study in a law library, but the time must be endured before the new barrister may accept her own cases. During the first six months of the pupilage the new barrister may not accept briefs, but even during the last six months she is not likely to have many briefs. She usually will have to plan on supporting herself during the pupilage, and quite possibly for another year as well until her workload increases. Criminal legal aid has provided the means of support for many young barristers, who otherwise could not have found work in the private sector.

Once a barrister is settled into chambers after completing the year of pupilage, he begins his practice of advocacy, of drafting documents and of rendering opinions. Under the "cab rank" rule, a barrister is required to accept briefs when asked by a solicitor, and a highly regarded barrister will have a heavy workload. But the cab rank rule does not require a barrister to take a case the barrister views as having no merit, although the barrister may prefer to reject it for other reasons, such as being fully booked. The barrister does not traditionally have direct contact with lay-clients, as opposed to clients that are solicitors acting on behalf of the ultimate consumer of the barrister's service. It is only since 2004 that the Bar Council has allowed barristers to have direct lay-client access. Before, when there was a need to confer with the client the barrister had met only in the presence of the solicitor, and usually in the chambers of the barrister. Now, lay-clients can contact a barrister directly to handle their concerns, without the added cost of the solicitor. For the more complicated litigation, however, it is expected that the traditional solicitor initiated and run system will continue. When contacted directly by a lay-client, the cab rank principle (discussed later) does not apply, though rules on anti-discrimination will be applicable. This new direct-access rule only applies for barristers of at least three years experience and where they have completed some additional training in order to be able to handle the new issues such direct access will inevitably entail.

Barristers may not form partnerships, as may solicitors, and barristers may not be employed by or form a partnership with solicitors, another restriction destined for extinction. Barristers will ultimately be able to form partnerships together, and most likely with solicitors. Although barristers may not form partnerships, they work together in chambers, sharing a clerk and the usual costs of a small law firm, such as secretarial assistance, books and a coffee machine. The clerk is more of an office manager; he negotiates his barristers' fees with solicitors and usually receives a commission as compensation. The fees are traditionally not fixed, but are set according to the complexity of the case and the reputation of the barrister, though since 2001 the Bar Council has allowed barristers and solicitors to fix their terms contractually. The fees are paid to the barrister by the solicitor, who may require an advance from his client to avoid having to pay the barrister without receiving the expected source of that payment, the fee owing from the client. As with solicitors, some barristers are employed by the government, industry, academia and so on. Particular barristers often are sought by solicitors because of the former's specialization, and a firm of solicitors will generally direct work to a select list of barristers. If the work is of only a nominal level of skill, a junior barrister may be associated. For a complex matter, a Queen's Counsel may be preferred.

Barristers, and now solicitor-advocates, with unusually good reputations and at least ten years experience may seek the role of a Queen's Counsel ("QC"). The grant of QC status is now conferred pursuant to a new independent selection process that aims to provide transparency and that seeks to ensure that only the most qualified and competent barristers and solicitor-advocates are selected to become QCs. Typically, about ten percent of the practicing Bar would become QCs. Becoming a Queen's Counsel is called "taking silk", substituting silk for stuff robes and adding QC to one's name. Those who do not choose to be Queen's Counsels remain junior barristers throughout their careers. Queen's Counsel (or leader) status, once limited to barristers working for the Crown, is now sought by barristers in general practice who hope they possess a sufficiently strong reputation to encourage solicitors to retain them for more complex and, consequently, more highly compensated matters, and to limit their work to advocacy and giving oral and written opinions. But a new QC may not be successful in attracting the higher compensated work. A Queen's Counsel not long ago had to appear in court with a junior barrister as an assistant, a requirement abolished in an attempt to reduce legal fees. This may assist some who have taken silk unwisely, who did not have a sufficient reputation to draw the higher fees necessary to pay both the Queen's Counsel and a junior barrister. A Queen's Counsel who does not succeed financially must not return to junior status. A way of alleviating an unwise choice is to seek and accept some minor judicial appointment. Seeking Queen's Counsel status thus is one more risk in a profession already filled with risks and obstacles. But if success is achieved as a leader, the financial rewards can be quite substantial.

Barristers do considerable office work, preparing wills, contracts, and drafts and written opinions. But their diminishing monopoly and the role which makes them so distinctive is as advocates in the Crown Courts, the Royal Courts (High Court and Court of Appeal) and the House of Lords. The successful barrister must be able to assimilate rapidly a great number of facts, possess a sound awareness of procedure and the rules of evidence, and use that knowledge in court where his capacity to think and respond immediately will determine his future. But what has often distinguished the barrister is shrouded in romanticism flowing from wigs and gowns and winged collars. The truth is that the average barrister is not necessarily an exceptional advocate. Critical observers often see pompous opening speeches, repetition in questions and comments, concentration on irrelevant details, and uncertainty over facts. Receiving briefs the night before trial is not a guarantee of adequate preparation, and many of the shortcomings appear related to a lack of preparation. The mist of perfection which has surrounded barristers for years is dissipating, and disclosing a profession like most other nations possess, with both exceptional and incompetent advocates. But it seems England has long done one thing right about advocacy, recognize that it is a skill not possessed by all lawyers, and require considerable training before one is permitted to step alone before the Bench. A divided profession, even if no longer a de jure divided profession, however, may not be the best way to assure the presence of advocacy skills.

## § 4.  The Lawyer in Public Service

Formalization of legal assistance began in the late 1940s. Initially rendered by a variety of associations, subsequent acts have brought it under a national, public scheme, administered by the new Legal Services Commission ("LSC"). But there is no profession of full-time legal assistance advisors. The English scheme of legal advice and aid draws upon the services of the general practicing solicitors and barristers, under contract from the LSC. A few neighborhood law centers have full-time, salaried solicitors, but the practice is nowhere nearly as extensive as in the United States. Other centers have a scheme of duty solicitors, adopted in several areas where participating solicitors are present at magistrates' courts to provide assistance.

The most critical problem facing legal aid in England is the reliance upon national financial support. Without immense government funding, the numerous individual legal advice and aid schemes which exist throughout the country are in jeopardy. The services which they provide are available effectively only to a small percentage of the population. Increased funding would proliferate neighborhood law offices with many new, young solicitors choosing to work full-time for the centers, rather than volunteering their services on a part-time basis in conjunction with their professional practices, as is the case with pro bono representations in the United States. But the services face decreased funding, and many options are presently under consideration, including limiting the availability of aid for certain cases, employing fixed fee arrangements and of funding some legal aid from contingency fees in successful legal aid cases. Looking to the continent fee is tempting for those who would reduce legal aid costs in England; for example Germany's legal aid system costs only a small fraction of England's. But the difference lies in the greater predictability of costs in Germany, and the popularity of legal insurance. Furthermore, legal aid is just one part of a legal system, and when the costs of the full system are viewed, Germany spends twice per capita on the justice system.

## § 5.  The Judiciary

Very young judges are not encountered in England. The route to the scarlet and ermine robes and cumbrous wigs of the judiciary is not an initial career choice, as in most civil law nations. The appointment of English judges to the superior courts from among the barristers is a convention dating to the 13th century. The absence of elected judges lends a consistency to the English judiciary which does not exist in the United States, where the selection practice varies between the federal and state judiciaries and indeed from one state to another, and even within a particular state with respect to different levels of the judiciary.

Advancing to the English bench is a long, orderly and traditionally secretive process with appointment rarely granted before the age of 40. If the slow and methodical process of progression to the judiciary is beneficial in its homogeneous experience and perceived competency, it has been at the cost of achieving diversity at any greater pace. While the process is often said to preserve judicial independence, what that judicial independence means is not well defined.

The English judiciary staffing the superior courts is a relatively small group, about 160, but increasing as more persons turn to the courts to resolve disputes. The increased number of judges in England has only modestly diminished judicial prestige. The enhanced role of legislation in contrast to judge made law has had a more severe impact. The judges of England with a lasting place in history—Mansfield, Coke, Bacon—thrived in an era where there were few judges and little challenge to the preeminence of precedent as the foundation of the common law. The judiciary in the United States may be associated with judicial activism, but the English judiciary tends not to issue rulings which grant to individuals rights that demand substantial national expenditure, believing that area to be the responsibility of Parliament, though as the judges increasingly encounter actions based on the Human Rights Act 1998 there may be a gradual change in this character.

Advocates, principally barristers, are drawn to the judiciary at the height of their careers, mostly from the position of Queen's Counsel. An invitation to judicial appointment is rarely rejected, because of the prestige, the challenge and a knighthood if appointed to the High Court or above. The move distinctly is not motivated by monetary gain. While it is true that judicial salaries are less than the earnings of a comparably qualified and successful barrister, judicial salaries have nonetheless intentionally been set at what is thought to be a high level, with the higher up the hierarchy the more pay. Law Lords may be paid around $300,000, high court judges around $270,000, circuit judges around $200,000, and district judges around $160,000, though it should be noted that costs of living in England and in particular in London are significantly greater than in most of the United States. Despite the differences is salary across the different levels of judges, it is generally thought that promotion is not sought for financial gain. Furthermore, traditionally there was no general expectation of periodic promotion, despite the fact that the selection of judges for the superior courts usually involved elevation from a lower judicial level. Today there is perhaps more of such an expectation. Still, there is a difference between the perception of the English barrister toward his role and future as a judge and that of the "civil servant" continental law judge, where promotion through the full hierarchy is a major expectation and, in fact, a necessity of the system since few judicial appointments are made from outside the ranks of professional judges. One benefit of a judiciary homogeneous in experience and reputation, both within a given level of the court system and from one level to another, is the lack of a sense of need for an appeal to reach a more experienced or competent judge. The English system tends to assure one of meeting competency at even the lowest level, thereby reducing the indispensability of an appeal for a fair hearing.

Judicial appointments had until very recently been made after secret "soundings" by the Lord Chancellor's office from judges and senior practitioners regarding who among the Queen's Counsels is most fit for appointment. Open advertisement and competition were absent. The process has, however, like so much else in the English legal system undergone radical reform. Pursuant to the Constitutional Reform Act 2005, judicial appointment nominations are now made by the independent Judicial Appointments Commission, based on a fair and competitive process, considering candidates from as wide a spectrum as possible. The nominations are then sent to the Lord Chancellor who may reject the nomination, but must provide the reason for any such rejections.

These recent judicial appointments reforms, however, are very recent, and as a result the judiciary has not yet been impacted by the likely diversification that will result from the new process. The judiciary thus has remained largely white and male. Women and racial minorities have received judicial appointments in embarrassingly small numbers. It was only in 2004 that the first woman was appointed to the House of Lords—Lady Justice Hale. Furthermore, recent figures for the rest of the judiciary do not suggest that it reflects British demographics.

Only around 20% of all judges are woman, while for the Court of Appeals and the High Court the figures are quite a bit less. Furthermore, despite the increasing multi-cultural and ethnic mix of modern Britain, the judiciary has very few identified judges of an "ethnic" background. Another sign of the lack of diversity is that graduates of Oxford and Cambridge still dominate the higher courts, and are a significant presence throughout the judiciary.

Although the face of the judiciary does not reflect the face of English society, the judiciary has an esteem unmatched in most other legal systems. The English legal system owes its reputation, and its reception by other nations, as much to its personalities as to its principles. The personality of the judge is a key element of this reputation. Entry into the judiciary only after long years as a barrister, or, alternatively, and most recently, as a solicitor-advocate, generally at least ten years for the High Court, illustrates that becoming a judge signifies the culmination rather than the beginning of a career. Few judges ever leave the bench to commence a new endeavor. The rare judge who steps down to enter business often elicits a negative response from the bar, partially because the prestige and a knighthood does not terminate with the judicial resignation.

Even though entry procedures to the legal profession have been significantly altered, the changes will not affect the judiciary for many years. As a result, the latent conservatism of the profession will likely continue for the foreseeable future. As an advocate progresses through the stages of the profession, from a junior bar member to Queen's Counsel to the bench, a measure of conservatism tends to evolve. Judges rightly appreciate that they have passed stern tests in achieving judicial appointment, and they are not given to very much self-criticism. A few have criticized this process as discouraging any judicial reform suggested from within the judiciary, and as constituting a body which often acts counter to parliamentary enactments by a severely restrictive approach to statutory interpretation. Such interpretation is an alternative to rendering criticism of the legislation during public debate; judges rarely speak out on issues of controversy.

The English judiciary certainly is not an aggregation of judicial activists, but that is largely viewed as one of the professions noteworthy strengths. The judge is independent in two regards, first from interference from the government and second from influence from social causes. The first is attributable from the structure, the second from the process of training and appointment. Proposed legal reforms are always tested by judges against the norm of judicial independence, which sometimes is used mostly as a diversion to block any serious analysis.

The English judge is not a case manager in the manner of the French or German judge, but an arbitrator of the contest—a "silent umpire"—between two advocates in a largely oral process. It was not always this way, judges before the Industrial Revolution played a more inquisitorial role. But since that era, with the increase in issue complexity and the inability of judges to understand all the issues of the times, the process assumed a more adversarial nature. The oral process has endured. But an oral process is a time consuming method, and there are pressures for the judge to again more actively manage cases and reduce time spent in oral debate. Such changes evolve slowly. As before, the nature of contemporary legal reform to address changing social needs in England better accommodates the gradual evolution and modification of current institutions rather than drastic alteration. The current structure has matured over centuries and is viewed from many areas of the world as a crucial structure to an orderly society, as an irreplaceable backbone to a just system. The British Empire may have disintegrated, but left in its ashes is considerable respect for its legal system.

Additional to the appointment to ordinary and special courts staffed by professional judges, lesser judicial appointments are available, such as appointment as a master. Masters undertake the duties of processing cases before trial, a task left to ordinary judges in many nations. The English master has developed a reputation for a remarkable expertise in passing judgment on pre-trial motions, and especially in reducing the issues to be heard by the judge by overseeing the collection of facts and seeking the agreement of the litigants on minor issues. Not infrequently is the work of the master so effective that the dispute is resolved without the need of a trial. If trial is nevertheless required, the master may assign it to a county court or determine that it should be heard in the High Court in London or on circuit.

A second minor judicial position is an appointment to a magistrates' court in a large city, sitting as an individual professional judge in contrast to the lay magistrates who convene in collegiate form in both cities and rural areas. The professional magistrate, called a district judge (magistrates' courts), and formerly called a stipendiary magistrate, undertakes repetitious and intense work, handling a vast number of minor (mostly summary) criminal cases. The "stipe" generally sits daily, which may produce a boredom that is less a problem for the lay magistrates, who serve mostly only for a day every second week.

Judges hold office for life, they may be removed by the sovereign only if in breach of good behavior and only at the request of both the House of Lords and House of Commons. Removal of an English judge from the superior courts has never occurred. Though in the nineteenth century an Irish admiralty judge was removed, and in the 1980s a judge from the inferior courts, a circuit court judge, was removed for "smuggling" tobacco and alcohol into Britain on his yacht. But these two exceptions show just how rare is removal from office.

Lifetime service is permitted of judicial appointees to age 70, virtually a decade longer than allowed other government officials. Before the age limit of 70 was placed on superior court judges, many served to a very advanced age; Lord Halsbury sat nearly until his death at 93, exceeding Oliver Wendell Holmes' service until 90. Permitting lengthy service does reduce the possibility of a judge retiring and returning to other full time work, although it may result in ineffective service by judges who become incapacitated in later years.

# CHAPTER 10

# PROCEDURE

## § 1. Civil Procedure

English civil procedure developed internally, that is, within the court system itself to meet immediate needs. Rules which resolved questions of how the course of an action would proceed were established ad hoc by the King's Courts. The development of English civil procedure, particularly since the 16th century, has constituted a process of continual refinement, reflected in the periodic alterations to correct immediate deficiencies which distract a court from reaching a just result. This development contrasts significantly with the more methodical, external development of civil procedure in most civil law nations, where procedure is guided by legislative enactments and by the writings of legal scholars, detached from any particular, current dispute. The civil law lawyer consequently views his system of procedure as more logical and rational in development.

An extraordinary transformation occurred in English civil procedure from its dominant role in the early stages of the formation of English law. That dominance was demonstrated by the inflexible forms of action in the writ process, reflected in the statement "where there is no writ there is no right." Comparatively little substantive law existed in the initial decades of the development of English law, it evolved over a long period of time through judicial pronouncements, each issued within a strict procedural framework. The legal relationships of ordinary persons, such as in contracts and torts, grew slowly from the aggregation of specific decisions. As substantive legal rules accumulated in the reported decisions, the dominant role of the strict procedural elements declined. Current English civil procedure is considerably more flexible than during the early centuries of its development. There is no longer any general attitude that procedure overshadows the substantive law. Once governed by an almost mystical unwritten scheme, for a little more than a century now English civil procedure substantially has been codified. Until recently, the Rules of the Supreme Court, originally authorized by the Judicature Acts 1873, regulated most civil proceedings in the Supreme Court, and there were corresponding rules for the county courts and for criminal proceedings in the magistrates' courts. But, like so much else in the English legal system in the last decade, there have been significant reforms to the civil procedure, beginning with the Civil Procedure Act 1997. Subsequent to that reform in 1999 the new Civil Procedure Rules and Practice Directions went into effect—though there has been a constant stream of amendments and additional directions since that time as the government expands and modifies the new rules and directions. Accordingly, the new civil procedure presents a somewhat new and supposedly more efficient procedural system— from the initiation of suits to the production of evidence and documents to eventual settlement or the award of damages.

For example, prior to the recent reforms, civil proceedings used to begin by the appropriate court office issuing a writ or a summons to commence the action, depending on which court was involved. The writ included only enough information to apprise the defendant of the nature of the action. It was, however, unlike the earlier, strict forms of action, which required a plaintiff to choose his form correctly or face dismissal. The writ was a command in the name of the sovereign to enter an appearance before the court. The "appearance" was accomplished by sending an acknowledgment of service to the court office which issued the writ. The reforms, however, replaced the writ and summons with a standard form, called a "Part 7 Claim Form." The claimant, as the plaintiff is now known, must provide a concise statement supporting the claim. Similarly, if the defendant responds (and if not, default may be entered), she must also state her side of the facts in sufficient detail. Furthermore, all statements submitted must be accompanied by a "statement of truth"—a signed statement attesting to the truth of the assertions submitted. If later it turns out that the statements were known to be false the party may be guilty of contempt of court. This applies to disclosures (previously called discovery) as well. Overall, the procedures are intended to encourage early settlement and resolution of disputes. To further encourage settlement, the new procedures include "pre-action protocols" for many of the more common suits in order to encourage more reasonable behavior between the parties and earlier exchange and disclosure of information, and, of course, pre-trial settlements. While compliance with these pre-action protocols is not mandatory, failure to participate may be taken into account when the court awards costs at the end of the trial. Thus an uncooperative or needlessly difficult party may be liable for additional costs, the "loser paying" principle as the usual rule in England, or may not be awarded the otherwise expected legal fees if victorious in the suit. These strict protocols and procedures bring to mind the earlier period in English legal history of strict procedural rules.

The English legal system contributes to the pre-trial ("interlocutory") stage in the High Court the expertise of a "master" ("registrar" in the Family Division, "district judges" outside London). They are former barristers or solicitors who accept this position of less prestige, but less pressure, than a judge, and who are as skillful in procedure as the judges who will try the final issues are in interpreting substantive law. Masters perform numerous functions intended to refine the case for trial, or bring it to an early conclusion by way of settlement or withdrawal. They rule on requests for interrogatories or the discovery of documents, proposed amendments to the pleadings and requirements for security. If the master has performed his task well, the issues will have been narrowed to those truly in conflict. Documenting evidence will have been collected, and the judge at trial will have been relieved of confronting many procedural conflicts which may burden the proceeding and confuse the participants. Acting in the quiet of her office or a hearing room, away from the publicity, openness and formality of the courtroom, the master plays an important role in preparing cases so that the oral, trial stage may proceed without delay, and in contributing to litigation a degree of uniformity which allows the trial stage to focus on the substantive issues. In one sense the master contributes to lessening the orality of the trial, by the Summons for Directions. The perceived success of the master and the slowness of the civil justice system at the trial stage contributed to the reforms of the civil procedure, reforms that now allow judges more discretion in disposing of cases by giving them a greater management role, much as they have in small claims courts where professional advocates are not present. For example, it is now possible for the judges to place some cases, assuming they satisfy certain criteria, on a fast-track judge-dominated process. Whether this has resulted in a more civil law-like management process remains to be seen, though it certainly raises the spectre of such a system.

The English trial is an oral process. This was necessarily so in earlier times when jury members were usually illiterate; presenting written evidence would have been futile. Although the oral process also is mandated by the nature of the trial today, the use of written witness and expert statements has diminished the oral adversary system. Continuation of the deliberate and often time consuming written procedures which dominate the pretrial stage may end when all the parties have gathered for the trial, but the greater the use of written submissions, the less the need for oral advocacy. The parties expect the trial to proceed without undue postponement. The English trial, as in most common law nations, is "an event." It begins with all parties present and proceeds to its conclusion while they remain. This oral proceeding exhibits the skills of the English advocate—be it the traditional barrister or one of the new solicitor advocates. The nature of the English trial, a predominantly oral hearing proceeding without interruption (in theory often more than practice) until its conclusion, does not always afford time for judicial study of complex issues. One reaction has been to create numerous specialized tribunals, each designed to deal competently with specific matters. However fragmented and unsystematic the tribunals may be, even as there is an effort to rationalize them, they offer a composition and procedure often both less expensive and less restricted by rules and conventions than the ordinary courts.

The oral process of an English civil trial is familiar to any common law system observer. Counsel for the plaintiff makes a statement of his client's case, and next calls his witnesses, each of whom may be cross-examined by defense counsel and reexamined by the plaintiff's counsel, if thought appropriate.

When the plaintiff's case has been presented, the defense initiates a similar presentation of witnesses, with cross-examination by the plaintiff. Both counsel give final summaries, and a decision then is rendered by the judge. But the English civil trial judge sometimes plays an active role in directly questioning the parties, to clarify conflicting or unclear matters, or even to commence a new line of questioning which the judge perceives as important, but which had been ignored by counsel. Judicial participation is important in a civil trial where either party may decide not to introduce evidence. The judge may be able to extract what one counsel prefers not to mention, and the other ignores.

Although England's civil procedure once followed extremely strict procedures, an English trial today appears less disrupted by the application of strict rules of evidence. Evidence precluded in the United States often is admitted unchallenged in an English proceeding, and an advocate certainly is more hesitant in objecting to a line of inquiry presented by the judge than by opposing counsel. Greater latitude in the presentation of evidence is certainly related to the predominance of bench trials versus jury trials.

English common law almost never affords the parties a trial with judge and jury in civil cases. The use of a civil trial jury varies throughout common law systems. The United States extends the right to trial by jury well beyond practice in England. Trial by judge alone has not always been the English practice. At early common law, a jury was the norm, except in the Chancery Court. The Judicature Acts of the late 19th century, fusing law and equity, initially were responsible for the reduction of jury trials in civil cases. Later laws specifically limited their use. They may still be used at the option of the claimant in cases involving libel and slander, false imprisonment, seduction, breach of promise of marriage, fraud, and malicious prosecution. They may also be used at the discretion of the court, though it is rarely granted. In fact, they tend to be used mainly in the libel/defamation arena. Overall, less than one percent of civil trials are heard before a jury, with most of those being in the county courts, involving coroners cases and actions against the police. Thus, most civil disputes in England are tried by a judge sitting alone. The concept that the essence of the common law system is trial by jury, appears to the English lawyer to be carried to an unnecessary extreme in the United States. The importance of the jury in the development of English common law is more correctly associated with the *criminal* legal process.

## § 2.  Criminal Procedure

English criminal procedure is a mix of concern for protecting the innocent and convicting the guilty, with both often overshadowed by a concern for judicial economy.

Changes in criminal procedure since the Conquest are no less striking than the demise of the forms of action and the merger of law and equity in civil procedure. Until the late 16th century, an accused was detained until trial with no opportunity to prepare a defense, and no knowledge of either the evidence to be introduced or the identity of witnesses for the prosecution. The accused could call no witnesses on his own behalf, and had to appear without counsel were the charge treason or a felony. The accused literally was isolated against the state. Changes in criminal procedure in the last few centuries, and most importantly since the mid to late 19th century, have almost without exception benefitted the accused. But those changes may appear quite nominal compared to the constitutional protections granted an accused in the United States during the last half of this century. Historically, there was far less public criticism in England than in the United States that the balance has swung too far in favor of protecting the interests of the accused, to the detriment of society, but public sentiment in this regard has changed of recent years, with increasing concern about the "rights" provided the accused as a result of modern reforms. But, if anything, many of the recent reforms, especially post 9–11, have resulted in increasing the power and abilities of the prosecutor and police, but then there has for a long time been a feeling that the English criminal procedure is biased towards the prosecution—a bias that is reflected not just in the pre-trial procedure, but also in the procedure employed during the trial itself.

The English and American systems have thus been subjected to their own separate stresses and reform movements. Significant differences have evolved, though the English system in particular is presently undergoing a series of significant reforms whose end is not yet in sight. The primary goals of these reforms appear to be an attempt to balance the dictates of the new Human Rights Act and the European Convention of Human Rights (especially Article 6), efficiency, handling the vast increases in cases, and providing justice for the accused and victims alike. The recent wave of reforms have not only been in response to human rights dictates, but also, and more specifically, in response to the governmental reports on the state of the criminal justice system. Though the government's response to the reports and other criticisms was to enact Criminal Justice Act 2003, which in the main simply reorganized aspects of the criminal procedure as opposed to engaging in wholesale reform, despite calls for the enactment of a modern criminal law code.

At this point should be reemphasized that the vast majority of criminal cases are disposed of at the magistrates court, often without counsel and under very relaxed procedures. The discussion here primarily concerns those more serious cases that end up in the Crown Court for trial—though in light of the fact that most plead guilty, it is the pretrial process that impacts the vast majority of criminal defendants. Furthermore, despite the development of the English criminal law, the impact of the European Court of Human Right's Article 6 jurisprudence cannot be ignored—for its requirements are, through the Human Rights Act, "supreme" over any English law to the contrary.

The contemporary English criminal process is accusatorial rather than inquisitorial. Pollock noted that, "Courts of justice are public; they judge between the parties, and do not undertake an official inquiry not even in criminal cases or in affairs of State." The case against an accused is investigated, prepared and directed through the courts by a party, usually a public official representing the Crown, not by the judges or magistrates as in an inquisitorial system. But the English judge or magistrate may actively participate in the trial, asking questions directly of the accused and witnesses, calling witnesses (rarely) and thus bringing an inquisitorial element to the trial to a greater degree than in the United States. But as issues have become more complex over the decades, judges have tended to leave questioning to the advocates, sitting more as silent umpires than an inquiring third party.

The decision to prosecute is not reserved by the state. With exceptions which are increasing in scope, *anyone,* not only public prosecutors or other officials, or even those with an interest in the matter, may act as a prosecutor. The system of prosecution is thus much more widely diffused than in the United States. But a privately initiated prosecution occurs only in exceptional cases (and is sometimes taken over by the Crown Prosecution Service) most often where the citizen (or more often a group opposed to something) believes public authorities have improperly refused to prosecute an action.

Private prosecution is discouraged, the costs must be borne by the citizen. Although private prosecution is used rarely, it illustrates the conceptual aspect of the common law criminal process, that a *citizen,* either public or private, must commence and pursue the action, and that the role played by the person or group which determines guilt or innocence is only a minor part in the preparation and presentation of the suit.

Civil procedure tends to be not greatly dissimilar between different courts, the amount in controversy usually determines the level of court with jurisdiction. In contrast, there is a greater variation of procedural characteristics in criminal proceedings in different courts, directly related to the seriousness of the offense. Seriousness is usually the basis in any legal tradition for determining which criminal procedure will apply. While the goal in civil litigation is to determine liability and damages, a criminal proceeding may involve, in addition to determination of guilt, an educational element, loss of freedom or physical retribution, or a mandated work requirement. Offenses are classified, the least serious (summary offenses in England, misdemeanors in the United States) may require nothing more than the payment of a fine by mail, with a notation in the court records of the financial satisfaction of the wrong. As the summary offense becomes more serious in England, persons must appear in person before the magistrates' court, to be tried by lay peers (or in the large cities a single professional district judge (magistrates' court) without a jury.

The procedure is less formal than more serious crimes demand (indictable offenses, not unlike the felony in the United States), where a jury will be convened and rules of evidence become stricter and more carefully followed. The complexity of the procedure in a criminal prosecution is directly related to the gravity of what society may demand as a consequence for one's guilt. No such indictable-summary classification existed during the early years of the development of common law. Other than trial by ordeal, all trials were by judge and jury. To use the current labels, all were indictable.

For many years the police most often prosecuted in the magistrates' courts. This function was the most distinguishing characteristic in contrast to the role of police in the United States. (The lack of an investigating magistrate is perhaps the most distinguishing characteristic in contrast with civil law systems.) Many towns appointed local solicitors as prosecutors, which alleviated some of the criticism of "police advocacy." Police prosecutors were thought to lack the indifferent attitude as to the outcome of the case, which is quite necessary if the prosecutor, as an advocate, were to assist the court in reaching a just conclusion. In theory, the state is not in a win or lose position, it wins as much if an innocent person is acquitted as when a guilty person is convicted. A prosecuting solicitor did represent the chief constable, but had a greater detachment than a member of the police force. This slow movement towards a more independent and unified prosecuting procedure accelerated with the creation of the Crown Prosecution Service in 1986, the first independent national prosecuting service. Additionally, as a result of the Criminal Justice Act 2003 the decision to charge defendants in serious cases was transferred from the police to the Crown Prosecution Service. Within the CPS today, some 2,700 professional prosecutors serve as prosecutors, handling around 1.2 million cases before the magistrates' and Crown Courts. The CPS has, however, had a very difficult gestation period, and was severely criticized by police, judges, magistrates and their clerks, and the probation service. But there has been an increasing acceptance of this very significant change to the criminal justice system. Perhaps the most contentious issue in its early years was the right of solicitor-CPS prosecutors to appear in the Crown Court, a right now allowed by the Access to Justice Act of 1999. The concern with that right of audience was that it would create an inherent conflict of interest between the promotion and job prospects of the CPS civil servants versus their duty to the court and justice. In other words, they might pursue improper prosecutions in their zeal to secure promotion or to achieve department set prosecution and conviction targets.

The English defense process is more similar to that in the United States than the prosecution, though with the increasing role of the CPS even that difference is diminishing. As Karlen has pointed out, the early American system ''was more generous'' in allowing legal representation to the defendant, but in terms of both allowance and funding of defense counsel, the two systems are not now greatly divergent. English legal aid does tend to exist more within the traditional professional structure than in the United States, where separate public defender offices have prevailed. That English professional structure, where barristers and judges have common roots and comprise a homogeneous fraternity, tends to give an American observer the impression that there is a closer bond between counsel and judge than between counsel and client, a bond that, as Karlen notes, may "inhibit the presentation of a strong defense."

The accused somehow must be brought before the authorities. How that is done varies; it may or may not involve a warrant, it may be by an arrest or a summons without arrest, and it may be accomplished by a public official, the police or by a private citizen. Of importance to criminal procedure is both the lawfulness of the act itself, such as the arrest, and the consequences of an unlawful act at this stage of the trial, particularly as to the exclusion of evidence obtained incident to an unlawful action. A **Miranda**-like "caution" warning is required, and the right to counsel has been enlarged. The emphasis for the police during questioning is on "investigative interviewing". The result of unacceptable interrogation practices disclosed during the reversals in the three IRA miscarriage of justice cases in the early 1990s, investigative interviewing involves hearing the full story repeated twice before questions—a contrast to the U.S. interrogation.

The English law of arrest may seem vague to an American observer, it has evolved from suits for false imprisonment and resisting arrest. Warrants are used less frequently in England, both because of the pattern of success in issuing summons (mostly limited in the United States to traffic violations) even for some serious crimes, and because the issuance of a warrant may require a concurrent decision as to bail, which is not part of the warrant process in the United States.

The English police officer is more limited in arresting for offenses committed in his presence; if a misdemeanor either it must constitute a breach of the peace, which is not clearly defined in English law, or the officer must rely on an increasing number of specific statutes. The limitations on the English police officer's powers reflects the historically relatively homogeneous nature of the population, and a perhaps outdated corresponding absence of fear on the part of a citizen stopped by a police officer. But that is changing rapidly as England becomes multicultural and with the large numbers of immigrants of recent decades, the negative caution an American feels if stopped by police increasingly is now shared by many persons in England. It affects the relationship at the time a police officer has little more than a suspicion, and it brings to the relationship the adversary element of the later stages of the criminal process.

There are disparities between criminal procedure in England and the United States in several regards. A major reason is that numerous rights in the United States have constitutional roots, those in England have legislative or precedential roots. One contrast is the use of evidence obtained in an unlawful search. Some systems, including that in the United States, exclude that evidence because of the method of its acquisition, regardless of its relevancy. England allows evidence if it is relevant, though with some exceptions. Were it illegally obtained, it may result in punishment of the police, but usually not in exclusion at the trial unless the judge believes its use would be unfair.

Disclosure by the defense, formerly absent of any obligation, has also undergone change. Most recently, as a result of the Criminal Justice Act 2003 the defense is now required to hand over all of its evidence to the prosecution prior to trial—including witnesses names and addresses, points of law to be relied on, and any expert witnesses consulted. The right of the accused to remain silent has a minor crack. The English tend not to view silence as a very fundamental right. For example, if an accused after being cautioned fails to mention a fact upon which he relies at trial, an adverse inference may be drawn from his silence during questioning. Also, whether or not an accused takes the stand is irrelevant to whether his past criminal record is admissible, but past records are usually not admitted for other reasons. The U.S. allows past records only when the accused does take the stand.

Although she does not prepare the case, it is the judge who determines the relevancy of evidence, her decision is guided by limiting statutes and a considerable bulk of precedent. The English judge must not only rule on what evidence counsel may admit, but, unlike an American judge, she may herself participate in molding the finished product, the final aggregate of facts upon which either she or the jury will decide guilt or innocence. The judge may recall witnesses or introduce new witnesses (rarely), and she may question witnesses either to remove doubt based on earlier testimony, or to inquire more deeply into matters which she believes were only superficially treated. Furthermore, the new Criminal Procedure Rules, enacted pursuant to the Criminal Justice Act 2003 also provide for a more active judge to ensure efficient case management.

The discretionary power of the judge in other common law nations, including the United States, is limited severely. American criminal verdicts are appealed far more often than in England. There is a sense that the process requires both trial and appeal, a view that has not existed in England, but one that is changing. The English criminal trial stage thus is the controlling location in the criminal process, but that control center shifts to the appellate stage in the United States.

The right to a jury trial, of some sort and character, exists in most common law nations. It has existed for 800 years, evolving from witnesses who were familiar with what had occurred to persons who were not at all familiar with the events. The use of the jury in England in criminal trials remains important, but not in terms of numbers. Most crimes are disposed of in the magistrates' courts.

But the more serious crimes continue to be tried before a jury in a Crown Court. There the procedural elements of the English jury vary markedly from the United States jury. The English jury long remained, as Lord Devlin has noted, "predominantly male, middle-aged, middle-minded and middle-class." It is changing, but pressures for a more representative jury have until recent years, been less visible than in the United States, and still have a long way to go to truly reflect the changing demographics in England. But the most notable distinction in the selection process is the absence of a voir dire examination, allowing counsel to challenge the fitness of prospective jurors. In theory, the English advocate may challenge for cause, but it is not done often. Preemptory challenges, of which 20 were allowed in 1530, were reduced in stages and eventually abolished in 1988. For years before their abolition, there was little evidence of their use. The rule is to accept those persons called to serve by the administrative machinery, however haphazard that process may be. Their elimination resolves one troubling use of them in the United States, racially motivated challenges. There is, however, a process of vetting an English jury, by checking police and security records and requesting that the person "stand by for the Crown." It does not occur very often.

The second striking difference in the jury procedure involves the verdict. But it is a difference which is diminishing. The verdict in English criminal law long mandated unanimity. Moving away from this sacrosanct characteristic was accomplished in the Criminal Justice Act 1967, which introduced the majority verdict. A jury is informed initially that it should reach a unanimous verdict. If it does not, it is then told that although it should continue to try to reach a unanimous verdict, a majority verdict will be accepted. The English majority verdict does not mean a bare majority, as is accepted in Scotland, however, but rather permits only one or two dissents depending on the size of the jury. This is thought to diminish the possibility of either a hung jury caused by a member who proves unfit to serve the role of a reasonable juror, or a jury which has been tampered.

The majority verdict in criminal cases may be a practice whose time has come. It has been adopted in several states in the United States, where the pattern has been to allow a smaller majority than the English view. The accused is believed to have enough in his favor under modern procedural rules, and the impact of a single (or small minority) obstinate juror is thought to justify this important change from the early common law adherence to the unanimous verdict. Thus the difference is not between or among common law nation systems, but between contemporary practice and the historical mandate of a unanimous verdict.

The criminal procedure of different common law nations may reflect very contrasting treatment of an accused, but there is a more common element to the sentencing process, namely the debate about the balance between judicial discretion and mandatory, fixed sentences. Judicial discretion in sentencing contrasting with the more strict trial procedures, and more broadly contrasted with judicial subservience to Parliamentary sovereignty. One additional concern in England about mandatory sentences is the impact they might have on the debate about plea bargaining. The English fear that mandatory sentences may lead to plea bargaining is perhaps even more relevant now that the Court of Appeals in R v. Goodyear, [2005] 3 All E.R. 117 overruled the Turner case prohibiting judges from providing an indication of a likely sentence if the defendant pleaded guilty. Now, the accused, his counsel, the prosecutor and the judge can all work together in structuring a plea agreement. The judge, however, is still not allowed to indicate what sentence would be handed down if the case went to trial and the accused were found guilty, as this is viewed as potentially placing too much pressure on the accused to enter a guilty plea. The issue is thus rather complicated.

Another feature in English sentencing which is unknown in the United States is that where a defendant, having been found guilty by a magistrates' court, is believed by the magistrates to have committed a crime for which the magistrates lack authority to grant sufficient sentencing, the magistrates may refer the matter to the Crown Court for the imposition of sentence. A defendant appearing before a magistrates' court must thus be aware that the sentencing limitations of the magistrates' courts are supplemented by those of the Crown Court. If a defendant before a magistrates' court believes there is a likelihood of a reference to the Crown Court for sentencing, he may well prefer to have the entire matter referred to the Crown Court for trial. The reason accused persons tend to avoid requesting a trial in the Crown Court, however, is an expectation of a modest sentence by magistrates in return for an almost certain conviction. Recently introduced is a requirement that the accused in a magistrates' court indicate his plea before the magistrates decide whether it ought to remain in their court, or be tried before a Crown Court. It is thought to allow disposition quickly in the magistrates' court of guilty pleas.

Criminal trials are much in the minds of American observers, willing or otherwise. They are given a heavy dosage of newspaper and television reporting of the accused and what he has done, and how the trial is proceeding. The public's right to know in the United States has little parallel in England, where it is balanced, or abused, by the unclear rules in the Contempt of Court Act 1981. Reporting of criminal (and civil) proceedings is restricted, though recently proposals to allow cameras in the court rooms for certain parts of trials was floated, but ultimately rejected (though the new Supreme Court may decide to allow recordings, although that decision will be made by the Supreme Court President when the court finally opens). Only formal, record matters, such as the names of those charged, the nature of the charge and the result is allowed at the committal proceeding. The evidence may not be discussed, unless permitted by the defendant, or unless the accused is not committed for trial. The same rule holds true during the trial, the media must await the verdict. Except in a few circumstances, the trial is open to the public. The limitation is not on the public nature of the trial, long an important part of English law, but on what use is made of information about the proceedings, whether or not that information is gathered at the trial or elsewhere.

## § 3.  Appellate Review

In the early development of the common law, an appeal lay only to challenge an error on the record. One sought a writ of error, and then pursued a process which to us seems unwieldy. A review of the judgment, alleging that the court reached the wrong conclusion, later was recognized in the Chancery Court. Thus appeals developed as part of the common law, recognized not by statute, but in the same manner as other rights, as the "way things ought to be" by the judiciary. When the rural courts were abolished, the right of appeal was incorporated into the statutory framework, the primary source being the Judicature Acts.

An appellant now seeks to reverse the judgment as incorrect in law, which in a narrow sense constitutes a rehearing since the judgment may be reversed or some other judgment substituted. But it is not a rehearing in the manner of the rehearing of a civil law appellate court, where new evidence will be heard and there is a de novo proceeding. New evidence may be presented in the English appeal, but it very rarely is, and is accepted only where it could not have been obtained for use at the trial, suggests an important influence on the result and seems reasonably creditable. The most frequent acceptance of new evidence is in an interlocutory appeal, not an appeal from the trial judgment. Although the appellate court does rehear the case, English judges are far more hesitant to interfere with the discretionary power of judges than in the United States. But they do often overrule procedural determinations.

As discussed earlier there are two courts that are appellate courts—the Court of Appeals and the House of Lords (the judicial committee), soon to be replaced by a Supreme Court. In addition, there are intermediate appeals that may be brought to the divisions of the High Court and to the Crown Court from the County Courts and the Magistrates' Courts. Until recently, the appeals process and the relationships between the different courts was exceptionally complicated—as one would expect from a system that developed through the common law and as a result of specific solutions to individual appeals issues. Furthermore, that system tended to allow appeals to easily reach the higher appellate levels—including reaching the Court of Appeals, or even the House of Lords. This had the effect of inefficiently employing very senior judges in matters that should not have merited their attention, and in allowing multiple levels of appeal, where one appeal should have been sufficient. The recent reviews of the justice system pointed out these issues and made recommendations for simpler more efficient appellate procedures.

On the civil side, the changes have come about through the Access to Justice Act 1999 and the regulations promulgated pursuant to that act. The system is still complex, but at least appears to make more sense. The new system tries to ensure that appeals only go to the next level, rather than taking up the time of judges much higher up the hierarchy. The system does allow, however, for some cases to "leapfrog" all the way to the Court of Appeals if there are important issues that need resolved by the Court of Appeals.

As in the United States, some appeals in England are a matter of right, others require judicial permission. Prior to the recent reforms, appeals as of right were quite common, and appeals that required "leave to appeal" were less common. The reforms reversed this situation, and now appeals generally require leave of the court from whose decision the appeal is being sought.

The criminal appeals process has also been the subject of recent review and change. It should be noted however, that prior to 1907 there was no right of appeal in criminal cases involving trials on indictment (as opposed to summary offense trials before the magistrates' courts). From 1907 the criminal appeals system was gradually constructed, statutorily and jurisprudentially, culminating in the Criminal Appeal Act 1995. Lord Auld nicely summarized the state of the law: "namely whether the conviction was wrong in law, 'unsafe or unsatisfactory' or there was 'a material irregularity' in the course of the trial, but all subject to an express proviso that, even if the appellant established any of those complaints, the Court could still dismiss his appeal if it considered that 'no miscarriage of justice' had occurred." While the English law seems settled on this issue, there is some concern that the interplay with Article 6 of the European Convention on Human Rights, especially as articulated in *Condron v. U.K.*, (2001) 31 E.H.R.R. 1, may require a new trial where it is found that the trial was unfair. Another approach may be to rehear the case itself. But, while appeals from the magistrates' courts go to the Crown Court for a trial de novo, appeals to the Court of Appeal are significantly more limited in the fact finding capabilities or desires. Though for both civil and criminal appeals, the court does have the power to receive fresh evidence. This includes the production of documents and the appearance of witnesses. It is a power which should be, according to the rules, and is, according to practice, exercised very sparingly.

Following the general tenor of the Auld Report and other official reports at that time, in its Criminal Justice Act 2003 the government essentially abrogated the double jeopardy rule. The new rule provides that the prosecution may make an appeal against decisions in the crown court having the effect of terminating the prosecution. The new rule allows for a new trial for serious offenses following an acquittal where new evidence comes to light. The offenses involved tend to be ones that would result in life sentences.

The centralized role of the Court of Appeal as the exclusive civil and criminal appellate court is further supported by its jurisdiction over appeals from courts of special jurisdiction and tribunals. These special courts do not have a full procedural hierarchy, including special appellate courts, such as exists in many civil law systems.

There are few appellate judges in England, less than 50 on the Court of Appeal and House of Lords. They sit in London, the appellate process is highly centralized. But the process does not require the presence of the clients, it is a written and oral documentary process. The centralization and limited number of judges does offer a consistency in decision making generally absent in the United States, further enhanced by the process of appointing appellate judges, discussed earlier, which creates a judiciary more consistently competent than in many common law systems where judicial selection more closely approximates that in the United States.

The relatively small number of judges in England is possible by the limited frequency of appeal. Although the incident of appeal has been increasing in the last decade, nevertheless it is correct to note that there remains a greater public belief in England than in the United States that issues are dealt with competently at lower levels and that there is correspondingly less likelihood of a reversal on appeal. The recent increase in appeals has placed a substantial burden on the appellate court structure, and was part of the rationale for many of the recent reforms.

The emphasis on an oral process and the infrequency of reserving judgment distinguish English appellate procedure from the process in the United States. The record of appeal, which is furnished to the judges from the lower court, provides much of the information that in the United States is included in counsel's briefs. The lower court judgment in England usually includes an outline of the evidence, the authorities which the judge relied upon in reaching the decision and his reasoned decision. The oral focus is most evident during the actual appellate argument before the court. It is not preceded by lengthy and sometime printed briefs, the cumbrous work product of the American attorney. A paper, the "case" or the "skeleton argument" is presented by each side. It is supposed to be concise and to follow the practice directive that lists the specific points that must be raised—with the emphasis on brevity. If the written process were to assume the full brief form of the United States, there would be little left for the oral hearing. Many U.S. jurists view the U.S. oral hearing on appeal to be little more than an opportunity for the lawyers to clarify what they might have better prepared in the writings. Perhaps it is little more than a time for the lawyers to make the process appear more oral than it actually is. The challenge for the English system is to preserve the benefits of "working out" a solution in an often lengthy oral process, without making the process unduly time consuming and costly.

The inordinately long time of the English oral proceeding was once attributable to the reading of the record of appeal and the authorities relied upon by counsel. It is now hoped that judges at the beginning of the oral arguments have read the pleadings, the order under appeal, the notice of appeal, the judgment below, and the submitted skeleton arguments.

The oral arguments are not limited in time, and may go on for days or even weeks. It is rarely predictable how long the oral arguments will last, but counsel is supposed to provide an estimate of her expected time. The court may interrupt counsel, accept her proposition and dispense with the reading of authorities. It may further, after the appellant's argument, immediately state that it has not been persuaded by the appellant and render judgment.

After the conclusion of the oral arguments, the view of each judge often is given orally, although in the House of Lords decisions are generally reserved and written. How very different from the United States, where judges invariably reserve judgment and counsel must wait weeks or even months to know the outcome of their efforts. Another distinction is that English judges each render a separate opinion, a clear contrast to the usual civil law style of single, unsigned opinions. Separate opinions are time consuming, their value thought to be in adding to the possible lack of clarity of only one opinion, in reducing the likelihood that sentences would acquire near statutory authority, and avoidance of superficiality or intellectual laziness. But the latter may be present in the many instances where the second and third judges accept the opinion of the first.

The nature of the English appeal requires the judge to spend most of his time on the bench, very little time is spent in chambers. He generally hears oral presentations morning and afternoon of every day throughout the term. The American judge in contrast works many hours in chambers and receives substantial aid from one or more clerks and personal secretaries. The use of law clerks has largely been absent in England. Since extensive briefs are not used and judges may render their opinions extemporaneously upon completion of oral argument, clerks serve little purpose prior to the appeal. But more recently the Court of Appeal judges have had as many as a dozen "judicial assistants", new solicitors or barristers who do much of the same work as U.S. clerks. Intended as a parttime and short-term measure to help clear the backlog of cases, the position has been well received and may remain.

Finally, another level of review beyond that of the Court of Appeals and the House of Lords/Supreme Court exists as a result of Britain's participation in the European Community. The European Court of Justice hears references from English courts. It is perhaps incorrect to call the European Court of Justice an appellate court, since a reference to the court is less an appeal than a request for a ruling on European law which will be binding on the referring English court. If it is appropriate to describe the European Court of Justice as part of the English judicial structure but not an appellate court, it may be appropriate to describe the European Court of Human Rights in Strasbourg as not part of the English judicial structure but as an appellate court!

# CHAPTER 11

## RULES

### § 1. Sources of Law

Sources of law pertain not to how an ordinary citizen believes his conduct is governed, but to where courts look for the legal rules applicable to resolve a specific dispute. Tradition often separates sources into written and unwritten. It is a confusing distinction, intended to contrast laws which have been formally enacted from such non-enacted sources as judicial decisions and customs, and, important in English law, conventions and the royal prerogative. The variety of sources of English law attest to its nature as a *method* of administering justice.

Classification of sources is less important than their assigned values, particularly when the sources represent conflicting rules. How judges perceive the value of different sources additionally affects the manner in which they will apply a governing source of law. Value allocation to sources within a system is a slow, evolutionary process. English judges traditionally have been less inclined to defer unquestionably to legislation, particularly social reform legislation, than United States judges. Disdain for social legislation has diminished slowly. The legal profession in England has bred an independent and pervasive sense of what is right. Paramount is a sensitivity for preserving an individual right to contract freely and to alienate property. Social change is thought to be better introduced by the adaptation of precedent to new circumstances, than by legislation. The judiciary believes that due accord to social change is illustrated by the development of common law decisions. Although there is no dispute that legislation is the source of law which has authority over all other sources, the fabric of the common law is its precedent, and the vast number of volumes of "unwritten" law is the foremost distinguishing feature of the common law tradition.

## § 2.  Precedent

In any legal system, the opinions of judges in disputes are likely to be of interest in subsequent cases with similar facts. If a judge assumes that earlier decisions in his court and in higher courts were dealt with competently, there is no reason to suppose, in the absence of changed circumstances, that a similar result would be inappropriate. Continuity and predictability of the law are positive attributes. The theoretical *usefulness* of prior case law should not be any less in a legal system where judges do not have to follow earlier decisions, than where they are compelled to follow them. This presupposes access to the substantive law in the earlier decisions by means of an effective reporting system. When the rules denominating sources of law in a system exclude precedent as the primary source of law, precedent nonetheless retains value. Precedent is often noted in a civil law decision as *teaching* something, a use which refers to the form of assistance written decisions provide in determining how statutory law ought to be interpreted. Where precedent becomes a primary source of law, as in common law systems, the case does more than teach judges something, it exists separately as law to be followed, or distinguished. For centuries English precedent not only existed as law, as it continues to do today, but it existed as the primary source of law, giving way partially only to legislative enactments of Parliament after the civil war, and later being overshadowed by legislation as a source of social reform in the mid–19th century. Much of the doctrine of consideration was developed in the English courts, as were such other areas as agency, and negligence in tort law.

Case law binding upon courts may have assumed a diminished role in the English legal system, but legislation faces a gauntlet of interpretation by the courts. Decisions which interpret legislation become as much a source of law as the laws which they interpret. The existence of interpretive decisions of a parliamentary act tends to arouse a sense of comfort with English lawyers and judges. Until judicially interpreted, laws are sometimes believed to lack the authority which arises with judicial sanctification. While this in no way diminishes the supremacy of Parliament, it illustrates that where the interpretations of statutes possess independent status and authority, the statute alone may be incomplete until it has been interpreted.

Certainty, precision and flexibility are viewed as characteristics of precedent as a binding source of law. Once a decision has been rendered, there is some assurance that in a subsequent identical fact situation a similar conclusion will be reached. Common law system lawyers nevertheless are exceptionally skillful at distinguishing fact situations when a client's case seems disadvantaged by an earlier case of uncommon similarity. The aggregate of judicial decisions in England constitutes an extensive framework of variations on common themes. To the English lawyer it is inconceivable that these variations could be foreseen, or included, in statutes. The most exhaustive code cannot offer solutions to all possible situations. It must of necessity have some measure of abstractness. A civil law system judge has the task of resolving a case from broad statutory principles and underlying theories of the "essence."

English common law has attributes both of flexibility and rigidity. A decision that might at first be assumed to establish a clear rule in specific circumstances, may be distinguished from what appear to be identical circumstances. Common law lawyers speak of a distinction without a difference. English judges appear more reluctant than American judges to ignore a decision which seems to mandate an inappropriate or unjust resolution. The English opinion may state that however regrettable the court's decision might appear, the law on the subject is settled by earlier precedent, and any change must come from Parliament and not the courts. The degree of rigidity of a common law system thus depends on judicial attitude. The greater homogeneity of judges in England, in contrast to the diversity that exists in the United States, with its extensive state court system, tends to identify the English judiciary with stronger judicial compulsion to follow precedent, and with fewer variances in attitudes towards the value of precedent.

No system possesses a written law governing all conceivable disputes. Judges must therefore fill gaps, and thus create new law. It may not be very obvious to an observer of a common law system that a judge has "made" law. What effectively is new judge made law may have some identity with elements of one or more previous decisions, minimizing the appearance of judicial law-making. But in a similar situation in a civil law system, judge made law may have a tenuous identification with abstract statutes. Gap filling is an important issue for the European Court of Justice. Unlike judges in domestic European courts, the European Court's civil law judges have not hesitated to fill gaps to further the cause of integration. The irony is that such gap filling has been criticized by many English "Eurosceptics", who oppose further integration of the Community, and dislike the same judge made law that is a foundation of the English system.

It is frequently very difficult to distinguish a legal principle in a case, or *ratio decidendi,* from additional rule-like statements which are ancillary to the decision and not binding, but considered only *obiter dicta.* If it is difficult for a civil law observer to separate law from dictum in reading a common law decision, some comfort should be found in the fact that persons trained in the common law often cannot agree on the distinction in a given case.

Judges must know which decisions are to be followed, and which at most have value as soundly reasoned judgments to be read for guidance or "teaching" in the civil law sense. Within the domestic court structure in England, House of Lords' decisions are binding on all other lower courts, even though there may be no line of appeal to the House of Lords. The Lords decided in 1966 to discard a practice more than half a century old, which had held the Lords bound by its own previous rulings. The House of Lords decided it would henceforth only follow "appropriate" earlier decisions. The source of this new rule was not a case, but a policy statement of the Lords. Whatever flexibility the House of Lords thus may have granted itself, it has continued in practice to adhere to its earlier decisions in all but a very few instances.

As one moves down through the court hierarchy the rule tends to remain consistent. Higher court decisions are followed by lower courts, both in the civil and criminal courts. Also, courts tend to accept their own earlier rulings. There are of course variations, for example the decisions of High Court judges sitting alone at first instance are not binding on other High Court judges, although they are of persuasive authority. And the decisions of the inferior courts are not binding within the inferior court system, not so much for the reason that they lack the value of decisions of the superior courts, but because they are generally not reported.

An unwritten or unpublished decision may have little or no future value. Precedents are only as functional as their reporting. English law reports developed very slowly, without government participation. They continue to be the product of a private enterprise system which chooses which cases shall be reported, often on the basis of the economics of including a particular judgment. Yearbooks developed in the late 13th century. They were notes compiled by advocates, but under no pretext that they were to be used by judges as precedent. But they were used for that purpose occasionally, increasingly so by the 15th century. When publication of the yearbooks ceased, private reports were produced, initially under the name of the particular law reporter. They proliferated for three centuries until, in the mid–19th century, a semiofficial council was formed for the purpose of reporting cases in England and Wales. Their Law Reports, which have now replaced most of the private series, are not the exclusive publication of cases, but convention suggests that they are the reports which should be referred to when citing decisions.

The system remains quite informal. Not all cases are reported, and citations often are made to unreported decisions, or to a series other than the Law Reports. Substantial duplication exists, a case may be reported in three or four different series, and

additionally included in periodicals. Recommendations have been offered to make reporting official,
and also to produce an authenticated transcript
filed with the court of record for a decision, a
practice prevalent in other common law systems.
English reports are produced by barrister-reporters
who are present in court to hear judgments. The
authenticity of the report thus occurs not from the
fact that it is included in the Law Reports, but
rather because a barrister was present at the deliv-
ery of the judgment, and has vouched for the accu-
racy of his work. Repetition is avoided. It is a very
different practice from the United States, where
reporting systems print most published decisions,
including many which add nothing new to what is
often a line of consistent opinions on a particular
point, usually the interpretation of a statute.

While the general environment in England with
respect to law reporting and precedent in the past
decades has largely remained the same, there have
been some notable changes. As an initial matter,
electronic reporting of some cases on official cites
has restored some control back to the courts,
though in England most courts are not yet at the
point, and may never be, of providing case reports
on line. Additionally, the proliferation of commercial reports and commercial databases has diminished the likelihood that important cases will not be
available. Finally, in response to concerns about the
use, and perhaps abuse, of excess citation and of
citing unreported cases, especially those culled from
the notes of barristers, the courts are seeking to

limit the sources from which cases can be cited. Following the lead of the House of Lords in *Roberts Petroleum Ltd. v. Bernard Kenny*, the Court of Appeals released a Practice Direction restricting and regulating the use of some citations.

A further issue with respect to employment of reported cases is that the format of reporting largely determines its usefulness as precedent. Effective employment as precedent is possible only where a decision is reported in a form which makes it usable by judges in future cases. The form of reporting has thus tended to develop in a style which assures the utility of these private ventures. Reported cases in England, as in the United States, briefly outline the facts and the legal issue which has been presented, and give reasons, often quite lengthy, for reaching a particular decision. But in English cases, facts are perceived differently than in the United States. Factual differentiation often is carried to an extreme in the United States, rendering "different" decisions indistinguishable. English precedent consequently is more likely to serve as a forceful value in future cases.

Participation in the European Union, and the consequent delegation of the interpretation of any EU instrument to the European Court, has added to the English system of legal rules the question of the binding nature of decisions of the European Court on English courts. Also of importance is how the English judge on the European Court will view and use earlier judgments of that Court. Decisions worded in the abstract, in the manner of civil law cases, may prove of relatively minor use in decisions in the national units. But decisions to date have not been abstract, and prior decisions are frequently referred to by the Court. While the judges seem uniformly to accept prior decisions, how each values them tends to be strongly influenced by their civil or common law training.

## § 3.  Custom

Custom as a source of law is present in every legal tradition. The English common law has drawn extensively upon local custom; the Normans did not bring to England a legal system from the continent. Local custom assumed an important function in aiding post-Conquest English judges in resolving specific disputes. Custom was a basis for much of the early criminal law, as well as for such family prescriptions as the rights of parents. In this sense custom was an integral part of the common law.

Some local custom also existed separate from and sometimes as exceptions to the common law, usually involving rules which were applicable to a very small group of people within a local community. Local custom separate from the common law included rules regulating local fishermen, such as where they could dry their nets. This was custom which was not inconsistent with common law, but which filled gaps. There was also custom which might conflict with common law, such as stipulating the characteristics of public access across private property. Custom in this form differs from custom which is part of the common law only in its narrow and limited application, and its variance to the common law. With the passage of time, local customs often come to be modified to evolve into general customs which are integrated as part of the common law.

The initial establishment of custom requires proof that it existed uninterrupted for a long time, and that it existed by common consent rather than by the use of force. Also, it must be consistent with other customs, be local in effect, contain certainty, be exercised as of right, and be accepted as obligatory and of significant importance. And finally, it must be reasonable, and, of course, can not conflict with a statute.

## § 4.  Conventions

Conventions are an influential source of English law, and, along with customs, constitute the principal unwritten legal sources. Convention dictates expected conduct in the functioning of the judicial system as well as other institutions. No act of Parliament specifies that there must be a Prime Minister, nor outlines the method by which the Prime Minister is chosen. It is according to convention that a Prime Minister is selected from the parliamentary or majority party, and that if the Prime Minister fails on a vote of confidence or a major government proposal, resignation should follow. Convention additionally limits the conduct of the sovereign. It was convention which caused King Edward to abdicate in 1936; at that time a monarch should not marry a divorced person. It is also by convention that the sovereign carefully limits any exercise of the royal prerogative, and follows the advice of the Prime Minister in making cabinet and ministerial appointments and in granting royal assent to acts of Parliament.

Within the judicial structure, convention has long played a role in determining the respect to be given to the decisions of other courts, the right to issue dissents and the commencement of certain disputes before a specific court, even though other courts possess concurrent jurisdiction. The several courts acts have codified and altered convention, but it remains an integral element of the structure of these institutions.

Convention exists in every society; it is a part of every legal system. It prevails more successfully in a system where there is little emphasis on the codification of rules, and thus is less important in civil law systems. A homogeneous society probably is more conducive to admitting convention where tradition plays an important role, where the expectations of one individual with regard to the conduct of others tend to be common throughout the population. Convention is a flexible source of law, but nevertheless a source of exceptional importance in the machinery of justice in England.

## § 5.  Royal Prerogative

Powers of the English monarch are severely limited. Sovereignty of the crown, as contrasted with sovereignty of Parliament, is essentially a sovereignty symbolizing loyalty to the monarch. The power of the monarch, called the royal prerogative, includes various rights exercised directly by the sovereign, and some rights exercised by the executive—theoretically on behalf of the sovereign.

The judicial system was highly centralized in the beginning years of Norman rule in England. The king was the supreme source of justice. Various devices such as the writ system allowed the royal courts to increase their jurisdiction at the expense of local, rural courts. The king went unchallenged until the Magna Carta 1215, the first formal check on royal power acceded to by the king. The will of the king was no longer the law, though several centuries later civil strife occurred over the issue of the scope of royal power. The use of the royal prerogative surged in the 16th century with the establishment of the Star Chamber. The Stuart kings extensively enlarged the royal prerogative, based on their conceptions of the king's divine right. This challenge was met by common law advocates, and by the end of the 17th century the prerogative was returned to a state of diminished exercise. The royal prerogative was never again the source of authority for the creation of new courts, such as the Star Chamber. The question was becoming not what the sovereign could do to the citizenry, but what the citizenry could do to the sovereign. The royal prerogative became further eroded as the sovereign's immunity from civil proceedings diminished, by the mid–20th century ancient rules restricting civil actions against the sovereign were all but eliminated.

Comparatively little remains of the royal prerogative, although the monarch plays a role in the functioning of the government. A few formal powers remain, essentially summoning and dissolving Parliament, rendering royal assent to bills, presiding over the Privy Council, conferring honors, granting pardons, appointing some state officers, approving cabinet and minister appointments, appointing leading clerics, and concluding treaties. Many of these are illusory powers—thus, the monarch does not personally select the Prime Minister, but acts according to the will of the leaders of the parliamentary party. It is unlikely that the royal prerogative will increase in scope in the future. The monarchy is more a symbol than a source of authority. Today, the royal prerogative is at the command of Parliament.

## § 6.  Legislation

The authority of legislation in England or the United States, or in any other common law nation, may appear quite fundamental to observers in each nation. Enactments of the principal legislative bodies become law which must be followed. In the United States, complex questions about the effectiveness of the legislation may arise because of the existence of both federal and state legislatures and constitutions. Is the matter at issue enumerated in the Constitution for the federal congress? Is the matter one of specific residual delegation to the states, and thus not for federal action? These questions do not arise in England; parliamentary enactments are not questioned by challenging legislative competence. With few, though increasing exceptions, Parliament is sovereign in legislating domestic law. Of course, for Scotland, Northern Ireland and Wales, this is no longer the case in post-devolution Britain.

Parliament may enact unwise laws which the courts nevertheless in theory are bound to apply. As a theoretical matter, the English constitution does not contain fundamental rights which may lead to parliamentary decrees being invalidated by the courts as unconstitutional. However, the role of the Human Rights Act 1998 has provided the courts with the ability to issue "declarations of incompatibility" where statutes are inconsistent with certain human rights. Furthermore, membership in the European Community has allowed the courts to note inconsistencies between parliamentary enactments and superior obligations under EU law which are then later reconciled by the Parliament.

Outside of the human rights and EU context, however, there are other issues and obstacles that may confront legislation. Indeed, the vast amount of statutory law is thought by some to be inconsistent with and a threat to the stability of this common law system. Legislation gains greater respect, and perhaps authority, when judicially interpreted; English judicial interpretation is more highly refined than in the United States. Absent the ability to rule legislation unconstitutional, the English courts have developed a finely tuned system by which legislation is interpreted. Courts thus have significant influence on the post-enactment development of statutory law, since enacted law is only as effective as its judicial application. In the last few decades judges appear to have become more critical of legislation. Whether judges believe that there are more gaps in recent statutes, or they are attempting to consider public opinion, or just view the enactments as ill-conceived, is unclear. But the view that judges simply interpret and do not make law is simply inapplicable to contemporary England.

What interpretive rule is adopted may depend on what is the responsibility or role of the judiciary in interpreting statutes. But in specific cases and with regard to certain legislation, there may also be a strong personal antipathy by a judge to a particular statute, but no judge would simply rule that it is not binding. He might, however, emasculate the statute by his method of interpretation, just as he might a previous case with which he disagrees. The English have developed several rules and approaches to interpretation: the "literal" rule; the "golden" rule; and the "mischief" rule.

One may approach statutory interpretation through a strict rule, a literal interpretation of the statute without regard to what such ruling does to reason or justice. The literal approach has much support in the English cases, but even the concept of a "literal approach" may be subject to different interpretations of what literal may mean for statutory interpretation. Furthermore, where the literal approach leads to an absurdity, a repugnance, an inconvenience or an inconsistency, then another meaning may be sought. The admission of an absurdity as the result of a literal application of a law led to the creation of a second approach, the "golden rule". But what degree of absurdity, or inconvenience, will allow the search for a better meaning? The rule may thus open the door, as far as the judges wish it to open, to a decision based on social policy or political preference. What must be stressed, however, is that the rule does not permit one to open the door quickly and widely and to enter the domain of unfettered justification. It is a rule applied only after the literal rule is first attempted—and because an undesirable conclusion arises. Then, the golden rule permits a search for a more reasonable meaning, but only to the degree necessary to avoid such a conclusion.

In the event that a proposed interpretation continues to appear absurd, the provision may be considered in the context of the entire enactment, not just in the light of the purportedly applicable portion. To consider what the legislature was trying to correct or achieve is called the "mischief rule". This "purposive" approach to statutory interpretation is now well entrenched in England. But, having established the legitimacy of purposive interpretation when a literal approach will not work, the courts are then faced with the problem of identifying that purpose. Historically judges were not permitted to consider parliamentary materials in order to consider the social, political and economic circumstances which led to the enactment. That situation has now changed, though the issue of access to parliamentary materials is still in flux and quite controversial. The question concerning the use of parliamentary proceedings when interpreting statutes is really part of the larger issue of what are considered legitimate "aids to construction". There are essentially two types—internal and external aids.

Internal aids include all that may be read on the official printed version, the Queen's Printer's copy, of the statute. That being said, some parts such as headings and marginal notes may only used when the words of the statute are ambiguous or confusing. With respect to punctuation, another potential internal aid, before 1850 statutes were not punctuated, that was left for later. Accordingly, the traditional rule, no longer followed, was that punctuation could not be used in interpreting the statute. The contentious issue today largely concerns the question of which external aids may be employed by the courts. In other words, what evidence of the meaning of the statute not found on the printed version of the statute may be used. As a general rule, external aids are excluded. Most surprising was the historic ban on the judge's use of parliamentary proceedings. The rule was created by the courts themselves in the eighteenth century. Originally this included commission reports and White papers, though that prohibition was reversed in the nineteenth century.

In part, the reasoning for the prohibition of using parliamentary proceedings was that the original reports were unreliable. This was true even of the early reporting service, the initial versions of Hansard's Parliamentary Debates. Later, after 1909 even though Hansard's was subject to governmental editing, they still were not allowed. From that point forward, the argument against use of Hansard with its records of parliamentary debates resembles that employed today in the ongoing concern over the use of legislative history in statutory interpretation in the United States—that one may find what one wants within the legislative history. For example, with statements made by both sides of an issue declaring the meaning of the statute, which one should be allowed to govern. This was even more so in the English Parliament, where debate is more vigorous and responses are often made on the spur of the moment, without clear articulation or even clarity—half sentences and utterances being not uncommon. Another reason, based on English constitutional grounds, was that the English Bill of Rights 1689 provides that "the freedom of speech and debates or proceedings in Parliament ought not to be impeached or questioned in any court or place out of Parliament". This, provision, it was argued, served to bar the courts from delving into parliamentary proceedings when interpreting statutes.

Finally, in 1993 the House of Lords in *Pepper (Inspector of Taxes) v Hart* reversed the long held rule and allowed that in some instances courts could refer to parliamentary proceedings. The court rejected the constitutional argument against their use, and allowed their use where a statute is "ambiguous or obscure, or leads to an absurdity" and the statements to be relied on are "clear". The new rule, however, only applies to the passing of a statute, not parliamentary statements about the state of the law then existing. The decision was controversial and has been under attack since that time. Indeed, the House of Lords has itself retreated somewhat and noted that Hansard should be employed sparingly. An exception to this retreat has been in the context of court's interpretation of statutes in lights of the Human Rights Act 1998 and EU Law and the corresponding duty of the courts to consider whether later statutes are "incompatible" with the protected human rights and EU commitments.

## § 7.　The Constitution

Defining the constitutional law of the United Kingdom is made complex by the absence of a single constitutional document. Most nations have a constitutional document, although this does not mean it includes a bill of rights or that the constitution grants the judiciary the power of judicial review of legislation for constitutional inconsistencies. But the absence of a single document of British constitutional law has led to the creation of a myth. British constitutional law is frequently noted as being based on an "unwritten constitution." It is true only in the sense that constitutional law is not contained in a single document; the complex and abstract nature of the British Constitution results from it being an aggregation of numerous sources, mostly written, but all identifiable. The essential principles of the British constitution are "the separation of powers, the supremacy of Parliament, and the rule of law." Changes in any of the sources which comprise the British Constitution will alter its total structure, making it more flexible than many constitutions.

The Constitution is affected by most traditional sources of English law, including the royal prerogative, conventions, common law, a few of the more important acts of Parliament, the addition of acts of the European Communities and its various courts, and, more recently, the Human Rights Act 1998 and Devolution. Clarity of identifying the British Constitution is dependent upon recognizing its sources. The existence of custom, conventions and the royal prerogative do not render this an easy task.

The most important elements of the British Constitution are the Magna Carta, the Petition of Right 1628, and several statutes enacted by Parliament. The Act of Union with Scotland 1707, while classified as a parliamentary act, has a special status over most other acts, a status given also to the Bill of Rights 1689. The Act of Settlement 1700, and the Habeas Corpus Act 1679, are additionally constituent elements of British constitutionalism. Similarly, the acts devolving power to Scotland, Wales and Northern Ireland. Uniquely important is the European Communities Act 1972, which joined the United Kingdom to the European Communities. This added a new source of law, the law-making bodies of the Communities. Community law takes precedence over domestic United Kingdom law. If not applied by the United Kingdom courts, it will be by the European Court of Justice. The role of the European Court of Justice and its jurisprudence and the Human Rights Act should also be considered part of the constitutional landscape.

A final element of the British Constitution is that part of custom referred to as conventions, an important part of the framework of both the Constitution and ordinary English law. The source of conventions and their enforcement is less identifiable than other constitutional elements. Convention evolves principally from a non-judicial precedent established over decades if not centuries, of consistent conduct. Pressures for continuance are the expectations of the public and the convenience of the existence of the conventions. A considerable part of the body of conventions applies to government structures and functions, even to the existence of a Prime Minister. Conventions tend to become sanctified as the years of their recognition and observance accumulate.

In addition to the absence of a single written constitutional document, there is no court with authority to rule on the issue of the constitutionality of acts of Parliament. A parliamentary act is supreme. If it conflicts with an earlier act of Parliament, or with precedent, the earlier law is modified, not violated. This might suggest that it is absolutely clear that no act of Parliament can be challenged. For Parliament to pass an act inconsistent with the Act of Union with Scotland, or with the European Communities Act, but which was not intentionally directed to altering those important acts, a court would face the difficult problem of construing them as abolishing or amending those earlier acts, or being unintentionally in violation of those acts and thus invalid. What measure of parliamentary activity is necessary to amend or abrogate an important earlier parliamentary act is unclear, particularly where that earlier act is part of the aggregate which collectively is known as the British Constitution.

There is a fair amount of "euro-skepticism" within Britain. But if EC law were to become unacceptable in the United Kingdom, the only method to renounce that law would be political, not judicial, mandating a withdrawal from the EC by repealing the European Communities Act and any other English statutes associated with the EU treaties. The effect of any action less than withdrawal, such as an act of Parliament in conflict with the European Communities Act, remains a matter of debate, though considerably less so since the recent high profile case of *Thoburn v. Sunderland City Council*, [2003] Q.B. 151. Parliament has been sensitive in avoiding passing laws in conflict with the Acts of Union and of emancipation of the colonies and dominions. It would seem similarly aware of problems associated with passing laws in conflict with participation in the EU, though it may at times pass a law and be unaware of the conflict subsequently created.

Nations which have adopted the common law have usually chosen to have a written constitution. That should not be surprising. The unwritten constitution of Britain is the product of centuries of accretion of a variety of rules from diverse sources. A nation granted or grasping independence tends to reject the idea of an unwritten constitution not because that form has not worked in England, but because the newly independent nation usually has ideas of what the fundamental law should state—and a writing is a natural consequence of the circumstances of modern nationhood.

## § 8.  Human Rights

Typically, countries have provided in their constitutions or in a separate document for the specific protection of individual rights. What about in England? Well, in England it was argued that it was the judiciary that stood firm in protecting civil liberties. The judiciary did so despite the fact that the 17th century Bill of Rights does not guarantee individual liberties. Indeed, until recently, where such rights were protected, the sources of law relied upon to protect them were various conventions, judicial decisions and statutes. Consequently, a contemporary, written bill of rights in England had been sought by many for years.

In 1951, Britain ratified the European Convention for the Protection of Human Rights and Fundamental Freedoms (ECHR). The ECHR was an international treaty designed to provide human rights for the post-war Europe. Britain, however, argued that it did not need to do anything additional in order to have implemented the Convention as British law already provided the protections found in the ECHR. Nonetheless, from 1966, British citizens were permitted to take ECHR violation cases against the British Government to the European Court of Human Rights (ECtHR) in Strasbourg.

Finally, in 1998, Britain implemented major parts of the Convention through special domestic legislation, the Human Rights Act 1998 (HRA). The HRA provides domestic enforcement, through the courts in Britain, for significant parts of the ECHR. The rights protected by the HRA include the right to: life; be free from torture; liberty and security; freedom from slavery and forced labor; a fair trial; no punishment without trial; respect for private and family life; freedom of thought, conscience and religion; freedom of expression; freedom of assembly and association; to marry; and freedom from discrimination. Of course, the details of each right are spelled out in the HRA and must be applied in light of their interpretations by the European Court of Human Rights-and so are vastly more complex than this list might suggest.

The HRA further requires the judiciary to interpret legislation, even subsequent legislation, so that it is in conformity with the HRA, even through employment of the jurisprudence emanating from the ECtHR in Strasbourg. The cases resolved there, however, include not just British cases, but cases involving all forty-plus signatories to the ECHR. It has thus been suggested that the HRA thereby operates as an "interpretive act."

Nonetheless, and problematically for enforcement by the courts, within the British constitutional structure the HRA is not formally supreme over other legislation, regulations, or constitutional principles. The HRA, however, provides a device for the courts to signal to the government when the government's actions are in conflict with the requirements of the HRA—a "Declaration of Incompatibility." These Declarations can only be issued by the highest courts, and when they are considering such a declaration, the government has the right to be joined in the case in order to defend its actions (be they executive or legislative actions). While the Declarations do not formally act as a form of judicial review, they nonetheless have a powerful moral impact on the government, Furthermore, the government has stated that it will typically change the law when faced with such Declarations. The courts will, nonetheless, seek to interpret conflicting laws in such a way that there is no need for the Declarations.

Despite the potential for complexity and confusion as such a body of law is incorporated into the English legal system, the implementation of the HRA appears to have gone quite smoothly and successfully.

## § 9.  The Law of the European Union

Ratification of the Treaty of Accession and the European Communities Act 1972, initiated England's entry into the European Communities ("EC") (European Economic Community, European Coal and Steel Community, and European Atomic Energy Community), later renamed the European

Union by the Maastricht Treat in 1993. But England follows the dualist theory of international law; a treaty does not by accession become the law of the United Kingdom. As such the Treaty of Accession was thus not self-executing; Parliament had to act to give England's participation legal standing. Parliament not only accepted EC law existing at the time of the Act, but it agreed to adopt directly applicable EC legislation of the Council or Commission enacted subsequent to entry. Parliament thus delegated law making power to EC institutions, although limited to rights and obligations created by the text of the treaties.

EU legislation which is not directly applicable requires parliamentary action to become effective in the United Kingdom. Such legislation may be implemented by statute or, the more likely course under the 1972 Act, by subordinate legislation adopted by the English executive under delegated authority.

EU law includes sources beyond the treaties and secondary legislation. Decisions of the European Court of Justice may become an important source of law, both as precedent in that Court and in courts in the United Kingdom. A decision of the Court of Justice does not nullify a member state law, but the decision must be followed in member state courts if it pertains to the meaning or effect of the treaties, or the meaning or validity of an EU instrument. United Kingdom courts are bound by European Court of Justice decisions.

EU legislation, drafted by persons trained in the civil law, tends to be general, without either the precision identified with English legislation or useful interpretation clauses. But even though EU law does not contain the precision of words and sentences more typical of English law, English judges have been willing to speculate as to what was intended by the drafters. The noteworthy English decisions in the first decades of membership, guided considerably by the rulings of former Master of the Rolls Lord Denning, illustrated a distinct preference to reach conclusions without the participation of the European Court. But even though interpretive rulings were not the norm, the rulings of the English courts tended to comply with the spirit of the European treaties. In more recent times, however, the courts have been more willing to refer cases to the ECJ for interpretive rulings.

The Treaty of Rome and the subsequent treaties, as is customary with law-making in European nations, were drafted with broad general principles. They are subject to many different interpretations. The English courts thus confront legislation quite different from English legislation. It requires them to do what they are usually disinclined to do—to fill the gaps. The European Court of Justice may help by giving an interpretation of EC law—indeed, that is what the Court exists for (it does not decide individual cases). The role of the European Court remains quite different when it fills gaps. An English court may, in the absence of legislative clarity, retreat to the common law. It may suggest that it is applying a principle of the common law, though it may challenge the best of minds to find that principle anywhere in the foggy parameters of the common law. The European Court has no such latitude. They talk rather in terms of general principles of law as they create new rules. Both are involved in judge made law, but with different justifications to assuage the fears that the judges are stepping beyond the line which limits their authority.

The entry of the United Kingdom into the European Communities has required a most important submission of domestic law to an external law-making body. Other treaty obligations have raised similar issues touching upon the sensitive question of English parliamentary sovereignty, including Britain's participation in the WTO, the United Nations and the European Convention on Human Rights.

## § 10. Reception of Roman Law

Roman law is not a direct source of law of the English legal system. There has been an indirect effect on the development of the English legal system from the Roman law, however, principally from the area of canon law. Early English ecclesiastical courts were attended by advocates and presided over by Chancellors whose educational experience at Oxford and Cambridge included the study of civil law. English family and succession law, including the formalities of wills, thus demonstrate some rules not dissimilar to those of Roman law.

Where early English courts were not aided by precedent and turned to opinions of such writers as Bracton, there was a further indirect application of Roman law principles. Bracton's treatise reflects his knowledge of and respect for Roman law, influenced by the writings commissioned by the late Roman ruler Justinian. Bracton's classification of bailments follows directly the later Roman categorization. It subsequently was adopted in an early English decision. In other instances, judges have considered Roman doctrines when difficult questions were presented, and there was no direct, traditional source of English law as a guide.

All legal systems tend to benefit from others, particularly as comparative legal study becomes more prevalent. Where there has been no attempt to codify vast areas of the law, there are bound to be gaps which require judges to seek guidance from other sources. Other legal systems in civilized nations, whether they are common or civil law systems, may provide that guidance. If the Roman law has been considered appropriate guidance in a particular case, that should not suggest that there has been a reception of the Roman law. Reception means a direct acceptance of the Roman law as a principal source of law. That has not been a characteristic of the development of English common law.

## § 11.   Divisions of Law—Law and Equity

Where alternative systems of justice exist, conflict is bound to occur. Equity supplemented the common law by offering compatible remedies in some cases, but in others it produced a direct conflict with the common law. The Court of Chancery often issued an equitable injunction ordering an individual to cease an action which had been commanded by a common law court. The success of the equitable remedies depended upon the ability of the sovereign to exercise prerogative powers. Objections to the injunctive power of Chancery ultimately waned in the early 18th century, when the rules of equity had become nearly as rigid as those of the common law. The Judicature Acts 1873, finally abolished the conflict by transferring the powers of the common law courts and courts of equity to the newly established Supreme Court of Judicature. No division of the High Court may issue an injunction to restrain a proceeding in another division, ending the most controversial conflict between the two systems. The fusion nevertheless was not absolute. Traditionally legal remedies remained a matter of right, those of equity continued to be discretionary. But the administrative conflicts were abolished, the systems no longer possess any substantial measure of conflict. This was reinforced statutorily when equity was fused in the nineteenth century, Parliament provided in the Judicature Act 1873, and then again in the Supreme Court Act 1981, that where equity and law are in conflict—equity would be supreme.

## § 12. Divisions of Law—Public and Private Law

Division of common law systems into private and public law is referred to infrequently. A division is more often noted in terms of the law of torts or the law of property, all part of what is known as substantive, as opposed to procedural, law. Were the system to be classified as public and private law, private law would include the law of contracts, torts and property. Additionally so categorized would be family law, succession and trusts. Criminal law would constitute a major part of the public law, which would further embody constitutional and administrative law, and procedure. Civil law nations often employ entirely separate hierarchies of courts for public and private law. While there are specific common law courts in England for criminal law, the principal criminal law courts, the Crown Courts, are part of the Supreme Court of Judicature. Appeals may lie to different divisions, but both civil and criminal matters are heard in the same appellate court. With the passage of the Human Rights Act there is yet another area of public law, though it is still in its early days and it is not clear that the courts will recognize that its "public" nature requires different treatment than is accorded to private law matters. The other major section of public law, the law of the constitution, is allocated in the main to administrative tribunals, but the common law appellate court system retains jurisdiction over most administrative appeals.

Public law has had a tough time establishing itself in England. The problem of not having a centralized and cohesive constitution makes the role of public law particularly problematic. Additionally, the ad hoc growth of the administrative tribunals has fostered a myriad different mechanisms that deal with public law issues. While it appears that some of those issues are in the process of being resolved through the gradual systemization and amalgamation of the various tribunals, there is a long way to go. The growth of the Human Rights Act claims will only complicate matters, as will the simultaneous and on-going transformation of the English welfare system. Finally, the interaction of public law and the rest of the English system will continue to be problematic inasmuch as public law is as an essentially civilian construct. It has been transplanted without much thought, and so will continue to have a difficult time interfacing with the English common law tradition.

## § 13. Divisions of Law—The Law Merchant/Commercial Law

Commercial law is often separately administered in civil law nations. It evolved within the fairs and markets of the Middle Ages, creating what became known as the law merchant. Commercial law might have developed within England as a largely separate system existing parallel to the common law. But it substantially had assimilated into the common law by the 17th century, although it retained a separate significance, because judges recognized that commercial rules chiefly were based on the practices of merchants and traders. Commercial usage constituted custom. The common law rule requiring proof of the existence of a custom from a very early time was not required in commercial litigation. Current custom was acceptable as long as it did not conflict with common law decisions. In the late 19th century, most of the law merchant was incorporated into statutes, including the Bills of Exchange Act of 1882, the Partnership Act 1890, and the Sale of Goods Act 1893. While the law merchant had its own separate and important origin, little of that isolation remains today in English law.

From these English commercial acts the United States evolved a set of its own commercial laws, the 1896 Uniform Negotiable Instruments Law, the 1909 Bills of Lading Act, the 1906 Uniform Warehouse Receipts Act and the most important commercial law, the Uniform Commercial Code, adopted first in Pennsylvania in 1953. Because commercial law was assimilated into the common law and did not develop as a parallel subject of law, the term "commercial law" has quite a different meaning than that on the continent. There are no separate courts in most common law countries for commercial law problems, although there are special courts for certain commercial matters, such as the bankruptcy courts in the United States and the Restrictive Practices Court in England. But there is in England a Commercial Court, which is part of the Queen's Bench Division of the High Court. The judges are High Court judges assigned to the Commercial Court because of their expertise in commercial law. The Court has gained popularity and respect, though private commercial arbitration is still the preferred mechanism for resolving commercial disputes. But the Commercial Court is not a separate, specialized court outside the civil court structure, as in some civil law nations. Thus, while commercial law is a distinct field of law in England, with an associated court within the Queen's Bench division of the High Court, one should not assume that the field carries with it the significance of the similarly named fields in Continental Law legal systems.

## SELECTED BIBLIOGRAPHY

B. Abel–Smith and R. Stevens, *In Search of Justice* (Penguin Books Ltd.1968).

The Right Honourable Lord Justice Auld, *Review of the Criminal Courts of England and Wales* (HMSO 2001)

Bailey, Ching, Gunn & Ormerod, *Smith Bailey & Gunn on the Modern English Legal System*, Fourth Edition (2002).

Sybille Bedford, *The Faces of Justice* (NY 1961).

Harold J. Berman, Law and Revolution: *The Formation of the Western Legal Tradition*, 7–10 (Harvard Univ. Press 1983).

Penny Darbyshire, *Eddey & Darbyshire on the English Legal System*, Seventh Edition (2001).

Lord Denning, *The Discipline of Law* (Butterworths 1979).

A. Dicey, *Introduction to the Study of the Law of the Constitution* (London 1924).

Catherine Elliott and Francis Quinn, *English Legal System*, Seventh Edition (2006).

Jeffrey Goldsworthy, *The Sovereignty of Parliament: History and Philosophy* (2002).

W.S. Holdsworth, *A History of English Law* (London 1913–1966).

R.M. Jackson, *The Machinery of Justice in England* (7th ed.) (Cambridge 1977).

Sir Andrew Leggatt, *Tribunals for Users, One System, One Service: Report of the Review of Tribunals* (HMSO March 2001).

F. Pollock & F.W. Maitland, *History of English Law* (Cambridge 1898).

Dawn Oliver, *Constitutional Reform in the UK* (2003).

Martin Partington, *Introduction to the English Legal System*, Third Edition (2006).

Richard Ward & Amanda Ragg, *Walker & Walker's English Legal System*, Ninth Edition (2005).

The Right Honourable the Lord Woolf, *Access to Justice—Final Report* (HMSO July 1996).

The Right Honourable the Lord Woolf, *Access to Justice—Interim Report* (HMSO June 1995).

# PART 3

# SUPRANATIONAL EUROPEAN LAW AND INSTITUTIONS

In the last several decades, supranational legal norms and institutions in Europe have increased markedly in scope, authority and significance. While developing their own salient characteristics, the European-wide regimes also reflect the national legal traditions out of which they arose. At the same time, they have added significant new dimensions to their member states' national legal traditions, affecting relevant institutions and actors and their respective political roles, the tools and methods of legal culture, and even the normative foundations of national and international law. Through this dynamic process of drawing from and at the same time transforming the legal traditions of European nation-states, supranational European law and institutions have become an integral part of each of those legal traditions. In important ways, they also further the convergence of the diverse legal traditions of Europe. The two most far-reaching regimes in these respects have been those founded by the treaties establishing the European Union and by

the Convention on the Protection of Human Rights
and Fundamental Freedoms.

# CHAPTER 12

# THE EUROPEAN UNION

## § 1. Founding and Expansion

What is now known as the European Union was born in the wake of World War II as six European countries (Belgium, the Federal Republic of Germany, France, Italy, Luxembourg, and the Netherlands) joined to pool their coal and steel industries under the jurisdiction of a supranational High Authority, pursuant to the 1952 Treaty of the European Coal and Steel Community (ECSC). In 1957, the Treaties of Rome established the European Atomic Energy Community (Euratom) and the European Economic Community (now known more simply as the European Community or EC). Together, the three treaties establishing the European Communities sought to create a single, common market in Europe and, more broadly, to bring the European states into ever closer union. In 1993, the Maastricht Treaty on European Union integrated the three European Communities into a new and broader political and economic structure, the European Union (EU). The 1997 Treaty of Amsterdam subsequently made some important changes to the structure of the EU. The Treaty of Nice, which entered into force on in 2003, reformed the institutions so that the EU could function efficiently after its enlargement to 25 Member States. The Treaty of Nice, the Maastrict Treaty, and the Treaty of the EC have been merged into one consolidated version Consolidated Treaty on European Union or Consolidated TEU). Most recently, in 2007, the Heads of the Member States signed a new agreement, the Treaty of Lisbon, which will make further, significant changes to the constitutional structure of the EU if it is ratified by all of the Member States.

Denmark, Ireland, and the United Kingdom joined the original six states of the European Communities in 1973. Greece acceded in 1981, Spain and Portugal joined in 1986, and in 1995 Sweden, Finland and Austria joined the EU. Ten more countries—Czech Republic, Cyprus, Estonia, Latvia, Lithuania, Hungary, Malta, Poland, Slovenia and Slovakia—became members of the EU in 2004, and most recently, in 2007, Bulgaria and Romania brought the total membership of the EU to twenty-seven countries. Croatia, the Former Yugoslav Republic of Macedonia, and Turkey are currently candidates for membership. Norway had signed a treaty to become a part of the EU in 1994, but (as they had once before, in 1973) voters rejected the proposal in a national referendum. The citizens of Switzerland have also rejected the idea of membership, although the country formally applied.

Just as the EU broadened geographically, it also broadened functionally. Originally, the ECSC and Euratom were essentially restricted to specific economic sectors, and the EC was limited primarily to economic liberalization. By virtue of its generality, the EC has had far greater importance than the other two basic treaties. Within the context of the EC, the Member States gradually yielded more of their sovereignty to give the European Community extensive authority over other related matters, such as social, environmental, and regional issues. The Maastrict Treaty expanded the European Union's influence further to cover areas such as immigration, border, and drug and crime control, and cooperation in justice; public health; education; culture; consumer protection; research and technological development; development cooperation with developing countries; trans-European networks; and political cooperation among the nations of Europe. In 1999, the Euro was introduced as a common currency in the EU, and is accepted as legal tender in 15 of the Member States.

## § 2.  Institutions of the European Union

The EU has four principal institutions of legal import: The Council of Ministers, the European Commission, the European Parliament and the European Court of Justice (ECJ).

The Council of Ministers (formally designated in the TEU as the Council of the European Union) is responsible for making the major policy decisions of the EU. Consisting of one representative of each of the Member States (usually the minister of the central government responsible for the particular matters under consideration, such as Agriculture or Labor), the Council meets regularly in Brussels. Although legally a single institution, in practice the

Council meets in a variety of specialized groups which are responsible for certain types of issues. For instance, different Council groups focus on particular matters such as agriculture, the environment, transportation, or the budget of the EU. The Council is assisted by a Committee of Permanent Representatives (COREPER), which coordinates the Council's multiple decision-making meetings, and a general secretariat. The Presidency of the Council rotates among its members every six months.

In general, the Council is the EU's principal lawmaking body. Some sensitive areas such as taxation or the rights and interests of workers require unanimity, but otherwise decisions of the Council are reached by majority vote. A simple majority with each State having one vote is used when Council adopts its own rules of procedure or votes to request the European Commission to present a proposal for legislation. In areas such as the establishment and functioning of the internal market, research and technological development, consumer protection, and the environment a "qualified majority" is required. This procedure accords more voting power to larger states than small ones. The bigger the country's population, the more votes it has, but the numbers are weighted in favor of the less populous countries.

The European Commission has several functions in the EU. The first is to draft and present legislative proposals for the Council to adopt or reject. This "right of initiative" has been inferred from the numerous treaty provisions that authorize the

Council to act "on a proposal of the Commission." The Commission's right of initiative is exclusive in most areas. Under the TEU, however, the Member States have concurrent, and in some cases exclusive, powers to initiate action to be taken by the Council with regard to common foreign and security policies and cooperation in judicial and home affairs.

A second important function of the Commission is enforcement of EU norms. As the guardian of the treaties, the Commission ensures that their provisions, as well as the measures adopted by the EU institutions, are properly implemented. When there is a violation, the Commission can refer cases to the European Court of Justice; it can also grant Member States temporary waivers or derogations from EU rules. The Commission can also do investigative work in some areas, and can impose fines on individuals or companies who violate EU regulations.

Third, the Commission has a quasi-executive function for the implementation of EU policies. Its executive powers apply to certain specific economic sectors or activities, the creation of administrative rules for the implementation of Council decisions, the negotiations of treaties and trade agreements and representation of the EU in international organizations, and the management of agricultural markets. The Commission is also in charge of most of the EU budget.

Unlike members of the Council, Commission members must be independent of any government or other body, and must act solely in the interests of the EU as a whole. They are appointed by the common accord of the governments of the Member States for five years, subject to the consent of the European Parliament. There are currently twenty-seven commissioners, one from each of the Member States. The Commission is supported by a civil service, based mainly in Brussels and Luxembourg, divided into 36 departments, or Directorates–General, responsible for specific policy areas.

The Commission is answerable only to the European Parliament. The Commission must present its annual reports to Parliament and must defend its action in open sessions of the same. Parliament monitors, comments on and votes on the Commission's program and it can compel the Commission to resign by a two-thirds majority vote. Also, for the first time in 1995 the Parliament held U.S. Senate-style hearings on Commission nominees, including the President. The Parliament also must formally approve the nomination of the President of the Commission.

Legislatively, Parliament participates in the formulation of directives, regulations, and other EU legal decisions in a number of important areas. It does this through the consultation, co-decision, and cooperation procedures between it and the Council described below. Parliament's assent is also required for any further enlargements of the EU and for all international agreements. The Treaty on European Union gives the Parliament the extended legislative power to request the Commission to submit any appropriate proposals on matters on which it considers an EU act is needed.

Beginning with the Maastricht Treaty, the Parliament has also been given general supervisory powers. Through these, Parliament can set up Committees of Inquiry to investigate alleged maladministration in the implementation of EU law. This is done through an appointed Ombudsman who has powers of investigation. Any citizen of the EU or anyone within its jurisdiction may petition the Parliament on any EU matter which directly affects him or her.

Finally, the Parliament plays a significant role with regard to the budget. Whereas the Council has final word on "compulsory" expenditures in the Commission's draft budget (mostly agricultural policy), the Parliament has final say with regard to "non-compulsory" expenditures. Ultimately, Parliament can either approve or reject the entire budget; in the latter case, the process must start again with another draft budget from the Commission.

Originally, the members of the Parliament were drawn from the parliaments of the Member States. However, since 1979 the European Parliament has been directly elected by universal suffrage in each of the Member States. There are currently 785 Members of the European Parliament, or MEPs, roughly apportioned according to population. The direct elections are organized under national electoral laws in Member States, but once elected to their five-year terms, the deputies are organized into ideologically similar political groups rather than by nationality. The Parliament holds its sessions in Strasbourg; its 20 committees and its political groups meet in Brussels; its general secretariat is based in Luxembourg.

The main function of the European Court of Justice is to guarantee the proper interpretation and application of the treaties and other legal instruments adopted by the institutions of the EU. Its collective functions include reviews of EU legislation for compatibility with the treaties, consideration of enforcement actions against the Member States for noncompliance with EU law, and preliminary rulings clarifying the scope and interpretation of EU law at the request of national courts.

Based in Luxembourg, the ECJ is comprised of as many judges as there are Member States, but it usually sits in a Grand Chamber of thirteen judges or Chambers of three or five judges. The judges are assisted by eight advocates-general. The judges and advocates-general serve for renewable six-year terms. According to the EC Treaty, the judges and Advocates General must be "persons whose independence is beyond doubt and who possess the qualifications required for appointment to the highest judicial offices in their respective countries or who are jurisconsults of recognized competence." The resulting Court unites jurists from many different legal traditions.

The role of the advocate-general is to consider the parties' cases after all submissions have been com-

pleted and before the judges begin their deliberations, and to present the judges with a written,
reasoned, independent opinion in the case. The report includes all facts and issues, and recommends a
decision to the judges. While the recommendation of
the advocate-general is very influential on the
judges' decision, it also assures that the case will be
fully considered twice, just as a court of first instance and a court of appeals would work.

In addition to the ECJ, the EU judiciary has since
1989 included a Court of First Instance, created by
the Council for the purpose of relieving the increasing case load of the ECJ, especially in cases requiring more detailed and thorough fact-finding or expertise in complex economic issues. Its jurisdiction
include, for example, cases under the EU competition laws and under the anti-dumping laws, and
actions brought by natural or legal persons against
an act of a European Union institution.

## § 3.   Scope and Subject Matter of European Union Law

The European Union, as instituted by the Maastrict Treaty and modified by the Treaty of Amsterdam and the Treaty of Nice, is made up of three
"pillars". The central pillar consists of the previously existing Communities and their law. The side
pillars are, first, the common foreign and security
policy and, second, police and judicial cooperation in
criminal matters. The three pillars support the
over-arching constitutional order of the EU. The
central pillar, however, is predominant as it con-

tains all the Community policies from the original three treaties, and all legislation adopted since 1952. Although the EU is commonly referred to as a "constitutional" order, it has no comprehensive constitutional document as such, nor does it have many of the attributes of a fully developed constitutional state, most notably status as an independent sovereign. However, its broad, general competence over wide areas of economic and social life and its key underlying principles and values together define the scope of the EU's legal order.

The neoliberal philosophy of the founding Treaties of the Community was to promote peace, unity, and security for the peoples of Europe through the social and economic benefits of market unification. These goals are to be achieved through the progressive affirmation of the "four fundamental freedoms" of the EU: free movement of goods, workers, services, and capital. Also, these freedoms must be exercised on the basis of equality, without discrimination based on nationality.

Article 3 of the Consolidated Treaty on European Union lays out the specific objectives of the EC. These include: the elimination of customs duties and the elimination of quantitative restrictions on the importation and exportation of goods between Member States; the establishment of a common customs tariff and a common commercial policy towards third countries; the abolition of obstacles to freedom of movement for persons, services, and capital between Member States; a common policy toward agriculture; a common policy toward transport; a system ensuring that competition in the common market is not distorted; procedures by which the economic policies of Member States can be coordinated; approximation of Member State laws in order to assure the proper functioning of the common market; creation of a European Social Fund to improve employment opportunities for workers; creation of a European Investment Bank to facilitate economic expansion; and association with overseas countries to promote trade.

To achieve these objectives, Article 249 of the Consolidated TEU authorizes the Council and Commission to "make regulations, issue directives, take decisions, make recommendations or deliver opinions" in order to achieve its objectives. The treaties, however, do not give the EU general powers to promote its goals; rather, each chapter of the treaties lays down the extent of the EU powers to act upon the specific goal which the chapter covers.

These limited powers have been supplemented in two different ways. First, Article 308 of the Consolidated TEU provides that if action by the EU proves necessary to achieve one of the objectives of the EU, and the Treaty has not provided for this action, the Council may take appropriate measures through a proposal by the Commission and approval by Parliament. Second, the ECJ has allowed the expansion of EU powers through its development of a doctrine of implied powers. This doctrine requires that the treaties be understood to allow whatever means are necessary to attain the objectives legitimately within the EU's domain under the treaties.

Expansion of the scope of EU activity has led to a corresponding erosion of Member State powers. As the EU has regulated certain areas of activity more and more comprehensively, the residual concurrent powers of the Member States have diminished correspondingly. This process is encouraged by the EC Treaty's "principle of cooperation," which obliges Member States to take all appropriate measures to ensure fulfillment of the obligations arising from the Treaty or other action taken by the institutions of the EU and which prohibits Member States from doing anything that would jeopardize the attainment of EU goals. This principle has been called a fundamental principle of the EU legal structure by the ECJ, and has contributed significantly to the strengthening of EU powers over Member State powers.

The Maastricht Treaty on European Union further facilitated EU growth over Member State powers. The Treaty provided for the establishment of a common European currency; common rights of European citizenship; broad new powers for the EU in areas from public health to crime to industrial policy; and a common foreign and security policy. On the basis of these various powers, EU institutions can enact additional legislation independent of, and binding in, Member States.

While the scope of EU law increased in several important areas, the Maastricht Treaty also gave formal status to the doctrine of subsidiarity in the EU's constitutional structure. Subsidiarity requires that in areas in which the EU and the Member

States have concurrent competence, the EU will only act if the objectives of the proposed action cannot be sufficiently achieved by the Member States and can be more efficiently achieved by the Union. The doctrine of subsidiarity is intended to mitigate Member States' concerns that they will lose their national power and identities to the expanding scope and supremacy of EU law.

As implemented under the current treaties, however, subsidiarity has thus far had little tangible impact on the EU political and legal order. Subsidiarity applies only in areas that do not fall within the exclusive competence of the Union, but the EU has a high degree of discretion in determining whether to assume exclusive competence over a particular matter. According to the ECJ's doctrines of the supremacy of EU law (discussed below), in addition to the EU's exclusive competence over common commercial policy and fisheries policy, the EU is considered to have exclusive competence in all areas in which the Member States have transferred competences to the Union and the Union has issued comprehensive measures. Thus, notwithstanding the subsidiarity principle, within the scope of EU law the Union can decide that it is time to set a Union-wide standard in an area which would otherwise normally fall under Member State competence.

## § 4. Sources of Law in the European Union

There are three general categories of sources of law in the European Union. The first and foremost in authority is primary legislation, created by Member States themselves. This includes the founding Treaties of the EU with their various protocols, amendments, additions, and annexes (the "Treaties"). Secondary legislation, which is subordinate in authority to primary legislation but much more common as a source of community norms, includes the body of law made by EU institutions acting within the scope of the Treaties. Finally, there are sources of law beyond secondary legislation which include other treaties and international agreements, ECJ decisions, and general principles of law.

Secondary legislation can take the form of regulations, directives or decisions. The EU acts that encroach furthest on national law are regulations. Article 249 of the Consolidated TEU states that "a regulation shall have general application. It shall be binding in its entirety and directly applicable in all Member States." In this way, regulations do not need to be transformed into domestic law, but directly confer rights and create obligations within Member States. Regulations have the power to preempt national legislation in a particular area.

Directives, on the other hand, state an objective to be achieved within a certain time, but leave the means by which the objective is achieved to the discretion of the Member State. This form of legislation is designed to allow Member States to fashion rules which best suit their particular domestic circumstances while still implementing EU law and policy in a relatively uniform way. The overall result on a Union-wide basis is to help harmonize the domestic laws and policies of the Member States.

Since the EU has no single institution that constitutes its "legislature," directives and regulations are enacted through the interaction and cooperation of different EU institutions. The precise procedures of the legislative process depend on the Treaty article on which the legislative initiative rests, and thus vary according to the substantive area being addressed by the legislation. Most of the time, the Commission initiates legislative proposals. A particular department within the Commission will prepare a detailed draft proposal in its field of expertise, and present it to the entire Commission. If adopted by a simple majority, the Commission proposal then goes to the Council which will ultimately dispose of it through one of three procedures: consultation, cooperation, or co-decision.

In the consultation process, the Parliament must give its opinion on the Commission's proposal before the Council reaches a final decision, but that opinion is not binding on the Council. The more complicated cooperation procedure gives Parliament a more significant role. The Parliament is given two opportunities to read the proposed legislation. If it approves the proposal or is silent, the Council may pass the legislation by qualified majority, but if Parliament rejects the proposal, it can be adopted by the Council only by unanimous vote. If Parliament amends the proposal by absolute majority, then it is given back to the Commission to reexamine. If the Commission accepts the amendment, then the Council can pass the legislation by qualified majority. If the Commission rejects the amendment, then the Council can pass the legislation by unanimous vote only.

The Maastricht Treaty instituted the co-decision procedure and the Treaty of Amsterdam expanded its application to apply to a majority of the areas of EU legislative action. Like the cooperation procedures, co-decision gives the Parliament the ability to accept, reject or amend a proposal. However, if the Parliament rejects the proposal or the Council refuses to accept the Parliament's amendments after the Commission has examined them, a Conciliation Committee is convened, comprised of representatives of the Council and the Parliament, and in the case of amendments the Commission as well. If Parliament confirms its rejection, then the proposal will not go forward. If the Committee succeeds in producing a joint text, both the Parliament and the Council must each adopt the act for it to become law; rejection by either precludes adoption of the text. If the Committee does not come to an agreement, the Council may affirm its position, with or without Parliament's amendments, but Parliament may still reject the proposal. Thus, under the co-decision procedure Parliament always has the power to veto a proposal.

Unlike directives or regulations which are of a legislative nature, a decision, which is more of an administrative measure, can apply to individuals and corporations as well as to the Member State. A decision, which is binding in its entirety upon those to whom it is addressed, requires a particular Member State or person to perform or refrain from a particular action.

Closely related to the secondary legislation of the EU, but not legally binding as such and thus not formally a source of law, are the Commission's recommendations. These may suggest certain interpretations of EU law, or recommend detailed rules to be adopted by Member States, and can exert a powerful political influence which may lead to more formal legal results.

Treaties and international agreements have become sources of law in the EU through the doctrine of implied powers discussed above. Thus, although the Treaties themselves only grant very narrow treaty-making powers to the EU institutions, the implied power to negotiate and conclude international treaties with third parties has substantially increased the number of such agreements in recent years.

Court decisions are an additional important source of law in the EU. They are applicable to the parties before the European Court of Justice, to the referring national courts, and sometimes are valid *erga omnes*, such as a ruling on the invalidity of a European Union act. A prior ruling of the ECJ on a particular point of EU law can in some circumstances also extinguish national courts' obligations to refer questions of EU law on that matter. In some cases, national courts have explicitly recognized prior ECJ decisions as binding precedents. In these ways, the Court's rulings have acquired some of the attributes of precedent in the common law tradition.

Under Article 220 of the Consolidated TEU, "the Court of Justice shall ensure that in the interpretation and application of this Treaty the law is observed." This language implies that there is a higher law to be followed outside that of the Treaties, but that is applicable to the treaties. On the basis of this and similar provisions, the ECJ has judicially adopted "general principles of law" as an additional source of law within the EU legal order. The Court has drawn these unwritten principles principally from the constitutional traditions of Member States. Examples include the principles of legal certainty, proportionality, equal treatment or non-discrimination, and subsidiarity.

One particularly important example of the application of general principles of law is the Court's development of a jurisprudence of fundamental human rights within EU law. Prior to the Treaty on European Union, the Treaties made no reference to the application of human rights norms within the EU. However, starting in 1969 the Court began to assert the existence of fundamental rights guarantees as inherent in EU law. Human rights principles have been drawn from both the constitutional traditions of Member States as well as international treaties, especially the European Convention on Human Rights (references to which were later included in the TEU). The Court has come to recognize many fundamental rights, including the right to ownership, the general right to privacy and the privacy of correspondence and of the home, freedom of association, freedom of religion, the freedom to choose and practice a profession, the right to form trade unions, and the principle of democracy. IN 2000, the EU adopted a Charter of Fundamental Rights of the European Union, which codified those fundamental rights recognized in the jurisprudence of the ECJ as well as many other rights drawn from a variety of sources. Although the Charter is not part of the treaties, it has been used by the ECJ in the interpretation of general principles of law, and if the Treaty of Lisbon is ratified it will become formally a part of the primary legislation of the EU.

## § 5. Supremacy of European Union Law in Member States

The full impact of the EU legal order upon the legal traditions of the individual states of Europe depends not only on the scope and forms of EU law, but also on the manner in which that law is given effect in domestic legal systems. Of decisive importance in this respect have been the EU system of judicial review and the judicially-developed doctrines of supremacy, direct effect and indirect effect. Supremacy and direct effect, together with the doctrines of implied powers and the development of a jurisprudence of fundamental rights, have transformed the EU legal order from one of public international law to one of constitutional character, according to some EU legal scholars.

The doctrine of direct effect, first articulated by the ECJ in 1963, provides that primary and secondary legislation of the EU that is clear, precise and unconditional and that requires no further legislative intervention by the authorities of the EU or the Member States can be invoked as binding law in the sphere of EU competence. EU law having direct effect creates enforceable legal obligations both between individuals and Member States of the EU and also between individuals among themselves. Directly effective EU norms may be invoked by parties in national courts. As a result of the doctrine of direct effect, Member States' obligations under EU law are not limited to the international plane of inter-state relations but instead are invoked in domestic courts by the Member States' own citizens.

Even if a provision is not directly effective, a private party can still attain rights from it through the doctrine of indirect effect, which requires that even if an EU provision is not directly effective, it must be taken into account by national courts when interpreting national legislation. Although indirect effect applies mostly to directives, it also encompasses other forms of Union law, including treaty provisions, regulations, decisions, recommendations, and other forms of soft law which are not directly effective. The doctrine also applies to general principles of Union law, including the principles derived from the European Convention for the Protection of Human Rights and Fundamental Freedoms.

In addition to the doctrines of direct and indirect effect, the ECJ also developed the doctrine of the supremacy of EU law. Through a series of decisions beginning in 1964, the ECJ declared that in the sphere of competence of EU law, any EU norm takes precedence over any conflicting provision of national law, whether the latter was enacted before or after the EU norm. The doctrine of supremacy renders the conflicting national law automatically inapplicable. Moreover, the ECJ implicitly maintains the authority to determine which areas do fall within the EU's sphere of competence.

The application of the doctrines of direct effect and supremacy of EU law is ensured through the EU's system of judicial review of Member States' acts for their conformity to EU norms. At the EU level, legal actions for non-compliance with EU obligations may be brought in the ECJ against a Member State by the Commission or by any other Member State. At the level of national courts, the EC Treaty provides that when a question of EU law arises before a national court, that court may (and if it is a court of last resort, must) suspend the proceedings and refer the interpretation of the EU norm to the ECJ for a preliminary ruling (except in some circumstances where the ECJ has already issued a clear ruling on the same question). On the basis of the ECJ opinion, the national court then decides the case before it. The EU and national courts thus work together to ensure the consistency of national acts with EU law and to facilitate the uniformity of EU law in all of the Member States.

Direct effect and indirect effect are both intended to give provisions of EU law the widest possible application. In many cases, however, the Member States have delayed implementation of EU directives for extended periods of time. In such cases, the ECJ could hold that the EU provisions have direct effect and this can be invoked before courts even in the absence of implementing legislation. Since 1991, the ECJ has also held that in some circumstances individuals can claim compensation in tort from a state that has failed to implement a directive correctly, even in cases where the directive is not directly effective. Under Articles 226 and 228 of the Consolidated TEU, the Commission can bring an action against a Member State for breach of its obligations under the Treaties by failing to implement a directive in due time. Although this is at first a declaratory judgment only, the failure of a State to comply with a second judgment of the ECJ can lead to the imposition of a lump sum fine or a monthly monetary penalty on the Member State. The remedy depends on the gravity of the infringement and the need for an adequate deterrent. A lump sum is intended to have a punitive and deterrent purpose, whereas the monthly monetary payment is given to induce the State to implement the directive as soon as possible.

## § 6. European Union Law and National Constitutional Systems

In some cases, establishing the supremacy of EU law in the constitutional systems of Member States has entailed various degrees of legal struggle. The constitutional systems of Greece, Luxembourg, the Netherlands, Portugal and Spain generally provide that treaties, including those founding the European Union, are automatically part of the domestic legal system, without the need for independent national legislation to incorporate them into domestic law. Thus the application of EU law by the judiciaries of these countries generally has been unproblematic. The Netherlands and Luxembourg not only recognize the higher status of international obligations over national law, but also have enacted constitutional amendments to ensure the possibility of delegating sovereign powers to the EU. In Greece, it should be noted, the Constitution prohibits application of treaties violating "fundamental human rights and the foundations of the democratic system," but so far this reservation has apparently not led to Greek resistance to the supremacy of EU law.

The judiciaries of Belgium and France had slightly more difficulty completely accepting the supremacy of EU law. In particular, the question remained open regarding the continued applicability of EU law when it conflicts with a subsequent national statute. In Belgium, the issue was finally settled by the Court of Cassation in 1971, when it concluded that "the treaties which have created Community law have instituted a new legal system in whose favour the Member States have restricted the exercise of their sovereign powers in the areas determined by those treaties." In France, instead, the

Council of State long resisted the supremacy of Community law. The French Constitution establishes the superiority of treaty law over ordinary domestic law, but because the Council of State does not have the power to review acts of Parliament on constitutional grounds, it refused to apply treaty-based EU law over subsequent national statutes. Only in 1989 did it finally accept the doctrines of direct effect and supremacy of EU law. Separately, the French Constitutional Council in 1992 ruled that the Maastricht Treaty conflicted with the French Constitution with respect to voting rights, European monetary union and other more minor matters. In response, France adopted an amendment to its Constitution that explicitly recognizes France's membership in the European Union and resolves the conflicts raised by the Constitutional Council.

In general, the Scandinavian countries, Ireland and the United Kingdom require national legislation to transform international agreements into national law. Despite the potential difficulties this approach presents in principle (for instance, the possibility that a subsequent national statute will abrogate prior treaty obligations), courts in these three countries have thus far had no difficulty in applying EU law over conflicting provisions of national law. In part, this is due to the constitutional (in the case of Ireland and Denmark) or statutory (in the case of Britain) provisions enacted there at the time of accession.

In contrast, the constitutional courts of Italy and Germany have resisted more strongly the primacy of EU law. The constitutional systems of both countries require parliamentary approval of international treaties; once parliament has done so, a treaty becomes part of the domestic legal order. This leaves open the possibility that subsequent acts of parliament conflicting with the treaty will supercede it, and also puts into doubt the possibility of the direct applicability of EU legislation. After initial resistance, both countries' constitutional courts have come to accept the priority of EU legislation even over subsequent domestic law, albeit with some lingering reservations.

In Italy, the complex position of the Constitutional Court essentially rests on the acknowledgment that the autonomous nature of EU law obviates the need for its integration and transformation into domestic law. Instead, national law is understood to withdraw in favor of a substitution of EU norms, thus assuring the recognition and guarantee of EU law in Italy. But despite the Italian courts' substantial acceptance of EU law's supremacy, there remains a residual difference between their approach and that of the ECJ. Ultimately, the respect and guarantee of EU law as a higher norm within the domestic legal system still rests on the values and laws of the Italian legal system, in particular on the Italian constitutional requirement of state compliance with international obligations. Thus, the Italian Constitutional Court has forcefully affirmed that although it will not on an ordinary basis review

EU legislation for compatibility with the Italian Constitution, in principle if a rule of EU law violates a fundamental norm of the Constitution concerning human rights, it cannot be applied.

The German Constitutional Court has arrived at a similar position in its halting acceptance of the supremacy of EU law. Ultimately, it has based its decision to respect the supremacy and direct effect of EU law on its integrity as an autonomous system of law distinct from the domestic legal order. Like the Italian court, the German Constitutional Court also retained for itself the power to review the applicability in Germany of EU acts which could conflict with the fundamental rights protected by the German Basic Law. Since 1986, however, the German Constitutional Court has deemed that the EU legal order had developed a sufficient guarantee of the human rights safeguarded by the German Basic Law for the German Constitutional Court to suspend the exercise of its jurisdiction in this area so long as the Community continued to protect human rights at least at its then-current level. In 1993, the German Constitutional Court ruled that the transfer of Germany's sovereign powers to the EU under the Maastricht Treaty did not violate the German Constitution. At the same time, the Constitutional Court did assert its continuing jurisdiction to examine whether the legal acts of EU organs and institutions (and not just those of the German state) exceed their competence, putting itself in principle at odds with the ECJ's jurisprudence of EU legal supremacy and judicial review.

## § 7. European Union Law and National Legal Traditions

The broad and expanding scope of EU law and the forcefulness with which it has penetrated into the domestic legal orders naturally raises the question of EU law's influence on the basic legal traditions of the Member States. National judges are called upon to serve also as actors within the EU legal system; national legislatures are compelled to refashion their laws in accordance with the common policies of the EU. At the most general level, the structure, methods and content of EU law cannot help but infuse the legal consciousness of domestic actors (including law students who in many European countries are now required to pass an examination in EU law).

At the same time, the national legal traditions of the Member States have shaped the character of the European system. For all their differences, the judges and lawmakers in the European Union share the heritage of the Western legal tradition, which forms the political, historical, cultural and philosophical substratum of EU law. Indeed, it would be difficult to imagine fashioning such an intricate legal order without fundamentally similar ideas about law. Within the EU institutions, a majority of actors come from within the civil law tradition, and invariably bring with them a common education and practice in the concepts and grammar of civil law discourse. More concretely, the legislation of the Communities relies on national experts, and the Court draws its interpretive and gap-filling principles from common concepts in the law of Member States. When EU law is implemented by national courts, it is done in the context of national procedures, local legal language, and substantively national disputes. In short, the question is one of the reciprocal influence of intermingled legal systems.

One important example involves the role of courts and case law in the legal order. Some scholars of EU law have considered this to be a preeminent innovation of EU law which has had profound effects on the national legal systems, particularly with respect to private law. The ECJ's interpretive decisions, including the Court's use of general principles, have expanded the sources of law to which national judges must look far beyond the written sources of the EU treaties and other legislative acts. Until then, even limited acknowledgement of the binding precedential nature of another court's case law was, in continental countries, reserved almost exclusively for the special case of constitutional courts. In addition, based on EU law ordinary national judges have been called upon to disapply the acts of their national legislatures, and to exercise much broader powers than would be normally available under national law in order to ensure implementation of EU law by Member States. In all these respects, EU law entails a reconceptualization of the institutional balance within the constitutional systems of the Member States, including a revision of deeply rooted principles regarding Parliamentary sovereignty and its relation to the exercise of judicial functions.

At the same time, however, various elements within the EU legal structure mitigate the dominating force of courts and case law, reflecting the EU's predominantly civil law heritage. The European Court of Justice has stressed that the application of EU law by national judges is only a minimum, not a sufficient, guarantee of the full application of the treaties by Member States. The cooperation of other institutions is also required in order to promote greater respect for EU law, in particular through adequately publicized legislation helping to establish the legal certainty of EU norms in the domestic system.

Similarly, EU institutions other than the Court have used various administrative acts to clarify EU law and render it more certain and secure. For instance, the Commission has at various times used "general communications" to address the legal situation within a particular sector of EU law and to serve as a guide for both public authorities regarding their obligations and EU citizens regarding their rights. Although not creating an authoritative legal text, a general communication helps unite case law and written law and sets out the basis on which the Commission will exercise its regulatory and enforcement powers in a given area. Another example is the "negative clearance" in EU competition law, a procedure by which the Commission certifies that a particular business agreement or practice is outside the scope of the competition law without having to refer the matter to judicial decision. The procedure, form and content of a negative clearance essentially provide a form of quasi-judicial legal assistance to businesses. These and other "nonstandard" administrative acts do not diminish the importance of case law and adjudication in the EU system. Nevertheless, they do show how the civil law tradition continues to have important effects on the sources of law in the EU. In the view of EU legal scholar Paolo Mengozzi, "[t]he strongly felt need for legal certainty, the experience of codes and of a single text, as well as the limited analytical study of jurisprudence [i.e., case law] even in university law faculties, so typical and characteristic of the civil law culture of continental Europe, have led the Community institutions not to emphasize the law-creating role of Community jurisprudence by making it the central and privileged element of reference for legal actors."

Beyond the processes and methods of the different legal systems, a similar dialectic can be seen between the substantive law of the EU and that of the Member States. Until now, the EU legal order has most dynamically and innovatively interacted with the national law of the Member States in the area of public law. On the one hand, public law fields such as administrative law have historically been the most closely tied to the particular social, political and historical circumstances of the states of Europe, and therefore the least susceptible to either comparative study or to *rapprochement* or unification of any kind. Yet, on the other hand, precisely in these areas the ECJ has made the most use of its elaboration of the "general principles of law" discussed above. It has thus drawn most explicitly from the principles "common" to the Member States in this area and forged links between them.

In fashioning the general principles of law of the EU, the ECJ does not draw on the laws of the Member States in any mechanical way, such as a search for the highest or lowest common standard of legal protection, or the need to find a particular rule within a set number of Member States' laws to then be applied at the EU level. Instead, the Court has sought to extract broad principles from comparative analysis, which may find concrete expression in very different ways, or perhaps not at all, within any given Member State. The Court then applies the principle to the EU context as it deems most appropriate, not with a view to establishing how any other jurisdiction might decide the same matter. In this way, the Court does not simply replicate particular rules of national law, but interacts with them dynamically, developing the principles in question while drawing from the foundation of national law.

Crucially, these principles and their application, now in altered form, seep back into national legal systems from which they came through the operation of EU law domestically, particularly through national judiciaries. For example, according to a judge of the Supreme Court of the Netherlands who had also served as a judge of the ECJ, "English courts will thus be checking whether a certain government measure was really 'proportionate' to its aims, a concept unknown to the common law. And French courts are starting to get worried about the right to a hearing of a private company in administrative matters, just like a common law court might be."

In those areas of law traditionally governed by the common law or great 19th century civil codes, EU law both reflects and helps to further European law's progressive recognition of the economic and political organization of contemporary society. Most directly, EU law has formally established certain legal regimes at variance with traditional civil law constructs, especially in areas such as labor, banking, insurance and consumer law. Various examples can be found of EU legislation or ECJ decisions departing from the contracts or torts principles of the civil codes. With regard to consumer contracts, for instance, a 1985 EU directive both requires a written contract, and at the same time makes it easier for the consumer to repudiate the contract and be refunded any payment that has already been made. Such developments constitute exceptions to the strict principle of consent traditional to the civil law. Similarly, in an attempt to minimize the competitive distortions of different liability insurance rates for companies operating in different Member States, the EU has regulated the legal regime of liability for defective products. At the national level, such EU constructs have resulted in decisions such as that of a German court refusing to hold a German company in breach of its contract with an Italian company, even though clearly not complying with the express terms of the contract, because those terms violated an EU directive. The court essentially affirmed the primacy of EU private law over the express intent of the parties and national law which would have enforced that intent. Examples such as these reach to the heart of the principles upon which the civil law has been built.

In a more indirect way, EU law is destined to have an even greater impact on national legal traditions. The ECJ has ruled that even where EU law does not directly determine the rights of parties before national courts, nevertheless national courts are required to interpret their national law in the light of the wording and the purpose of relevant EU law. Even where EU law does not formally establish variations from domestic private law, therefore, it is bound to weigh heavily on the interpretation of all national law.

Even more broadly, EU law and the civil codes may have their most complex interactions at the level of the fundamental structure and conceptual framework of private law. The civil codes have traditionally viewed social and economic relationships in very individualist terms. For example, they have focused on individual employment contracts instead of the collective aspects of labor, such as collective bargaining or strikes. Civil law systems have gradually evolved to accommodate such more collective phenomenon. EU law reflects and reinforces the progression, particularly in areas of commercial law. Its development of competition law is perhaps the most striking example. A difference between "good" and "bad" competitive practices based on consideration of a broader market was a concept largely foreign to traditional private law, but is now finding a place in domestic law as well as at the EU level.

Competition law also illustrates the increasing application of functional approaches, especially involving the use of economics, to juridical constructs. This marks a significant divergence from the formal foundations of the civil codes. It is indicative of a broader movement in private law away from dogmatic and toward functional understandings of law, which has found a clear expression in EU law. European Union law, in turn, exposes and encourages this movement in domestic law. For instance, national judges addressing disputes involving EU law as well as national law in France appear to consider themselves more free to compare and balance the policy interests involved openly, and to weigh explicitly the practical effects of their judgments, instead of (at least outwardly) limiting themselves to formal interpretive concerns.

At the same time, EU law accelerates the increasing obsolescence of dogmatic categories of law such as the traditional distinctions between civil law and commercial law or between public law and private law. The very subjects of EU law—freedom to establish a business or provide services, the status of workers, including their rights, social security and freedom of movement, or insurance, competition, and other areas—all constitute intersections of "public" and "private" law, and therefore underscore the disutility of the distinction.

In light of each of these ways that EU law affects the structure of European legal traditions, one can see an evolution of new substantive categories of law, which cut across traditional divisions of private law and develop the law loosely around certain forms of economic activity, like consumption, competition, employment, or professional activity. The EU order is in this respect only a more stark model of a system which has been evolving for some time at the national level. For instance, at least since 1968 there has been an increasing tendency to teach law in French universities according to functional categories rather than dogmatic ones. But some scholars of European law, emphasizing that these new categories still lack internal coherence and autonomy, believe that part of the common future of EU law and national law includes the need for European jurists (including but not limited to private law specialists) to unite the diverse sectors of contemporary law and establish the essential foundations of a true European law, perhaps through a new European Civil Code.

# CHAPTER 13

# THE EUROPEAN HUMAN RIGHTS SYSTEM

## § 1.  Introduction

In the aftermath of the second World War, the countries of western Europe agreed to establish a regional Council of Europe for the development of European unity. Impetus for the creation of the Council came in large part from two related goals: the desire to ensure that the horrors of the Nazi dictatorship would never be repeated, and the desire to fortify the West in the face of the expanding power of the Soviet Union. The Statute of the Council of Europe, signed in London in May 1949, accordingly places particular emphasis on human rights and democratic governance. The Preamble declares that the parties are "Reaffirming their devotion to the spiritual and moral values which are the common heritage of their peoples and the true source of individual freedom, political liberty and the rule of law, principles which form the basis of all genuine democracy." Article 3 of the Statute goes on to make these principles a condition of membership in the Council: "Every Member of the Council of Europe must accept the principles of the rule of law and of the enjoyment by all persons within its jurisdiction of human rights and fundamental freedoms.''

To this end, one of the first tasks of the Council, including both its Consultative Assembly and the Committee of Ministers, was to create a normative and institutional system for the guarantee of human rights in Europe. Their efforts culminated in the Convention for the Protection of Human Rights and Fundamental Freedoms (the "Convention"), signed on November 4, 1950.

When it entered into force in 1953 (after having been ratified by ten states), the Convention established the first supranational institutional system in the world for the protection and promotion of human rights. Its particular innovative strengths lay not so much in making the relations between a state and its own citizens the object of international obligations (for which there had been modest precedent earlier in the century) as in the Convention's enforcement mechanisms. The Convention gives individuals as well as states the right to petition for redress of human rights violations, and confers on the European Court of Human Rights jurisdiction over cases concerning the interpretation and application of the Convention. Given the limited European experience of judicial review until then, the Convention thus marked a significant step toward acceptance of the judicial enforcement of fundamental rights. Substantively, the Convention has also helped to develop a common stratum of foundational principles for the legal and political systems of

Europe. At least 47 European states are party to the Convention.

## § 2.  Rights Protected Under the Convention

The Convention, affirming in its Preamble its foundation in the contracting states' "common heritage of political traditions, ideals, freedom and the rule of law," is largely limited to classic civil and political rights and freedoms. It guarantees the right to life, freedom from torture and inhuman or degrading treatment or punishment, freedom from slavery or servitude, the right to liberty and security of person. It provides for extensive rights to procedural fairness in the determination of a person's civil rights and obligations or in criminal charges, including a presumption of innocence in criminal matters. The Convention further protects the right to respect for family and private life, freedom of thought, conscience, and religion, freedom of expression, freedom of peaceful assembly and association with others, and the right to marry and have a family. Finally, the Convention requires that the parties provide an effective remedy for a violation of the rights and freedoms of the Convention, and requires that the rights and freedoms of the Convention shall be secured without discrimination with regard to sex, race, color, language, religion, political or other opinion, national or social origin, association with a national minority, property, birth, or other status. Many of the rights articulated in the Convention may be subject to such limitations as are necessary in a democratic society for the protection of public order, health or morals, or the rights and freedoms of others.

Additional rights, some of which were considered and subject to negotiations in the drafting of the Convention but did not immediately command a consensus, were left to subsequent additional protocols. The First Protocol to the Convention, opened for signature in 1952, provides that everyone is entitled to the peaceful enjoyment of his possessions, guarantees the right to education to every person, and requires the contracting parties to have free elections at reasonable intervals by secret ballot. The Fourth Protocol, concluded in 1963, recognizes freedom from imprisonment for debt and freedom of movement, including the right to leave any country and the right to enter one's own country. The Sixth Protocol of 1983 abolished capital punishment in times of peace. In 1984, the Seventh Protocol established five more guarantees: protection of the due process rights of aliens being expelled; the right to appeal in criminal cases; the right to compensation for miscarriages of justice; freedom from being tried twice for the same offence; and the equality of the rights and responsibilities of spouses.

## § 3.   The European Social Charter

The Convention's drafting and negotiating also included substantial discussion about how to address various economic and social rights, in addition to the civil and political rights agreed upon in the Convention. Many of the post-war constitutions of the European states recognized such rights. In the decade following the adoption of the Convention, the Council of Europe sought to elaborate a set of common social and economic goals for the Member States. The Social Committee of the Council of Europe drafted the European Social Charter, which was signed in 1961 and came into force in 1965.

The Charter's 19 rights and principles include, among others, the rights of workers, the right to education, health, social security and social welfare services, and protection of the family, especially mothers and children. Four additional rights were added to the Charter with the entry into force of the Additional Protocol to the European Social Charter in 1991: the right to equal opportunity and equal treatment in employment without discrimination on the grounds of sex; the right of workers to be informed and consulted within business enterprises; the right of workers to take part in determining and improving their working conditions and working environment; and the right of the elderly to social protection.

Supervision of the Parties' compliance with the Charter is entrusted to a Committee of Experts, who receive and examine biannual reports from the Contracting Parties. This Committee forwards its conclusions to a Governmental Committee comprised of a representative of each of the Contracting Parties and responsible for preparing decisions of the Committee of Ministers. The latter can then adopt, based on the Governmental Committee's report, a resolution including individual recommendations to the Contracting Parties involved. Recently, an Additional Protocol was opened for signature, which upon its entry into force will also provide a mechanism for submitting collective complaints to the Committee of Experts.

## § 4.   The European Court of Human Rights

Until November 1998, the institutional supervision of compliance with the Convention's norms was divided between a European Commission of Human Rights and the European Court of Human Rights. With the entry into force of Protocol 11 to the Convention, the European human rights system now has a single, permanent court, the European Court of Human Rights, which has replaced the prior, part-time Court structure as well as the Commission. The Court consists of a number of judges equal to the total number of members of the Council of Europe, no two of whom may be nationals of the same state (although they need not be necessarily from one of the Member states at all). They are elected by the Committee of Ministers of the Council of Europe from lists of names submitted by each member's delegation to the Consultative Assembly of the Council of Europe. The candidates must be of "high moral character and must either possess the qualifications required for appointment to high judicial office or be persons of recognised competence in national or international law." The judges serve in full-time positions for renewable nine-year terms, and sit in their individual capacities, not as representatives of their states.

The Court is organized into committees, Chambers, and Grand Chambers. The committees are set up by the Chambers for a fixed period of time and are comprised of three judges. The Court sets up the Chambers of seven judges each for a fixed period of time. The Grand Chamber is made up of seventeen judges. The President of the Court, the Vice–Presidents, the Presidents of the Chambers, and the judge elected in respect of the State against which the application is lodged are always members of the Grand Chamber. The other judges completing any particular Grand Chamber are appointed by the Court on a case-by-case basis.

The only power the committees have is to declare a case admissible or to strike it from the list. For a claim to be admissible, the petitioner must have exhausted all domestic remedies available and must not present substantially the same matter which the Court has already examined. Individuals may bring a case before the Court, as well as Member States. If the committee declares the case to be admissible, it then goes to the Chamber which reviews admissibility and also decides the merits of the case. Once the Chamber gives its decision, the Grand Chamber can reexamine the case at the request of one of the parties or in exceptional circumstances. For the Grand Chamber to reexamine a case, it must raises serious questions concerning the interpretation or application of the Convention or its Protocols, or raise an issue of general importance. The Grand Chamber's judgment is final and binding in international law, as is the Chamber's judgment if the case is not brought before the Grand Chamber. A friendly settlement can be reached at any time during the proceedings. The plenary Court only deals with organizational matters.

## § 5.  The Convention and Domestic Legal Systems

How deeply and effectively the Convention norms have penetrated into domestic legal systems has been dependent in some measure on the relationship between the Convention and the domestic constitutional system of the state in question. In Austria, for example, the Convention expressly has the rank of constitutional provisions, and requires no secondary legislation to give it formal constitutional status. In the great majority of Member States of the Council of Europe, however, treaties in general and the Convention in particular have a formal status below that of the constitution in the domestic legal order. In some, treaties may still have a position superior to that of ordinary legislation. This appears to be the case under the French Constitution, Article 55 of which provides that "Treaties or agreements duly ratified or approved shall, upon their publication, have an authority superior to that of laws." In other states, including Germany, the Convention formally has the same rank as ordinary legislation, and thus later legislation in conflict with the Convention would prevail over the treaty's norms. In practice, however, even in states such as Germany the Convention still retains a degree of superiority through common principles of statutory interpretation, especially the principle that a state's statutes should wherever possible be interpreted in harmony with the international obligations of that state. Accordingly, the German Constitutional Court has given priority to the Convention even over later-enacted statutes where the legislature has not clearly stated an intention to deviate from Germany's international obligations.

In a few states, the Convention in not considered to have any internal legal validity unless and until it is introduced into the internal legal order through domestic law. This is the case in the United Kingdom, Ireland and most of the Scandinavian countries. Where such states have not enacted any implementing legislation to give the Convention internal legal validity, as in the United Kingdom, the Convention's internal effect is consequently more limited. Even in the United Kingdom, however, courts have begun to give a small degree of internal effect to the Convention and to the European Court's case law by using them in modest ways as interpretive guides to certain statutory and common law rights. Ongoing debate over this lack of incorporation of the Convention in the United Kingdom has created a very strong possibility of formally enacting the Convention as a domestic statutory bill of rights in the near future.

The case law of the European Court of Human Rights has addressed nearly all of the substantive provisions of the Convention and its Protocols, and has developed into a substantial body of jurisprudence. Some scholars have referred to it as a sort of "Constitutional Court of Europe," since it deals principally with cases, in the words of a former President of the Court, "of a constitutional nature: it embraces the age-long and sensitive balance to be struck between the general interest of the community and the protection of the individual's fundamental rights." In some cases, the Court's decisions have indeed reached deeply into the constitutional orders of European states, requiring them to conform to such "constitutional" principles of the Convention. While beginning cautiously, over time the Court's decisions have come to be accepted by the States Parties as authoritative law even on such diverse and sensitive topics as the use of force against terrorists, corporal punishment in schools, the freedom of the media, and the legal status of transsexuals. In the areas of law traditionally governed by civil codes, the Court's jurisprudence has had the most profound effect on family law, through the Convention's guarantee of respect for private and family life.

Steadily, the Court has continued to expand the reach of the Convention's norms. The Court has consistently said that the Convention's norms must be interpreted dynamically, to evolve with changing social conditions. Thus, new or more extensive norms can emerge over time. For example, through its evolutive interpretation the Court has ruled that the criminalization of consensual adult homosexual activity violates the Convention, as does discrimination in the law of inheritance against children born outside of marriage, although clearly such norms were outside the scope of the Convention in 1950. At the same time, the Court has consistently tempered this dynamic interpretation with its development and application of the "margin of appreciation" doctrine. The margin of appreciation is the degree of discretion that the Court accords to national authorities in the implementation of the Convention before it finds a violation to have occurred. Where the Court finds a broad margin of appreciation, it will accord greater latitude to the States to determine the proper implementation of the Convention's norms in that State's domestic context.

Through the decisions of the Court as well as through the more overtly political process of European governments and legislatures seeking to conform their internal acts to the requirements of the Convention, the European human rights system has undoubtedly come to have a significant harmonizing effect on the public law of European legal traditions. It is fair to say that the European Convention, especially in conjunction with the fundamental rights jurisprudence of the European Union, now constitutes one of the central pillars of the European legal tradition, strengthening the common foundations of Europe's diverse national traditions.

### SELECTED BIBLIOGRAPHY AND SUGGESTIONS FOR FURTHER READING

R.C. van Caenegem, *European Law In The Past And The Future: Unity And Diversity Over Two Millennia* (Cambridge University Press, 2002).

Volkmar Gessner, Armin Hoeland, and Csaba Varga, eds., *European Legal Cultures* (Aldershot, 1996).

Bruno de Witte and Caroline Forder, eds., *The Common Law of Europe and the Future of Legal Education* (Kluwer, 1992).

Paul Craig and Gráinne de Búrca, *EU Law*, 4th ed. (Oxford University Press, 2008).

Paolo Mengozzi, *European Community Law*, 2nd ed. (Kluwer, 1992).

Joseph H.H. Weiler, *The Constitution of Europe* (Cambridge, 1997).

Anne–Marie Slaughter, Alec Stone Sweet and J.H.H. Weiler, eds., *The European Court and National Courts—Doctrine and Jurisprudence* (Hart Publishing. 1998).

Mark W. Janis, Richard S. Kay and Anthony W. Bradley, *European Human Rights Law*, 2nd ed. (Oxford University Press, 2000).

\*

# INDEX

---

**References are to Pages**

---

†

9/2015
JA Kelly
I move yours
its the only title we
have comparing
legal systems